Paul Robeson

To Henry Foner and Lawrence Lamphere

Paul Robeson

Essays on His Life and Legacy

Edited by Joseph Dorinson *and* William Pencak

WITH A FOREWORD BY HENRY FONER

McFarland & Company, Inc., Publishers
Jefferson, North Carolina, and London

Library of Congress Cataloguing-in-Publication Data

Paul Robeson : essays on his life and legacy / edited by Joseph Dorinson
and William Pencak ; with a foreword by Henry Foner.
     p.   cm.
    Essays that were presented at a conference held at Long Island
University's Brooklyn campus, Feb. 28, 1998.
    Includes bibliographical references and index.
    ISBN 0-7864-1153-8 (illustrated case binding : 50# alkaline paper) ∞
    1. Robeson, Paul, 1898–1976 — Congresses.   2. Robeson, Paul,
1898–1976 — Influence — Congresses.   3. African Americans —
Biography — Congresses.   4. African American political activists —
Biography — Congresses.   5. Political activists — United States —
Biography — Congresses.   6. Singers — United States — Biography —
Congresses.   7. Actors — United States — Biography — Congresses.
I. Robeson, Paul, 1898–1976.   II. Dorinson, Joseph, 1936–
III. Pencak, William, 1951–
E185.97.R63P375   2002
790.2'092 — dc21   2001052111
[B]

British Library cataloguing data are available

Manufactured in the United States of America

Cover photograph: Paul Robeson in 1933 as *The Emperor Jones* (photograph
by Edward Steichen)

McFarland & Company, Inc., Publishers
  Box 611, Jefferson, North Carolina 28640
   www.mcfarlandpub.com

Table of Contents

Music, Film, Theater

Legacies

Foreword

Keynote Address from the 1998 Long Island University Paul Robeson Conference

Henry Foner
Brooklyn, New York

Paul Robeson was born on April 9, 1898, in Princeton, New Jersey, the son of an escaped slave. He rose to heights unparalleled in the century in which he lived. Here are just some of his accomplishments:

He was hailed for more than three decades as one of the greatest singers and actors in the world, fluent in twelve languages, and conversant with the cultures of Europe, Asia, and Africa.

In 1918 he was elected to membership in the Phi Beta Kappa honorary academic society.

He was twice winner of All-American football honors at Rutgers College, in 1918 and 1919. He also starred in baseball, basketball, and track, and earned fifteen athletic letters in four sports.

Early in his career he was recognized for his important contributions to the Harlem Renaissance of the 1920s as the first who made the Negro spiritual an accepted art form and for his performances in two plays by Eugene O'Neill, America's foremost dramatist — *The Emperor Jones* and *All God's Chillun Got Wings.*

He was the recipient of honorary degrees from Rutgers College in 1932, from Hamilton College in 1940, from Morehouse College in 1943, and from Howard University in 1945.

In December 1943 he led a delegation of African American newspaper publishers that met with baseball commissioner Kenesaw Mountain Landis and the top officials of all the major league baseball clubs to urge the breaching of the color line in baseball — which paved the way for the historic breakthrough, three and a half years later, when Jackie Robinson was signed as the first African American player in baseball's major leagues.

This address was delivered on Saturday, January 28, 1998; it is here edited for publication.

In 1944 he received the Donaldson Award for outstanding male actors for his performance in Shakespeare's *Othello*, which held the record as the longest running Shakespearean play on Broadway up to that time. It eclipsed the record held by Orson Welles' production of *Julius Caesar.*

He appeared in eleven feature films in America and England, including *Show Boat* and *The Emperor Jones.*

In November 1939 he introduced on CBS Radio the *Ballad for Americans*, which received such a tumultuous response that for a while it possessed the status of a second national anthem. In 1940 the *Ballad* was sung at the conventions of the Democratic, Republican and Communist parties—and you can't get more universal than that!

During World War II he became a national symbol of unity in the fight against fascism abroad and racism at home, giving benefit concerts for war relief agencies, touring war plants, and speaking at war bond rallies. In 1945, while the United States armed forces were still segregated, he sang to U.S. troops in Europe as part of the first interracial USO-sponsored overseas show.

In November 1943 he received the Lincoln Medal from Abraham Lincoln High School in Brooklyn as the citizen who had rendered the most distinguished service to New York City. Recently I met an elderly woman who had been at the Lincoln presentation, and she said it was an event she would never forget. The auditorium was packed to the doors. Robeson spoke and sang, without accompaniment, and she estimated that his voice was heard in far-off Sea Gate!

He also received the prestigious Spingarn Medal from the NAACP in 1945 for "his active concern for the rights of the common man of every race, color, religion, and nationality."

He played a leading role in the major civil rights struggles of the United States in the 1940s—to end the crime of lynching, to eliminate the poll tax, and to fight against job discrimination—all of which laid the basis for the groundbreaking civil rights victories of the 1960s. In 1946 he led a delegation that met with President Harry Truman to demand passage of a federal anti-lynching law. To the nation's shame, that year there were a total of 54 lynchings perpetrated against African Americans, some of whom had just returned from fighting for their country against fascism. When Truman was asked to make a statement against lynching, he refused on the ground that it was not "politically opportune."

Robeson was also a firm and unwavering supporter of the American labor movement during the period of its greatest growth and influence in the 1930s and 1940s. He marched on picket lines, assisted in organizing drives, sang in union halls, and was awarded honorary lifetime memberships in more unions than any other public figure of his time. His speeches and writings played a decisive role in the successful campaign in 1940 of the United Automobile Workers to organize that bastion of the open shop—the Ford Motor Company.

He helped focus the attention of the nation and the world on the struggles of all colonial people for freedom. He founded and later chaired the Council on African Affairs where he worked tirelessly, along with his good friend Alphaeus Hunton, in the cause of African freedom.

At the height of his career he earned the highest income of any concert performer in the world and was an internationally renowned American second only, perhaps, to President Franklin D. Roosevelt.

He was inducted in 1972 as the only African American charter member of the National Theater Hall of Fame, which is housed in New York City's Gershwin Theater.

He was inducted into the National College Football Hall of Fame in 1995, almost fifty years after it was established. It is something of a commentary that it took almost half a century to recognize the greatest college football player of his time.

And finally, in February 1998 he was the recipient of one of the lifetime achievement awards from the National Academy of Recording Arts and Sciences, otherwise known as a lifetime "Grammy" Award.

A person with this almost incredible record of accomplishments became, in effect, a non-person as a result of a campaign of intimidation and harassment conducted by the FBI and other agents of the government that was only matched, some years later, by the attack on another great fighter for freedom — Dr. Martin Luther King, Jr.

Let me tell you about just one of the essays in this collection. I was asked to deliver a talk to the Brooklyn Chapter of OWL — the Older Women's League — on the subject (understandably, in view of the nature of the organization) "Paul Robeson and the Women Who Influenced His Life"—his mother, Maria Louisa Bustill Robeson; his wife, Eslanda Cardozo Goode Robeson; and his sister, Marion Robeson Forsythe. In the preparation of that talk, I relied to a great extent on the work of a scholar who lived in Park Slope, Brooklyn — Robert Schaffer — whose paper is entitled, appropriately enough, "Out of the Shadows: The Political Writings of Eslanda Goode Robeson." It tells the story of the woman Robeson married in 1921, who not only had a profound influence on his life, but also carved out a career of her own — in the course of which she helped immeasurably to heighten the United States' awareness of Africa, its people, and their contributions.

Let me conclude by relating my own personal contact with Paul Robeson. In 1949 I was an officer of the International Fur and Leather Workers' Union, one of the unions that had bestowed honorary lifetime memberships on Robeson. That summer he was invited to perform at our union's Fur Workers' Resort at White Lake in upstate New York. I was asked, and gladly agreed, to write a radio script that would be used to introduce him. I did so, and I shall always treasure his inscription on the first page of the script — "Thanks a million, Paul." A few weeks later I was part of the cordon of World War II veterans assigned to protect him during the second Peekskill concert (about which you will be hearing from one of the principal figures at the concert, the distinguished writer Howard Fast). When the concert was over, I was asked to drive Ewart Guinier, then an outstanding labor leader and the father of law professor Lani Guinier. We had to run a gauntlet of a jeering mob, armed with rocks and other missiles, while hundreds of state troopers stood by and did nothing. Because Mr. Guinier was a stately African American, some in the mob mistook him for Robeson and our car was the object of a special venom.

I had one more link with Paul Robeson, and that was through my late brother, Dr. Philip S. Foner, who was introduced to Robeson by Eslanda's mother, the daughter of Francis L. Cardozo, one of the leading figures of the much-maligned Reconstruction period. Together, Robeson and Phil made tentative plans for him to record some of the speeches of Frederick Douglass, on whose biography my brother was working. That project never reached fruition, but it was carried through by another great African American, Ossie Davis.

I am sure that these essays, along with other publications and events commemorating Robeson's centennial, will restore this giant figure to the recognition he so well deserves.

Preface

WILLIAM PENCAK

The volume before you has a complicated history. I first met Joe Dorinson at the conference he organized at Long Island University in February 1998 to honor Paul Robeson's memory on the hundredth anniversary of his birth. It was more than a conference, however. With participation by the New York City Labor Chorus (including a stirring rendition of "Ballad for Americans"), high school students, singers, poets, and dancers, it combined the usually scholarly presentations with the enthusiasm of several hundred people, both audience members and performers. In the process, at least for a day, Joe orchestrated a recreation of what Paul Robeson himself had, in fact, done. He placed scholarship and art in the service of a responsive public in the hope of building a better world. The event symbolically brought back to life the spirit of a giant upon whose shoulders we may, if we wish, choose to stand.

The scholarly papers themselves, apart from the general celebration surrounding them, were of very high quality. I arranged with Joe to publish several of them in the journal I edit, *Pennsylvania History: A Journal of Mid-Atlantic Studies*.

They appeared in the winter 1999 issue, volume 66, number 1; despite the additional copies we printed, we soon sold out.

We decided that our next step would be to publish the essays in book form. Besides allowing for wider distribution, the new format offered space for additional essays. We added the work of conference participants Lawrence Lamphere, Sheila Boyle and Andrew Bunie. While attending the Mid-Atlantic African American Group, which, thanks to Nell Painter's sponsorship, meets twice a year at Princeton, I recruited articles by Mark Naison, chairman of African-American Studies at Fordham University, and Jeffrey Stewart, curator of the Robeson Centennial Exhibit based at the National Portrait Gallery in Washington that traveled around the country. Joe Dorinson and I each wrote an additional article, each on our own premier passion (besides history): Joe about Robeson the athlete, I contrasting Robeson's approach to political activism with that of Marian Anderson, the other great African-American singer of the age. At the eleventh hour, Joseph Illick, a leading historian of childhood, offered me an article on African-

American childhood whose connections to Robeson's life cried out for adaptation and inclusion in this volume.

With few exceptions, we decided to use different illustrations than those that appeared in the *Pennsylvania History* issue, largely because a wealth of new photographs became available. Among those generously offering contributions were Paul Robeson, Jr., Ron Becker (Special Collections Librarian at the Rutgers University Libraries), and Carolyn Rummel of the *People's Weekly World*. Anne Easterling of the Museum of the City of New York and Martin Desht — a photographer and activist of whom Robeson would be proud — also went out of their way to provide illustrations. While we were not able to use all the illustrations, we were honored by the generosity and goodwill of all who offered material.

The Council of the Pennsylvania Historical Association, especially my friends Treasurer Bob Blackson (who handled the financial paperwork with good cheer), Susan Klepp, Leslie Patrick, and Randall

Miller, consecutive presidents of the society, were not only willing but eager for the articles to be reprinted, as were the authors, without exception. And it is an honor to reprint, thanks to Esther Jackson, a poem Pablo Neruda wrote in honor of Robeson that, to our knowledge, has previously appeared only in *Freedomways* magazine.

We dedicate this volume to Larry Lamphere and Henry Foner, both of whom made heroic contributions: Larry of his essay despite ill health, and Henry, who just turned eighty, for neverending encouragement and help with a million details.

As Mark Naison so eloquently tells us, we could use Paul Robeson today. In an age when he is commemorated by museums, and centers at universities are named after him, it would be salutary to remember that he did not struggle so hard that a great man might be memorialized, but so that people could speak their minds, fill their bellies, and do meaningful work in a world that respects human dignity.

Introduction

JOSEPH DORINSON
Long Island University

Paul Robeson is the greatest legend nobody knows. April 9, 1998, marked the 100th birthday of this brilliant, complex, athletic actor-singer-activist who was, arguably, the most prominent African American from the 1920s through the 1950s. He was the quintessential Renaissance man whose talents and achievements far transcended his first national arena, the football field. In fact, heavyweight boxing champion Joe Louis once said that he and Jackie Robinson, the first African American to play major league baseball in 1947 (with the Brooklyn Dodgers), owed everything to Robeson.[1]

Paul Robeson's life ended in loneliness and despair. His tragedy was the fact he was born too soon. To honor this man for all seasons on the centennial of his birth, a number of educational and cultural institutions—the New York Historical Society, Rutgers University, and Long Island University, to name only a few—sponsored programs celebrating his life and evaluating his legacy. Many of the essays in this volume were first presented at a one-day conference held at Long Island

University's Brooklyn Campus on Saturday, February 28, 1998. They cover many aspects of his life: His significance as a singer, his political activism, his effort to achieve solidarity between blacks and Jews, the important part his wife Eslanda played in his struggle, and the way conservative Americans rioted against him, refused to discuss him in the press, and attempted to silence his voice. Courses on Robeson are offered at colleges and high schools: A final essay explains how Robeson's multifaceted career can serve as the core of a course on African American or twentieth-century United States history.

Robeson gives us so much to celebrate, to mourn, and to ponder. Growing up in a segregated society, Robeson enjoyed a spectacular career as an athlete at Rutgers University. He won varsity letters in football, among other sports, despite being brutalized by teammates and opponents who often deliberately stepped on his hands with their metal cleats. Ever resilient, he picked himself up many times and went on to be named to Walter Camp's All-America Team, the first black so distinguished. Robeson might have won these honors at Princeton University, where his father, an ex-slave, was pastor at the African Methodist Episcopal Church. But then–President Woodrow Wilson of Princeton University refused to admit a black student. Today the street on which Robeson grew up is named Paul Robeson Place; his father's church still stands.

Robeson also towered above his Rutgers classmates academically: He was elected to Phi Beta Kappa and was class valedictorian. After graduation from Columbia University Law School, where he met his wife Eslanda Cardozo Goode (a political activist in her own right), he practiced law briefly before deciding to pursue the acting and singing careers that brought him critical praise and international fame.

It was Robeson's eloquence as a spokesman for human rights and social justice, however, that made him a true hero. Speaking twelve languages, he used his great bass-baritone voice and the lessons that he had learned on the gridiron to break down barriers of race, class, and ignorance. A natural ambassador of good will, he traveled the world over, championing peace and equality. He was also extremely generous: He donated his profits from Eugene O'Neill's play *All God's Chillun Got Wings*, in which he starred in 1934, to Jewish refugees fleeing Hitler.

But the Cold War marred the Hollywood happy ending. Because of his deep (like the river he exalted in memorable song) love for the Soviet Union and reverence for her people, coupled with his belief that the USSR was committed to equality for all races and cultures, Robeson spoke out spiritedly in defense of American-Soviet friendship.

Perhaps the greatest tragedy of the Cold War is that it led people with good intentions to side with ruthless leaders who placed ends before means, and support for a cause ahead of reasoned consid-

erations of alternative social visions. In the 1930s thousands of Americans joined a Communist Party committed to racial equality and organizing unskilled workers into labor unions, unaware they were serving the interests of Joseph Stalin, whose regime was secretly funding the party. When politics took a turn toward the right in the 1940s and '50s, politicians in the United States stifled freedom of expression and persecuted not only Communists, but liberals and socialists who shared some of their programs. Well-meaning Americans concerned about the Red Menace became the tools of the House Un-American Activities Committee (HUAC), Senator Joseph McCarthy, and a Republican Party anxious to demonize President Harry Truman and the Democrats as the men who "lost" China and Eastern Europe. If we are to condemn Robeson for defending an indefensible Soviet Union, his sin is no greater than every president from Truman to Reagan who supported murderous dictatorships in Asia, Africa, and Latin America simply because they were anti–Communist.

Robeson's international prominence made him a logical target of the zealous anti–Communists. He was red-listed and his passport was revoked. Like the protagonist in a Greek tragedy, he was marginalized, ostracized, and exiled in his own land. A victim of Cold War politics, he failed to receive the recognition that he richly deserved for his extraordinary achievements. Many young people today have never heard, or heard of, Paul Robeson. Older Americans remember him either as a singer or a victim of McCarthyism.

A year before the Robeson Conference, on April 3–5, 1997, I organized a three-day conference to honor Jackie Robinson on the fiftieth anniversary of the Brooklyn Dodger hero's historic breakthrough into major league baseball. (The proceedings of this conference have been published by M. E. Sharpe of Armonk,

New York.) Ironically, Robeson and Robinson crossed paths, if not swords, over remarks Robeson allegedly made in 1949. The great singer implicitly warned that American Negroes would not fight against the USSR if the Cold War turned hot. Exhorted to respond, Robinson went to Washington where, at a HUAC hearing, he criticized Robeson's stance. Overlooked by the national press was that he joined Robeson in denouncing segregation in both society and the armed forces in which he had served.

At the Robinson conference, Paul Robeson, Jr., discussed his father's famous exchange with Robinson. He offered new information, as did noted journalists Lester Rodney and Bill Mardo. Just before he died, Robinson, in fact, recanted his denunciation of Robeson and, in effect, apologized. Now that the Cold War is over and the former enemy is a newly-minted capitalist ally, despite a free-falling ruble, it is time for the nation as a whole to follow Robinson and reappraise Robeson, appreciate his achievements without justifying his Stalinism, and assess his entire persona, warts and all.

On balance, Robeson emerges as a giant whose flaws—and his unwavering defense of the Soviet Union even after Stalin's excesses came to light is a major flaw—are outweighed by his genius. In the face of rampant racism, young Paul triumphed at Rutgers as scholar and athlete. He invested the characters that he portrayed on stage and screen with a nobility invariably denied the Negro at that time. He spoke out against racism when it was neither fashionable nor safe. He went to the Spanish front in 1938 to show his solidarity with the freedom fighters against Franco's fascists. He introduced the *Ballad for Americans* (which the New York City Labor Chorus reprised at the conference) in 1939 on CBS radio. He helped the fledgling Congress of Industrial Organiza-

tions (CIO) organize black workers into the union in the early 1940s. In 1943 he reaped awards for his magnificent interpretation of Shakespeare's *Othello*. That same year he addressed major league baseball moguls and urged them to open the doors of the national pastime to meritorious men of color.

Then the Cold War came. Robeson was caught in the cross-fire. He went from national hero to national pariah. He slipped into obscurity. But a handful of unrepentant radicals, civil libertarians, and black activists remembered him. During the 1950s they sought to have his passport restored. Success greeted their efforts in 1958. Robeson reprised his Othello in 1959, which I witnessed at Stratford-on-Avon in England, and enjoyed two years of triumphant acclaim all over the world.

Ill health, perhaps triggered by a confrontation with Soviet Premier Nikita Khrushchev (whom he rebuked for continued anti–Semitism in the USSR) that may have produced a massive psychic breakdown, plagued his twilight years from 1961 until his death.[2] Unable to sing or appear publicly, Robeson was pushed aside by a throwaway culture. Robeson died in 1976, a shadow of the towering figure he had once been.

The place of Robeson's death was Philadelphia, his final home. Despite major studies of his life by Philip Foner and Martin Duberman, most school textbooks slight Robeson. To fill this void, I contacted Henry Foner, labor leader and trustee of the Paul Robeson Foundation, to set the springs of the Robeson Conference in motion. The youngest of four famous brothers, Henry contacted that amazingly prolific author, Howard Fast, who was also blacklisted and defied the agents of McCarthyism, serving time in prison rather than naming names. Not only did Fast conjure up a vivid recollection of the riot against Robeson at Peekskill, New York, in

1949, he also refused to accept payment for his appearance. The supremely energetic Foner also contacted the New York City Labor Chorus and gained the support of Paul Robeson, Jr. "Let a thousand flowers bloom," he exhorted, urging us to explore all aspects of his father's life.

I must at this point confess to a family skeleton rattling in the closet. Raised as a "Red-Diaper Baby," I was weaned on Robeson's music and inspired by his deeds. At Camp Kinderland, an interracial summer sleep-away facility for the children of radicals, Paul Robeson appeared as a frequent visitor. He would sing on Sundays for us with his unforgettable voice.

I remember the McCarthy Era with fear and trembling. Patriotic Americans hurled stones and tomatoes when I marched in May Day parades. Worse, in 1951 a right-wing, red-faced (from excessive drink, not political coloration) junior high school administrator ousted me from the school presidency and revoked the American Legion medal I had won on merit. At age fifteen I learned a painful lesson which propelled me to identify with other victims of the era, including Paul Robeson.

Imagine if Robeson had been born in 1958 instead of 1898. Alive today, he would be an athlete, scholar, lawyer, singer, actor, and political leader in an era when the doors of opportunity are open to African Americans that were closed tight during his lifetime. Such reflections are a way of measuring how far we have come in race relations in the past three hundred years.

And while we still have a long way to go, Robeson's heroic efforts to batter down those closed doors remind us how far back we started.[3]

Notes

1. As quoted by Ira Berkow, "Joe Louis Was There Earlier," *New York Times,* April 22, 1997, and cited in Joseph Dorinson, *The New York Times Newspaper in Education Curriculum Guide* (1997), 97.

2. As reported by Robert Robinson, *Black on Red: My 44 Years Inside the Soviet Union: An Autobiography,* with Jonathan Slevin (Washington, D.C., Acropolis Books, 1988), 319.

3. Much of this introduction appeared in an op-ed article, Joseph Dorinson, "Paul Robeson, All-American," *New York Daily News* (April 6, 1993), 33. For details of Robeson's multifaceted life, see especially, Philip S. Foner, ed., *Paul Robeson Speaks: Writings, Speeches, Interviews 1918–1974* (New York: Braziller, 1978); Lenwood G. Davis, *A Paul Robeson Research Guide and Selected Annotated Bibliography* (Westport: Greenwood, 1982) and *A Paul Robeson Handbook: Everything You Wanted to Know About Paul Robeson* (Kearney: Morris Publishing, 1998); Martin Bauml Duberman, *Paul Robeson* (New York: Knopf, 1988); Susan Robeson, *The Whole World in His Hands: A Pictorial Biography of Paul Robeson* (New York: Carol Publishing, 1981); Jeffrey C. Stewart, ed., *Paul Robeson: Artist and Citizen* (New Brunswick: Rutgers University Press for the Paul Robeson Cultural Center, 1998). Sheila Tully Boyle and Andrew Bunie generously allowed us to reprint chapter three of their biography, *Paul Robeson: The Years of Promise and Achievement* (Amherst: University of Massachusetts Press, 2001).

The Early Years:
Childhood, Sports,
and College

African Americans: Childhood in Slavery, Childlike in Freedom … and Paul Robeson as Child and Parent

JOSEPH ILLICK
San Francisco State University

All of us have been children, and many of us have raised or are raising children. We cannot doubt how difficult it is to understand this stage of life, how elusive its complexities are. Yet we try, as historians, to capture the worlds of the young, governed as we are by our prejudices and hampered by the meager sources available to us.

What was it like to be a child in slavery? Was the situation unique, virtually unavailable to us through our own experience, or were its characteristics universal enough to lie within our comprehension? One way to answer these questions is to study the attempts of earlier Americans to present slave childhood, since we may be better aware of their limitations than our own.

Frederick Douglass, the best known of many escaped slaves who published narratives before the Civil War, probably said more about his childhood than any of his peers. Writing in 1845, he recalled that his mother was black and his father was white — and unknown to him. His mother was almost unknown, since he was with her, but briefly, only four or five times. She died when he was about seven; he did not know the date of his birth. He witnessed whippings of slaves, and he heard their songs ("a testimony against slavery, and a prayer to God for deliverance"). He was inadequately clothed, fed with the other children "like so many pigs," and schooled in the cruelties of masters. He learned to lie, and he was taught to read by a mistress who was unacquainted with Southern custom (soon enough her "tender heart became stone," the effect of slavery). Education led him to "abhor and detest" his masters. He was sold at ten or eleven and became a field hand. He was whipped and finally fought back, an act which "revived within me the sense of my own manhood."[1] He was no longer a child.

Douglass remembered his childhood at three different times in his life — and in three different ways. William McFeely, his biographer, observes that in 1845 his account "is the brief, pungent declaration of freedom of a runaway slave writing a powerful antislavery tract." In 1855 "a mature writer gives deeper reflections on slavery. By then, Douglass could pause longer over the story of his life as a slave, but voids in it suggest that there were unbearable memories that had to be omitted." In 1881, revised in 1892, his was "the memoir of a famous man relishing his honors while smarting from those denied him."[2] It is only in the second volume that we meet his grandmother and learn that she was his primary caretaker, hear the story of his wrenching separation from her, and discover that he had siblings who were strangers to him. The life becomes larger and, perhaps, slave childhood becomes more familiar. But for all the details Douglass provides us, we would be hard put to say we understand him.

Popular as Douglass's *Narrative* was — it sold 30,000 copies in America and Europe in the five years after its publication — it hardly matched the celebrity of *Uncle Tom's Cabin*, which was serialized in the *National Era* (Washington, D.C.) in 1851 and 1852, and published as a book that sold 300,000 copies during its first year on the market. Harriet Beecher Stowe's novel was surely the way most Americans above the Mason-Dixon line learned about slavery and African-American childhood. Although it is most often remembered, at least popularly, for the characters it presents — Uncle Tom, of course, the God-fearing slave who submits to his masters, expecting his reward in Heaven; Simon Legree, who goads Tom to insubordina-

tion and then sends him to the hereafter; Sambo, who mimics master Legree until Tom converts him — it has not been a story immediately associated with children. But the death of Little Eva (like Tom, a model of Christian belief) and the antics of Topsy (susceptible to Eva and devastated by her death) provide vivid memories. In fact, children play a critical part in its plot development.[3]

The first third of *Uncle Tom's Cabin* is focused not on Uncle Tom, who unhappily but dutifully submits to his sale away from his Kentucky family into the lower South, but on Eliza's escape from slavery, the catalyst for her unexpected behavior being the pending disposal of her child Harry. Tom's wife Aunt Chloe observes about the trade in children: "Don't dey tear the suckin' baby right off his mother's breast, and sell him, and der little children as is crying and holding on by her clothes, — don't dey pull 'em off and sells em?" And only then: "Don't dey tear husband and wife apart?"[4] The planter's wife, Mrs. Shelby, confronts her husband with the same sentiment when she learns of the sale: "I have taught them [the slaves] the duties of the family, of parent and child, and husband and wife; and how can I bear to have this open acknowledgment that we care for no tie, no duty, no relation, however sacred, compared with money?"[5] Eliza is propelled to escape by maternal love, and Mrs. Shelby applauds her for the same reason.[6] Three other mothers and their respective children are separated by sales in the novel, and in one of these instances the mother commits suicide.[7]

In the second part of the novel the major character is the exemplary Little Eva, daughter of Uncle Tom's new owner St. Clare, a kindred spirit with Tom, an opposite number to the slave child Topsy. "They stood as representatives of their races. The Saxon, born of ages of cultivation, command, education, physical and moral eminence; the Afric, born of ages of oppression, submission, ignorance, toil, and vice."[8] While Miss Ophelia, cousin to St. Clare, asserts that Topsy's kleptomania can be remedied only with the whip, Eva cures her with kindness. She then tries unsuccessfully to convince her cousin that whipping is cruel and wicked, an issue then debated by her father and her uncle, the former suggesting the slave system carries the potential for rebellion (led by the enslaved sons of *white* fathers), the latter lamenting the difficulty of training planters' children under the system — "It gives too free scope to the passions"— and yet asserting that it had made his son "manly and courageous."[9]

The third and shortest part of the novel commences when kind master St. Clare dies and Tom is passed on to the brute Legree. Although the tension between the slave and his new owner dominates this section, a complementary theme is the emerging alliance between cynical Cassy, Legree's mistress, and Emmeline, a girl sold at auction (along with Tom) to Legree. Cassy, who turns out to be the long-lost mother of Eliza, succumbs to the "child-like spirit" of Emmeline, and they are able to escape together when Tom refuses to reveal their whereabouts to Legree, who murders Tom in response.

At the time *Uncle Tom's Cabin* was written, many slave narratives existed, though most of them said little about childhood.[10] Stowe drew upon these accounts, especially those of Josiah Henson and Henry Bibb, and she wrote to Frederick Douglass for information about the lower South. *Uncle Tom's Cabin*, like those narratives, stressed a major theme: the slave's will to be free.[11] Comments one of Stowe's biographers: "seeing heroism in black slaves was a new experience for the nation."[12] We can agree upon the nobility of Stowe's goal while recognizing that it would not contribute to her understanding of slave childhood unless she had been intent on explaining the youthful origins of the will to be free, which neither the slave narratives, she, nor Douglass investigated.

Even more than these accounts, Stowe drew upon Theodore Dwight Weld's *American Slavery as It Is*, which also includes little material about slave childhood. This antislavery tract does concede that immediately previous to and after childbirth a women was given an easier work load. She then carried her infant to the fields, sometimes accompanied by a young child attendant (Weld included a story of a six year old who purposely suffocated her charge); otherwise, she placed the infant under a tree or simply carried it on her back as she toiled. The growing child was depicted as insufficiently fed and clothed, often running naked, and in danger of being sold away from its mother.[13]

In addition to the slave narratives, Weld's book, and some press accounts, Stowe drew upon a brief visit to Kentucky, experiences of fugitives (and abolitionists) traveling through Cincinnati while her husband taught at Lane Seminary, and her employment of colored domestic servants. Despite (or because of) these limited contacts with slavery, she was sensitive to challenges to her reliability. When critics questioned the authenticity of *Uncle Tom's Cabin*, Stowe documented her work in *The Key to Uncle Tom's Cabin*— not a list of her sources but a corroboration of her facts. In this lengthy tract she drew on legal opinion to demonstrate that no parallel existed between the parent-child and the master-slave relation. She devoted a major chapter to the separation of families.[14] But in *The Key*, as in the novel itself, Stowe did not much illuminate the actual living conditions of enslaved African-American children, however much she may have captured their plight through their parents' eyes— which, it seems fair (and perhaps obvious) to say, meant through her own eyes.

Uncle Tom's Cabin is very much a novel of its times, a product of the moral prejudices and emotional boundaries we associate with the Victorians. Unsurprisingly, it displays the Victorian perspective toward childhood, granting children special qualities *along with the black slaves.* Stowe observes: "Now, there is no more use in making believe [to] be angry with a negro than with a child; both instinctively see the true state of the case, through all attempts to effect the contrary...."[15] This stance must not be confused with the proslavery argument that slaves were indeed childlike and, hence, bondage was their appropriate state. (This had not been the initial European perception of the African. As George Fredrickson notes: "Prior to the 1830s, black subordination was the practice of white Americans, and the inferiority of the Negro was undoubtedly a common assumption, but open assertions of *permanent* inferiority were exceedingly rare."[16]) However, the abolitionist attack on slavery led to the Southern white defense that blacks were inherently suited to the institution and unfit for freedom, that they were, in fact, happy only under the guidance of white masters. While white servitude had naturally disintegrated, permanent black slavery was compatible with white liberty and equality. By the 1840s scientific evidence was marshaled to show that blacks constituted a separate, biologically inferior species.

Stowe's position was akin to that of the Unitarian pastor in New York who, on determining that the Negro's "nature is singularly childlike, affectionate, docile, and patient," concluded that it was un–Christian to oppress such a person. Indeed, weren't Negro characteristics Christian virtues?[17] Contrast this with the message Frederick Douglass meant to convey — that resistance characterized his passage from childhood to adulthood. My simple point is that white writing, Northern as well as

Southern, about black childhood was unable to transcend prevailing stereotypes. (That white Northerners could not shake their ideas of black inferiority is a message that even our most conventional history books now embrace: When Republicans embraced the idea of Negro franchise after the Civil War it was not a consequence of believing in racial equality but, rather, a matter of political expediency.)

White leaders in the postwar South, in an expression of *their* understanding of the consequences of slave childhood, adopted a paternalistic attitude toward blacks, expecting that these newly created citizens would turn as children to their political fathers. These leaders simply assumed segregation and, in fact, were essentially racist. As Darwinism became popular, they — and most other Americans of European stock — accepted it as a newer justification for hierarchical assumptions. This was, in fact, a more benign point of view than another late nineteenth-century opinion: that blacks had degenerated since being freed from slavery.[18] In either case, in the postwar period childhood was seen as the whole stage of Negro life, and no effort was made to understand it.

In the American family the black-as-child was, at best, a *foster* member. This status was graphically illustrated in D. W. Griffith's film *The Birth of a Nation* (1915), based on the Negrophobe Thomas Dixon's novel *The Clansman* (1905), where the African American is described as "half child, half animal." Griffith, whose father had fought for the Confederacy and later lost the family fortune, looked back fondly to a paternalistic South where all black slaves acted as children; after the War, freed blacks (save for a few "old faithful") behaved like animals, most notably the predatory males, until put in their place by the Ku Klux Klan.

This enormously popular movie, characterized by President Woodrow Wilson as "writing history with lightning," set the stage for the many films in which blacks, or rather black *men*, performed as inferiors, their characteristic depiction until World War II.[19] Even whites who considered themselves friends of the African American promulgated this stereotype, such as the prominent Atlantan who wrote in 1906: "The Negro race is a child race. We are a strong race, their guardians." In Walter Hines Page's novel *The Southerner* (1909), a character observes: "the Negro is a child in civilization.... Let us train him.... Let us teach him to do productive work, teach him to be a help, to support himself, to do useful things, to be a man, to build up his family life."[20]

The use of the male pronoun in this last passage, the admonition "to be a man," points to the assumption implicit in the white discussion of blacks ever since the word "child" had been introduced in the pre–Civil War years: not the African American but the African American *male* was the subject. This focus might be attributed to the exclusivity of male suffrage in defining an American citizen or to the fact that men primarily created the image of black-as-child.

Deeper feelings also contributed to the focus on the male. The child/animal dichotomy suggests that a savage who is feared must be domesticated — into a child who is either permanently immature (the Negrophobe viewpoint) or educable (the Negrophile perspective). The dichotomy was perpetuated into the twentieth century. Donald Bogle entitles his "interpretive history of blacks in American films" *Toms, Coons, Mulattoes, Mammies, and Bucks.* Toms are, of course, faithful and submissive, while coons are lazy and unreliable; but both exhibit childlike characteristics in contrast to the undesirable, animal-like bucks.[21]

But what of mammies and mulattoes? Both are women, the former portrayed as dark, fat, and omnicompetent, the latter light, curvaceous, and sexy. One raises boys, the other tempts men — the madonna and the whore. Historian Catherine Clinton asserts that the mammy is almost absent from the documents of ante-bellum America; she "was created by white Southerners to redeem the relationship between black women and white men ... a counterpoint to the octoroon concubine, the light-skinned product of a 'white man's lust' who was habitually victimized by slaveowners' sexual appetites."[22] Probably Clinton is guessing about the motive, but she is correct in pointing to the post–Civil War emergence of fond Southern white memories of the mammy as child rearer and household organizer.[23]

Indeed, it is undeniable that Southern white children in the prewar years were cared for by black mammies (or whatever they were called), just as white children had black playmates. Eugene Genovese, who is convinced of the *real* presence of the mammy, captures both her strength and her weakness. "More than any other slave, she had absorbed the paternalist ethos and accepted her place in a system of reciprocal obligations defined from above." Strong because she operated resourcefully and responsibly within the system, she was weak because she could not pass her power to other blacks without making them even more dependent.[24] She was domesticated, though hardly made childlike, from the beginning and, hence, even more reassuring than a tom or a coon. Unlike the mulatto, she was neither a reminder of interracial sex nor a prod to the libido. That the most famous rendition of her character came from a white man in blackface — Al Jolson singing "My Mammy" — adds irony to the perspective.[25] The second most famous, by Hattie McDaniel in the 1939 film *Gone with the Wind,* won the only Oscar awarded to a black before Sidney Poitier in the 1960s.

A turning point in understanding the black male character came in 1941 when anthropologist Melville Herskovitz published *The Myth of the Negro Past*. Herskovitz accused scholars and policy-makers of basing their work on myths that supported race prejudice, the first one of which was "Negroes are naturally of a childlike character...." Pointing to the sophistication of an African world view, he concluded that "such maladjustments to the American scene as characterize Negro life are to be ascribed largely to the social and economic handicaps these folks have suffered, rather than to any inability to cope with the realities of life."[26] Such reasoning was, of course, lost on people such as George Wallace, a segregationist when he began his four terms (elected in 1962, 1970, 1974, 1982) as governor of Alabama, who reportedly gave barracks lectures during World War II defending his white supremacist position: "I don't hate them. The colored are fine in their place. But they're just like children and it's not something that's going to change. It's written in stone."[27] When it proved not to be, Wallace recanted.

The courage demonstrated by African Americans during the civil rights struggle surprised most white Americans, as indeed it should have. The long and concerted effort to marginalize blacks and rationalize such treatment on the basis of their being essentially childlike, weak and vulnerable was confounded by their willingness to confront their enemies at lunch counters, schools, and court houses, to create public demonstrations where sometimes their very lives were at stake.

History students should have been among those surprised Americans. The most popular college text, *The Growth of the American Republic* by Samuel Eliot Morison and Henry Steele Commager (4th edition, 1950; 6th printing, 1955), under the heading "The Slave," observed: "As for Sambo, whose wrongs moved the abolitionists to wrath and tears, there is some reason to believe that he suffered less than any other class in the South from its 'peculiar institution.' The majority of slaves were adequately fed, well cared for, and apparently happy.... Although brought to America by force, the incurably optimistic Negro soon became attached to the country, and devoted to his 'white folks.'"[28]

Nevertheless, the mainstream historical view was changing. Yet the two historians who had such a profound effect on post World War II writing about slavery, Kenneth Stampp and Stanley Elkins, offered few observations about childhood. "Parents frequently had little to do with the raising of their children; and children soon learned that their parents were neither the fount of wisdom nor the seat of authority," noted Stampp. He pointed out that slaves were to be governed by maintaining strict discipline and placing them in awe of the master's power, while making them aware of their own inferiority and helplessness, but supplied no details as to how these principles would be practiced in raising children.[29] Elkins's interpretation is somewhat different: "For the Negro child ... the plantation offered no really satisfactory father-image other than the master ... the mother's role loomed far larger.... She controlled those few activities—household care, preparation of food, and rearing of children—that were left to the slave family."[30] Like Stampp, Elkins supplied no details of child rearing, but theoretically these were unnecessary to his explanation. American slavery paralleled the Nazi concentration camp where "infantile personality features could be induced in a relatively short time among blacks...."[31]

Stampp and Elkins emphasized the power of the white master and his institutions. John Blassingame focused on the slave community and, quite logically, turned to the slave narratives among other sources.[32] He asserted that planters often yielded to parents "complete control of their children," even to the point of delegating punishment. Although work schedules prevented parents from providing much care for newborns or securing them adequate diets, they could and did lavish love upon their young. Early years in slavery were relatively pleasant. Parents tried to serve as role models, instill morality, and "shield their children from abuse and teach them how to survive in bondage."[33]

Eugene Genovese, who wrote not from the vantage point of the slave community but from the perspective of a patriarchal system he claimed was pervasive, told a story similar in some ways to Blassingame's. Slaveholders "could not abide their slaves' living together without outside interference," thus depriving adult males of a provider's role. Masters refused to dignify slaves' marriages or legitimize their offspring, and abused them in front of their families — indeed, raped men's wives and took away their children. Nevertheless, most male slaves somehow "overcame all obstacles and provided a positive male image for their wives and children ... even in those cabins without resident fathers." Women had a harder time than the men because the burden of childbearing was added to that of field labor. But they showered love on their newborns, nursing as long as the master would allow, and though they saw their growing children only briefly in the evening and on weekends, the youngsters reciprocated their love, a feeling articulated in the narratives. Children had the pleasure of long childhoods, not being assigned any chores before the age of eight, often enough free of serious labor until twelve or even longer. Though cared for only casually (the nursing of small children by larger ones was dangerous), dressed without regard for sexual decency, and fed like animals (but well enough nutritionally), they played games involving whipping and auctioning (often with their white counterparts) designed to parry the brutal aspects of the system, while being taught survival tactics by their parents and doted upon "as if they were playthings or pets" by their masters and mistresses, whom they frequently idolized for life.[34]

The novel approach of Robert Fogel and Stanley Engerman lifted the slave system out of a pre-modern setting and set it in the context of modern capitalism, focusing on the functioning of the slave economy, quantifying the sources, and noting, for example, that the typical field hand was a more efficient worker than his white counterpart. (Actually, Fogel and Engerman saw the economy as capitalistic but labor relations as medieval.[35]) Denying that the "plantation regime ... was so cruel, the exploitation so severe, the repression so complete that blacks were thoroughly demoralized by it," Fogel and Engerman asserted that slaves were well fed, sheltered, and clothed, received more than adequate health care (the death rate of slave infants was the same as that of white infants), and lived in families highly respected by planters, whose economic interest was to preserve domestic stability. Thus: "Most slave sales were either of whole families or of individuals who were at an age when it would have been normal for them to have left the family."[36] Miscegenation was not sanctioned and seldom occurred. Motherhood typically began after age twenty among women who were mature and married. Children were well cared for by mothers in families dominated not by women but by their husbands. True, whipping persisted, but only because "the cost of substituting hunger and incarceration for the lash was greater for the slaveowner than for the northern employer of free labor."[37]

Herbert Gutman devoted a book to

refuting *Time on the Cross*, which he termed "a profoundly flawed work" both conceptually and evidentially. Gutman disputed the assertion that slave behavior could be understood solely as a response to the masters' economic incentives, as Fogel and Engerman would have it. More specifically, he took sharp issue with the contention that slave sales did not break up families, pointing out not only that even if older children were involuntarily separated from parents and siblings the family was indeed broken, but also that the quantitative evidence failed to support the contention that fathers, mothers, or younger children were not sold away from one another. Indeed, he challenged the declaration that there was a stable nuclear family among slaves, again citing the absence of evidence.[38]

Gutman was not simply at odds with the quantitative methodology used by Fogel and Engerman but with the "prevalent 'models' of slave socialization and behavior that characterize much of the writing of slave history. Such 'models' usually greatly minimize and sometimes entirely ignore the adaptive capacities of African slaves and several generations of Afro-American slaves."[39] Adaptation could be seen only by studying behavior over time; the end result of such study would be an understanding of slave culture. Gutman gives several examples. Regarding the issue of slave separation through sales, he pointed to a dynamic situation wherein families could go through cycles of destruction, construction, and dispersal, which culminated in the creation of community and a slave culture.[40] Looking at the larger picture enabled him to explain how naming practices not only defined kinship but relationships to non-blood-related others, black and white.[41] Scrutinizing six communities, he observed slaves making similar choices and being moved by common customs, indicating that a social class was taking shape as its members adapted to the harsh circumstances of a century's enslavement.[42] As Gutman phrased it, it was first important to know *who the slave was*— or, while one should grasp how owners treated slaves, it was critical to recognize that how slaves behaved "depended on far more than their 'treatment.'"[43]

Thomas Webber soon demonstrated a problem of putting this admonition into practice. Gutman embraced a theory of biculturation (learning and practicing both mainstream and ethnic culture simultaneously). "What a slave child learned always depended upon how that child was taught and who [master? parent?] taught that child."[44] Webber, using a similar perspective ("the people of the [slave] quarter community are best understood as a society within a society"), argued that the planter class aimed to have slaves internalize values which would make them conscious of their own inferiority. "Overflowing with awe, respect, and childlike affection for the planter and his family," they would then cheerfully accept the rules of slave behavior and be convinced that slavery was not only right but the best of all possible worlds. Slaves were kept ignorant of the outside world and the written word, denied privacy, forbidden to recall their African past, and refused the very privileges that defined their white counterparts as adults.[45] While Webber argued that most of the values, attitudes, and understandings taught by white masters were not accepted by black slaves, he conceded that one must look deep into the slave literature to reach this conclusion. In other words, even if slaves were not convinced by their masters, they had to disguise their true beliefs. How long this masquerade persisted, whether it still goes on, is a matter of debate.[46]

Gutman also observed that, although most slave communities originated in the eighteenth century, no era of Afro-

American history had been so neglected. Obviously, an understanding of slave culture would depend on filling this void. Allan Kulikoff has played the major role in rising to this challenge, tracing family formation from the late seventeenth to the mid-eighteenth century in Tidewater, Maryland, observing that while white owners determined the external boundaries of slaves' lives, the blacks themselves determined relationships among family members. They adapted their African heritage — primarily, their experience with kinship — to a new environment and by the 1750s embraced a life cycle characterized by infancy (being nursed by mother), childhood (spent in the company of peers, often working part-time), and adolescence (leaving home but frequently living with kin and taking on full-time work, 10 to 14 years of age); women typically married in their late teens, men in their mid- to late twenties.[47]

The years since the mid–1970s have witnessed a scholarly outpouring of material on African-American children in slavery. Attention has been paid to the heritage of Africa — that is, west and west-central Africa where the great variation in climate and vegetation suggests the diversity in ways of living, not to mention the existence of several hundred mutually unintelligible languages. American scholars have searched out elements of continuity, those aspects of African life which could have been transferred to the New World. They have also been interested in kinship systems and community.[48] More specifically, newborn naming, infant care and mortality, and accessibility to mothers have been matters explored, as well as childhood disease and death.[49] Children's play, their education, and their nutrition have been examined.[50] So, too, has the sale of the young.[51] Finally, historians have differentiated slave children's situations by time and place.[52]

It is hardly a surprise — indeed, it is a matter of good fortune — that during the past five years two books on African-American childhood should be published: Wilma King's *Stolen Childhood: Slave Youth in Nineteenth-Century America* (Bloomington, 1995) and Marie Jenkins Schwartz's *Born in Bondage: Growing Up Enslaved in the Ante-Bellum South* (Cambridge, 2000). Both authors are quick to justify the demographic significance of their undertakings, pointing out that the bulk of the slave population in the pre–Civil War South was under twenty years old. Otherwise, they proceed from rather different perspectives. King argues that "enslaved children had virtually no childhood because they entered the work place early and were more readily subjected to arbitrary plantation authority, punishments, and separations.... Furthermore, parents tried to protect their offspring, who learned that mothers and fathers were also vulnerable to cruelties."[53] Schwartz observes: "By law, slaveholders determined the conditions under which bonded children grew to adulthood.... But the owners were unwilling to carry out the work of child rearing themselves and left these tasks to the slaves ... slaves gladly accepted the responsibility.... As they grew, children found themselves torn between the demands of owners and those of parents."[54] Seldom, however, are these two studies contradictory; often they are complementary. In breaking ground, they raise some interesting questions.

Stolen Childhood is arranged topically. In its opening chapter, which focuses on family, King notes: "If childhood was a special time for enslaved children, it was because their parents made it so."[55] Since most evidence, including King's ("early separation of mothers and children"[56]), points to parental inaccessibility, what were children doing — and with whom — during those early critical years? It seems unlikely that otherwise-engaged parents could communicate to children in any sustained way.

In her second chapter King points to "the quantum leap from childhood into the world of work" that occurred around the age of ten, although one former slave remembered that, "Us chillen start to work soon's us could toddle."[57] The distinctiveness of slavery is diminished when comparisons are made with other childhoods on this matter. Elliott West tells of frontier children toiling as early as three, while the experience of the working-class young in America's industrial cities was frequently to begin the grind by age ten.[58]

Concerning play, the heart of the third chapter (which no doubt provides a partial answer to the question raised in the first chapter about what children were doing and with whom), is it possible to know (or, at least, shrewdly guess) how white playmates in childhood conditioned the race relations in adulthood?

In considering education (chapter four), King attributes unusual accomplishment to parents who "taught their youngsters how to tolerate inhumane acts and degradation while maintaining their humanity and keeping their spirit intact," and "how to forge a balance between social courtesies to whites and their own self-esteem."[59] Since parents were only occasionally accessible, how were they able to teach such delicate lessons? Not through corporal punishment (the subject of chapter five), though King observes that "some slave parents" whipped their children.[60] A comparison with the treatment of white children might be illuminating, since corporal punishment remained common practice.

Born in Bondage, the beneficiary of *Stolen Childhood*, answers some of these questions. Its perspective is developmental. "Slavery was a relationship between people, the terms of which had to be ne-gotiated and renegotiated to reflect child development."[61] Owners held primarily economic goals, but to realize these goals they had to negotiate with parents determined to protect their children who, in turn, learned to protect themselves. Of course, the bargaining was not between equals, but that any negotiation was necessary may come as a surprise; even though Blassingame had asserted that planters ceded control of children to parents, Gutman had pointed to Afro-American adaptation as a means to the creation of a distinctive culture, and Webber had emphasized black resistance to white efforts at education.

According to Schwartz, the master-slave negotiations began with pregnancy, when slave women sought special accommodation for their condition, and it continued with childbirth, when they resisted the meddling of the owners. And so it went with housing, post-natal work schedules, nursing and weaning, infant care. Financially driven planters wanted females in the labor force, but they also needed to respond to slaves' wishes if they were to have healthy children in a future work force. (One of Schwartz's contributions is to distinguish here, and in other sections of the book, between practices in Virginia's mixed farming economy and procedures on the cotton and rice plantations farther south.)

Owners considered early childhood (ages two to five) to be a crucial time; "confident of their right to interject themselves between parent and child," their goal was "to transfer the love and allegiance of the children from parents to themselves."[62] Parents resisted, but faced a dilemma: "how could they teach the rituals that passed for racial etiquette in southern society, without imparting to their children a sense of inferiority and without diminishing their own worth in the eyes of their sons and daughters?"[63] King raised the very same question. Schwartz argues that parents taught by example: They deferred to owners who wanted work habits speeded up or improved, only to return to their own pace and methods when the owners were out of sight. "Such scenes, played out repeatedly, required no explanation." Yet, "youngsters saw little of their parents during the six-day work week."[64] Must we assume that young children were fast learners?

Some black and white children who played together at this age "produced friendships that lasted a lifetime."[65] However, inequality was inherent from the outset, as each learned to play the roles which would govern their lives, roles Schwartz labels the myth of Southern paternalism. The question is how deeply the myth penetrated consciousness on either side. Some of the sources (both slaveholder records and slave narratives,[66] especially those created by the WPA) strongly suggest that blacks were less persuaded than whites.

During the middle years, five to eight or ten years, owners switched from indulgence to the rod, and parents also relied on corporal punishment—the former for not working, rule breaking, property destruction, insolence; the latter out of concern for the health and safety of the children, who understood the distinction between masters' and parents' motives. The children resisted all adults, being intent on play. But work descended on them, gradually rather than as a "quantum leap," since they were already physically capable of working alongside adults in the field.[67] Their parents opposed their being pushed into this heavy toil, however, while owners denied them food and clothes if they refused to work.

"Adolescence held special perils for young slaves," says Schwartz. "As they took up the hoe and the plow, and donned the clothing of adults, teenagers entered a world characterized by hard work, but also by the threat of sale and, for girls, sexual exploitation."[68] The separation from families, the focus of *Uncle Tom's Cabin*, involved about ten percent of adolescent slaves from the upper South. But parents were so affected by the potential loss of their children that they might refuse to complete the planters' work.

In *Uncle Tom's Cabin* Stowe generally characterized slaves as victims, most of whom passively accepted their fate despite their desire for freedom (which, of course, several acted upon). Schwartz has depicted slaves as active in determining their own destinies; their choices were not simply bondage or freedom but a negotiated role within slavery. It is a convincing interpretation, for it explains slaves' survival without diminishing the obstacles they faced. And it includes a persuasive perspective on how slave children were prepared for adulthood.

Paul Robeson's father was born a slave in Martin County, North Carolina. In 1860, at the age of fifteen, William Drew Robeson escaped across the Maryland border to Pennsylvania, worked for the Union Army during the Civil War, attended elementary school after the War and went on to Lincoln University, where he received an A.B. (1873) and a Bachelor of Sacred Theology (1876). At Lincoln he met Maria Louisa Bustill, born in Philadelphia in 1853 to a distinguished family. William and Maria married in 1878. Paul was born in 1898, the youngest of six children who survived infancy.[69]

No specific information survives concerning Maria's childhood. Her grandfather, Cyrus Bustill, was in 1787 a founder of the Free African Society, the first mutual aid society for American Negroes. Paul knew that there were artists, teachers, and scholars on his mother's side of the family, but he could not remember her, only the circumstances of her funeral when he was six. Many years later he recorded an album entitled "Songs of Free Men," one of which was "Sometimes I Feel Like a Motherless Child." Yet, he observes in his autobiography: "There must have been moments when I felt the sorrows of a motherless child, but what I most remember from my youngest days was an abiding sense of comfort and security." His father, his siblings, nearby kin, the close-knit community — all contributed to his upbringing.[70]

But far more than anyone else, it was his father, the ex-slave, who shaped his early life. "The glory of my boyhood years was my father," he recalled in the opening line of his autobiography. "I loved him like no one in all the world."[71] Loved also by the members of his community (he was pastor of the Witherspoon Presbyterian Church in Princeton when Paul was born), William Drew Robeson commanded the respect of whites as well, according to his son. The text of William's life was, in Paul's words, "loyalty to one's convictions," and he appears to have taught that lesson in the most durable way — by example. Widowed father and semi-orphaned son, separated by more than half a century in age, lived alone together. "I readily yielded to his quiet discipline." In public Paul walked proudly by the older man's side. "There was no hint of servility in my father's make-up. Just as in his youth he had refused to remain a slave, so in all the years of his manhood he disdained to be an Uncle Tom. From him we learned, and never doubted it, that the Negro was in every way the equal of the white man."[72]

That Paul Robeson was able to act on these principles in his adolescence and adult life is abundantly clear. But he was not unconflicted. Wilma King and Marie Jenkins Schwartz both observed that slave parents faced the delicate task of teaching their children racial etiquette without imparting a sense of inferiority. Reverend Robeson counseled his son to avoid confrontation yet be assertive. Paul was cap-

able of walking that line, yet he later confessed to a friend that some of his experiences "aroused intense fury and conflict within him." And he appears to have carried an added burden of guilt because he believed he had an easier time in white America than his fellow Negroes.[73]

He leaned constantly on the example of his father as a citizen — but not as a family man; he failed to be the parent his own father was. In 1921 Paul married Eslanda Cardozo Goode, whose lineage was even more distinguished than that of Paul's maternal ancestors. But, as one of his friends observed: "He let things happen, and she tried to make them happen." And even after they wed, Paul remained attracted for several years to another woman, the prelude to many affairs. The relationship ran hot and cold. Essie decided to become pregnant without consulting Paul, and when she succeeded he took the news with mixed feelings, somewhat resentful. When Paul Robeson, Jr., was born in 1927, his father was concertizing in Europe — and traveling with a young woman — but hurriedly returned six weeks later when he learned Essie was ill. Soon he was back in Europe with Essie; Paul Jr., or Pauli, stayed with his grandmother.[74]

At age two-and-a-half a series of illnesses led to Pauli's hospitalization; Essie thought Paul was uninvolved. "The only times you are the least bit interested in him," she wrote sometime later, "are the rare occasions when you deem it suitable or befitting the artist to mention such prosaic things as children and parenthood." In response to an angry letter from Essie about one of his affairs, Paul referred to his son simply as "the boy." Possibly because Essie also was having an affair, her next pregnancy appears to have ended with an abortion. Paul withheld money from his family when pressing the reluctant Essie for a divorce. Pauli continued to be cared for by Essie's mother, and Essie quoted

A beaming Paul Robeson is surrounded by family: wife Essie, son Paul, Jr., daughter-in-law Marilyn (far left), and grandchildren Susan and David (1957). Courtesy of Paul Robeson, Jr.

Paul as saying, "I have no fatherly instincts about him at all." At this time Pauli was seven and living in New York while his parents resided in the Soviet Union. When Essie next reported Paul was "interested in Pauli," the child was in Moscow, while she and Paul were in Cairo. The family reunited when Pauli was ten and soon settled in Harlem in 1939. But Paul was frequently away, once sending a wire to his son, which, according to Essie, thrilled him but also confused him "with the signature Paul Robeson. Pauli couldn't understand why it wasn't signed Daddy."[75]

Paul Robeson had fallen into the absent-father syndrome which, when it became noticeable among African Americans in the twentieth century, was often attrib-uted to the circumstances of slavery. Such reasoning could not be applied to the Robeson family. We might guess that the premature death of his mother contributed to his never-ending search for the right woman, which distracted him from his son; but it would be no more than a guess. Robeson's situation demonstrates the limits of generalization about the conditions of childhood.

Notes

1. Frederick Douglass, *Narrative of the Life of Frederick Douglass…* (1845); *My Bondage and My Freedom* (1855); *Life and Times of…* (1881). Quotes are from the *Narrative.*

2. William S. McFeely, *Frederick Douglass* (New York, 1991), 7.

3. This interpretation is mine. Consult Joan D. Hedrick's first-rate *Harriet Beecher Stowe: A Life* (New York, 1994) for other insights into the novel and the writing of it. Thomas F. Gossett, in *Uncle Tom's Cabin and American Culture* (Dallas, 1985), devotes several chapters to the writing of the book, several more to its reception (by Northerners and Southerners, whites and blacks, even historians), as well as some pages to its life on the stage, from the time of its publication until the 1970s. See also Eric J. Sundquist, ed., *New Essays on Uncle Tom's Cabin* (New York, 1986).

4. Harriet Beecher Stowe, *Uncle Tom's Cabin; or, Life Among the Lowly* (orig. pub. Boston & Cleveland, 1852; Garden City, NY, 1960), 73.

5. *Ibid.*, 49.

6. *Ibid.*, 67, 93.

7. *Ibid.*, 146–147, 156–159, 388.

8. *Ibid.*, 286.

9. *Ibid.*, 308–314.

10. These pieces of literature, written by ex-slaves or by white abolitionists, or dictated to abolitionists, are the subject of Marion Wilson Starling, *The Slave Narrative: Its Place in American History* (Boston, 1981) and Charles T. Davis and Henry Louis Gates, Jr., eds., *The Slave's Narrative* (New York, 1985). Both contain bibliographies. John Blassingame's Introduction to his *Slave Testimony: Two Centuries of Letters, Speeches, Interviews, and Autobiographies* (Baton Rouge, 1977) is a guide to the reliability of the narratives. Davis and Gates, and Blassingame as well, also take up the subject of the interviews with former slaves put together by the Works Progress Administration between 1936 and 1938; see George P. Rawick, ed., *The American Slave: A Composite Autobiography* (19 vols.; Westport, CT, 1972; 12 vols., supplement, 1978; 10 vols., supplement, 1979).

11. *Four Fugitive Slave Narratives* [Josiah Henson, 1849; William Welles Brown, 1847; Austin Steward, 1857; Benjamin Drew, 1855] (Reading, MA, 1969). Henson's father was sold when Josiah was very young, and Josiah himself was separated from his mother and siblings when he was five or six, at which time he began working. Henson asserted that Uncle Tom was modeled on him, but his claim is dubious according to E. Bruce Kirkham, *The Building of*

Uncle Tom's Cabin (Knoxville, 1977), 87–100, and Robin W. Winks, *Four Fugitive*, v–xxxiv.

Gilbert Osofsky, ed., *Puttin' on Ole Massa: The Slave Narratives of Henry Bibb* [1849], *William Welles Brown*, and *Solomon Northup* [1853] (New York & Evanston, 1969). Bibb's father was white; he had six step-siblings, all of whom with their mother were sold away from Brown when he was a child.

The letter from Stowe to Douglass, dated 7/9/51, can be found in Charles E. Stowe, *Life of Harriet Beecher Stowe* (Boston, 1889), 149–153.

Also of interest is *Narratives of the Sufferings of Lewis and Milton Clarke...* (1846; New York, 1969). At age 6 or 7, Lewis Clarke was transferred from the son to the daughter of his white maternal grandfather (Lewis's father was Scot), a woman who tortured him for ten years. He escaped from a different master as a young man and later claimed he was the model for the character of George Harris in *Uncle Tom's Cabin*, whose circumstances resembled his, but this claim is questionable according to Kirkham, 82–85.

12. Hedrick, *Stowe*, 211. The slave or freedom narrative, argues Hedrick, was primarily a male story which Stowe feminized (with Eliza's and Cassy's escapes) while turning the bondage narrative, previously a female experience, into a male one (with Uncle Tom). *Ibid.*, 212–213, 219. Hedrick also suggests that Eliza's flight compensated for Stowe's loss of a child only a few years earlier (p. 214).

13. Theodore Dwight Weld, *American Slavery as It Is* (orig. pub. New York, 1839; New York, 1968), 12, 18–19, 49, 58, 95, 106, 166–169. It was also reported that free colored children were kidnapped and sent into slavery (p. 140).

14. *The Key to Uncle Tom's Cabin* (orig. pub. Boston, 1853; New York, 1969), 134–135, 257–278. Gossett argues that since fiction was held in such low esteem in the mid-nineteenth century, a writer had to prove she had actual models for her statements. Gossett also points to the difficulty in getting specific evidence against slavery. Gossett, *American Culture*, 285–287.

15. *Uncle Tom's Cabin*, 94; see also 328. The Victorian perspective is presented in Bernard Wishy, *The Child and the Republic: The Dawn of Modern American Child Nurture* (Philadelphia, 1968).

16. George M. Fredrickson, *The Black Image in the White Mind: The Debate on Afro-*

American Character and Destiny, 1817–1914 (New York, 1971), 43. This observation is borne out in Winthrop D. Jordan, *White Over Black: American Attitudes Toward the Negro, 1550–1812* (Baltimore, 1969). Europeans were concerned with issues such as complexion, religion, and behavior (especially perceived sexuality), always viewing Africans as alien but not depicting them as children.

17. Fredrickson, *Black Image*, 102. On *Uncle Tom's Cabin* see pp. 110–117.

18. *Ibid.*, 198–282.

19. Actually, the first film about African Americans, in which (as in *The Birth of a Nation*) whites appear in blackface, was *The Pickaninnies Doing a Dance* (1894). James R. Nesteby, *Black Images in American Films, 1896–1954* (Washington, 1982), 14. And despite the popularity of *The Birth of a Nation*, there was simultaneously a strong undercurrent of criticism, causing Hollywood to refrain from casting Negroes in bad guy roles until *Sweet Sweetback's Baadasssss Son* (1971), save for the release of *Free and Equal* (1915) in the mid–1920s. Donald Bogle, *Toms, Coons, Mulattoes, Mammies, and Bucks* (3rd ed., New York, 1998), 16, 24–25.

20. Fredrickson, *Black Image*, 287, 295–296. A year before *The Southerner* was published, Jack Johnson became the world's first black heavyweight champion. The film of him kayoing white Tommy Burns was burned, reportedly, from fear of creating race riots. Bogle, *Toms*, 17.

21. Maybe the enormously popular radio show *Amos 'n' Andy* would fit this interpretation. For a different point of view, see Gerald Nachman, *Raised on Radio* (New York, 1998), 272–295.

22. Catherine Clinton, *The Plantation Mistress: Woman's World in the Old South* (New York, 1982), 202.

23. Leon Litwack suggests that such memories were prompted by white repugnance at the assertiveness of the now-freed blacks. Conversation with J. Illick, January 13, 1999.

24. Eugene D. Genovese, *Roll, Jordan, Roll: The World the Slaves Made* (New York, 1974), 360–361.

25. For an interpretation that Jews assimilated by appearing blackfaced in films, see Michael Rogin, *Blackface, White Noise: Jewish Immigrants in the Hollywood Melting Pot* (Berkeley, 1996).

26. Melville Herskovitz, *The Myth of the Negro Past* (New York, 1941), 1, 293.

27. *New York Times,* 9/15/98.

28. S. E. Morison and H. S. Commager, *The Growth of the American Republic* (2 vols.; 4th ed., New York, 1950), I, 537. For opinions of other American historians, see Gossett, *American Culture*, 355, 360.

29. Kenneth M. Stampp, *The Peculiar Institution: Slavery in the Ante-Bellum South* (New York, 1956), 144–147, 343.

30. Stanley M. Elkins, *Slavery: A Problem in American Institutional and Intellectual Life* (Chicago, 1959), 130.

31. *Ibid.*, 88.

32. Blassingame later faulted historians for not making extensive use of the narratives, though he excepted Eugene Genovese. John W. Blassingame, ed., *Slave Testimony* (Baton Rouge, 1977), xvii.

33. John W. Blassingame, *The Slave Community: Plantation Life in the Antebellum South* (New York, 1972), 92–103.

34. Genovese, *Roll, Jordan, Roll*, 482–519.

35. Robert William Fogel and Stanley L. Engerman, *Time on the Cross: The Economics of American Negro Slavery* (Boston, 1974), 129.

36. *Ibid.*, 5. The authors observe: "The abolitionist position on the black family, which has been accepted so uncritically by historians, was strikingly inconsistent." I.e., the anguish of family breakup did not square with the idea that slavery robbed family of meaning (p. 143).

37. *Ibid.*, 105–144, 147.

38. Herbert Gutman, *Slavery and the Numbers Game* (Urbana, 1975), preface, 9–10.

39. Herbert Gutman, *The Black Family in Slavery and Freedom, 1750–1925* (New York, 1976), 31. Gutman criticizes Stampp for ignoring historical development (304–305), Elkins for considering the slave in social isolation (305–308), Genovese for ignoring cultural adaptation (309–319, 592, n7), and Blassingame for misconstruing slave sexual behavior (61).

40. *Ibid.*, 129–133.

41. *Ibid.*, 185, 216, 230.

42. *Ibid.*, 102.

43. *Ibid.*, 259.

44. *Ibid.*, 261.

45. Thomas Webber, *Deep Like the Rivers: Education in the Slave Quarter Community, 1831–1851* (New York, 1978), 27–42.

46. *Ibid.*, 157–250. That blacks accepted

or rejected white values, attitudes, and understandings is not an issue with a single answer. Note the debate over slave personality, concisely summarized in Leslie Howard Owens, *This Species of Property: Slave Life and Culture in the Old South* (New York, 1976), 238, n8. Kenneth Stampp made the case for extensive role playing (1956); Stanley Elkins argued that slaves became the role they played (1959); Stampp conceded that some slaves became the role (1971), as did Blassingame (1972).

47. Allan Kulikoff in "The Beginnings of the Afro-American Family in Maryland," in Aubrey C. Land, et al., *Law, Society, and Politics in Early Maryland* (Baltimore, 1977), 176–182; and Kulikoff, *Tobacco and Slaves: The Development of Southern Cultures in the Chesapeake, 1680–1800* (Chapel Hill, 1986). See also Russell R. Menard, "The Maryland Slave Population, 1658–1730: A Demographic Profile of Blacks in Four Counties," *William and Mary Quarterly*, 3rd Ser., 32 (1975), 29–54; and Jean Butenhoff Lee, in "The Problem of Slave Community in the Eighteenth-Century Chesapeake," *William and Mary Quarterly*, 3rd Ser., 43 (1986), 333–361.

48. A good beginning is Donald R. Wright's synthetic and concise book *African Americans in the Colonial Era: From African Origins Through the American Revolution* (Arlington Heights, IL, 1990). In *Mandinko: The Ethnography of a West African Holy Land* (New York, 1980), Matt Schaffer points to the distinction between slaves captured or purchased and those born into already established slaves families, the basis of a slave caste system that persists to today (p. 2). See also C. C. Robertson and M. A. Klein, "Women's Importance in African Slave Systems," in Robertson and Klein, eds., *Women and Slavery in Africa* (Madison, 1983), 3–25. The European export market in slaves was 2:1 male at least, imposing larger than ever child care duties on the women left behind. See H. S. Klein, "African Women in the Atlantic Slave Trade" and John Thornton, "Sexual Demography: The Impact of the Slave Trade on Family Structure" in *Ibid.*, 29–48. Also, Claude Meillassoux, *The Anthropology of Slavery* (Chicago, 1991).

In *Africa and Africans in the Making of the Atlantic World, 1400–1680* (Cambridge, England, 1992), John Thornton downplays the heterogeneity among Africans coming to North America; see especially Chapter 7. Thornton takes issue with much of the orthodoxy surrounding Africa, the slave trade, and African American life, but does not discuss childhood. A clear and concise treatment of contemporary African child rearing is R. D. Whittemore's "Child Caregiving and Socialization to the Mandinka Way: Toward an Ethnography of Childhood" (Doctoral Dissertation, UCLA, 1989).

Sterling Stuckey, in *Slave Culture: Nationalist Theory and the Foundations of Black America* (New York, 1987), maintains that "the depths of African culture in America have been greatly underestimated by most nationalist theorists in America," but that "most Africans had to be detribalized to aspire nationally — a process set in motion more fully in antebellum America than on the African continent" (p. ix).

49. Cheryll Ann Cody, "Naming, Kinship, and Estate Dispersal: Notes on Slave Family Life on a South Carolina Plantation, 1786–1833," *William and Mary Quarterly*, 3rd Ser., 39 (1982), 202. See also Cody, "There Was No 'Absolom' on the Ball Plantations: Slave-Naming Practices in the South Carolina Low Country, 1720–1865," *American Historical Review*, 92 (1987), 563–596; Philip D. Morgan, "Slave Life in Piedmont Virginia, 1720–1800," in Lois Green Carr, et al., eds., *Colonial Chesapeake Society* (Chapel Hill, 1988), 452; and others (see Cody, "There Was No 'Absolom,'" note 3).

Herbert S. Klein and Stanley L. Engerman, "Fertility Differentials Between Slaves in the United States and the West Indies: A Note on Lactation Practices and Their Possible Implications," *William and Mary Quarterly*, 3rd Ser., 35 (1978), 358.

John Campbell found that four weeks after delivery was standard time for mothers to return to work. "Work, Pregnancy, and Infant Mortality Among Southern Slaves," *Journal of Interdisciplinary History*, 14 (1983/84), 807. L. H. Owens says mothers were back at work three weeks after childbirth, during which time they did their own cooking and cleaning — activity which contributed to the high infant mortality rate in the opinion of some observers. He also observes that child neglect was inseparable from work demands, *This Species of Property: Slave Life and Culture in the Old South* (New York, 1976), 39–42. Richard Dunn notes that on the Jamaican plantation of Mesopotamia, women with five or more children were allowed to stay home and raise them, an incentive for breeding a new generation of slaves, "Caribbean Versus Old South Slavery," Paper delivered at the University of Minnesota, 4/29/94, 21. A slave's testimony relating her work situation to her son's retardation appears in Brenda E. Stevenson, *Life in Black and White: Family and Community in the Slave South* (New York, 1996), 195. Kenneth F. Kiple and Virginia Himmelsteib King, *Another Dimension to the Black Diaspora: Diet, Disease, and Racism* (Cambridge, England, 1981), 96–116. Todd L. Savitt adds to the Kiple/King list neonatal tetanus, infanticide, worms, and overt sickle cell disease in *Medicine and Slavery: The Diseases and Health Care of Blacks in Antebellum Virginia* (Urbana, 1978), 120–129.

Richard Dunn found the death rate among black infants "shockingly high" on the Virginia plantation of Mount Airy; over one-third of the slaves who died, 1808–1865, were aged zero to four (108 of 487 babies recorded as born live), "Caribbean versus Old South Slavery," 15. Richard Steckel places the infant mortality rate at about "350 per thousand and total losses before the end of the first year (stillbirths plus infant deaths) at nearly 50 percent." See "A Dreadful Childhood: The Excess Mortality of American Slaves," *Social Science History*, 10 (1986), 791. Because the excess infant losses occurred by the end of the first month of life, Steckel argues that the important influences were "disease and diet, and especially work" (p. 429).

Regarding the practice of older children caring for younger, see R. D. Whittemore and Elizabeth Beverly, "Trust in the Mandinka Way: The Cultural Context of Sibling Care," in P. G. Zukow, ed., *Sibling Interaction Across Cultures* (New York, 1989), 26–53. See also Patricia G. Zukow, ed., *Sibling Interaction Across Cultures* (New York, 1989), Chapters 3, 4.

I am interested in considering these features of child care from the perspective of attachment theory; see J. E. Illick, "Childhood in Three Cultures in Early America," *Empire, Society and Labor: Essays in Honor of Richard S. Dunn* (Special Supplemental Issue of *Pennsylvania History*, 64 [Summer 1997]), 308–323.

50. Bernard Mergen, in *Play and Playthings: A Reference Guide* (Westport, CT, 1982, 42–43), disputes the contention of David K. Wiggins, author of "The Play of Slave Children in the Plantation Communities of the Old South, 1820–1860," *Journal of Sports History* 7, 2 (1980), 21–39, that slave children relieved anxieties and fears through play and thus more easily withstood bondage. An interesting essay comparing play in non–Western and Western societies is C. M. Eastman's "N. Z. W. Swahili child's world view," *Ethos*, 14, 2 (summer 1986), 144–173.

Webber, *Deep Like the Rivers*; Janet Cornelius, "'We Slipped and Learned to Read': Slave Accounts of the Literacy Process, 1830–1865," *Phylon*, 44 (1983), 171–185.

Richard H. Steckel, "A Peculiar Population: The Nutrition, Health, and Mortality of American Slaves from Childhood to Maturity," *Journal of Economic History*, 46 (1986), 721–741. In *Medicine and Slavery*, Todd L. Savitt, a medical student before he became a historian, questions the use of evidence by Fogel and Engerman (p. 113), as well as Owens (50–69), on the matter of diet (pp. 86–87, notes 8, 9). Savitt, unlike Steckel, argues for the substantiality of diet (p. 96).

51. On examining the records of a South Carolina planter, Cody found that no children under ten were separated from their parents, few children between 10 and 19 were, but at the end of the 20 to 29 age span, only 40 percent of men were still with their mothers; daughters were twice as likely to stay with mothers. "Naming, Kinship, and Estate Dispersal," 207–208. Other evidence of keeping a family together appears in Daniel C. Littlefield, *Rice and Slaves* (Baton Rouge, 1981), 71. To the contrary, see Morgan, "Slave Life," 448–449.

52. Ira Berlin, in "Time, Space, and the Evolution of Afro-American Society on British Mainland North America," *American Historical Review*, 85 (1980), 44–78, describes many different living situations, varying considerably by region and including households where there were but one or two slaves. Jean Butenhoff Lee, in "The Problem of Slave Community in the Eighteenth-Century Chesapeake," *William and Mary Quarterly*, 3rd Ser., 43 (1986), observes that 45 percent of the slaves in Charles County, Maryland, lived in groups of ten or less. Obviously the issue of attachment would be different in these situations than on plantations.

Changes in African American ways of life during the late eighteenth century are the subject of essays by Gary B. Nash, Richard S. Dunn, Philip D. Morgan, and Allan Kulikoff in Ira Berlin and Ronald Hoffman, eds., *Slavery and Freedom in the Age of the American Revolution* (Charlottesville, VA, 1983).

53. King, *Stolen Childhood*, xx.

54. Schwartz, *Born in Bondage*, 3, 9. This statement contradicts the argument made by Lester Alston: "Children learned to look to their owners for confirmation of their worth rather than to their parents...." Alston views the years after age two as critical insofar as children had little or no basis for developing self-esteem from their subjugated parents. "Children as Chattel," in Elliott West and Paula Petrik, eds., *Small Worlds: Children & Adolescents in America, 1850–1950* (Lawrence, KS, 1992), 211–214.

55. King, *Stolen Childhood*, 1.

56. *Ibid.*, 13.

57. *Ibid.*, 21, 23.

58. Elliott West, *Growing Up with the Country: Childhood on the Far Western Frontier* (Albuquerque, 1989), 73–94; Steven Mintz and Susan Kellogg, *Domestic Revolutions: A Social History of American Family Life* (New York, 1988), 83–95.

59. King, *Stolen Childhood*, 68, 71.

60. *Ibid.*, 97.

61. Schwartz, *Born in Bondage* , 208.

62. *Ibid.*, 77.

63. *Ibid.*, 78.

64. *Ibid.*, 82, 87.

65. *Ibid.*, 94.

66. See, for example, Gilbert Osofsky, ed., *Puttin' on Ole Massa* (New York, 1969).

67. Alston argues that for many slave children "work was a constant, and they may not have experienced changes in the work they did as mileposts in their lives." "Children as Chattel," 227.

68. *Ibid.*, 154.

69. Paul Robeson, *Here I Stand* (Boston, 1988; orig. pub. 1958), 6–8; Martin Duberman, *Paul Robeson* (New York, 1996; orig. pub. 1988), 4–5.

70. Robeson, *Here I Stand*, 7–8, 14–15.

71. *Ibid.*, 6. I would not deny the influence of his mother; children rarely remember any life details before age three, and it is likely that Paul formed an attachment with his mother in his infancy and toddlerhood, judging by the confidence that he displayed ever afterward. See John Bowlby, *Attachment and Loss* (3 vols., New York, 1969–1980), II, 322: "there is a strong case for believing that an unthinking confidence in the unfailing accessibility and support of attachmment figures is the bedrock on which stable and self-reliant personality is built." Paul's father, it seems important to note, twice returned during the Civil War to see his mother on the Carolina plantation.

72. Robeson, *Here I Stand*, 6–11.

73. Duberman, *Robeson*, 15–18.

74. *Ibid.*, 102–103, 106, 110, 112, 115.

75. *Ibid.*, 139, 142, 150, 152, 161, 189, 194–195, 209, 235, 246.

Paul Robeson:
Rutgers Phenomenon, 1915–1919

SHEILA TULLY BOYLE
The Houghton Mifflin Company
ANDREW BUNIE
Boston College

From the day he first arrived at Rutgers on September 15, 1915, with his friend and Somerville High School classmate, Art ("Foot") Van Fleet, Paul Robeson stood out. A black face at this small New Jersey school on the outskirts of New Brunswick was enough of an oddity, but Robeson — six feet two, almost 200 pounds, and strikingly black — was impossible to miss.

In the decade previous to Robeson's arrival, Rutgers had transformed itself from a rural "cow college" specializing in an agricultural-technical curriculum to a serious academic institution offering a variety of liberal arts programs. College President William Demarest began taking steps to effect the change from his first year of tenure in 1906. By 1915 the school's curriculum had been substantially enhanced, admission procedures completely overhauled, and a host of new buildings added on land north of the old Queen's Campus

(the Neilson Campus) and at the other end of the city on the Experiment Station Campus. Between 1905 and 1915 enrollments doubled, from 250 to 500, and Robeson's freshman class numbered 185, the largest in the college's history.[1]

Despite its growth, however, Rutgers had not lost its small-school flavor and was still dwarfed by giants like Harvard and Columbia, both enrolling close to 4,000, and neighboring Princeton, which boasted five times Rutgers' student population. Incoming Rutgers freshmen typically hailed from northern areas of New Jersey, most the sons of farmers and ministers, small-town doctors and bankers, many the first in their families to attend college. Forty percent relied on state grants, and others, like Paul, financed their tuition through a combination of college scholarships, work, and benefactor assistance (in Paul's case, Somerville contractor Louis P. Gaston).[2]

31

Robeson would remember his college years as among the happiest times of his life. At Rutgers he would earn the success he yearned for, and received more recognition as a freshman than he ever dreamed possible. But this bright, reserved, and earnest seventeen year old had significant hurdles to overcome first. By choosing to attend Rutgers, Robeson had elected a course few blacks before him had attempted. (In 1915 less than 50 blacks attended white colleges nationwide.) There were no rules and few role models to follow. Racially, the situation in America was as repressive as it had ever been. The year Robeson entered Rutgers, D. W. Griffith's spectacular *The Birth of a Nation*, the movie version of Thomas Dixon's *The Clansman*, made its debut in theaters throughout the country. A lurid tale of Negro emancipation, the subsequent debauchery of white womanhood, and the South saved from total devastation by heroic Klansmen, *The Birth of a Nation* portrayed blacks as stupid, occasionally vicious, brute animals. Off the movie screen, racism was equally oppressive. Jim Crow flourished, sanctioned by law in the South and custom in the North.[3] The sharecropping system and lily white unions kept blacks economically trapped. In the South, intimidation and ingenious legal devices prevented the vast majority from voting, and lynchings—the ultimate weapon for keeping blacks in their place—remained an accepted fact of life. In such a racial climate even those most impatient with the pace of change thought twice about pushing issues. At Rutgers, then, Robeson would spend much of his time watching, listening, and assessing. He said the "right" things, sang the "right" songs, and assumed the "right" self-effacing attitude toward his own accomplishments. In exchange, he was allowed to succeed in a white environment.

During his college years, Robeson was many things to many people, and he poured tremendous energy into living up to his own and others' expectations. If the inner Robeson, the adolescent with his own thoughts and feelings, appears shadowy and submerged, it is no accident. Paul kept those feelings hidden, to some extent even from himself. For the time being there was the white world of Rutgers to conquer, the challenge of proving himself and his race competent and capable. In that context, attending to his own thoughts and feelings was a luxury Robeson could not afford.

Robeson had come to Rutgers to study, and from the start he devoted himself to his classes. He had his father's respect for learning and was determined to prove himself a scholar. "In the beginning," remembered lifelong friend and Rutgers classmate Malcolm ("Mal") Pitt, "Paul was quiet, almost apprehensive. He was always in the library studying. It was clear right away he was going to be a good student, or die trying."[4] Classmate Steve White agreed: "You never saw Paul as a freshman hanging around the campus. When he wasn't on the football field, he was either in his room poring over the books or trudging to the old Voorhees Library to study there."[5] Mathematics was Paul's favorite subject freshman year, but he applied himself to all his courses: He could not slide by on half efforts as in high school. He would earn two As (algebra and public speaking), three Bs (English literature, Greek, and Latin) and one C (English composition) that first semester, and he worked hard for those grades. (Concerning the C in English composition, several of Robeson's friends remarked that while Robeson wrote easily and well, he lacked the patience to revise and rewrite, and, as a result, his writing was often not as good as it might have been had he been willing to give it just a little more attention.)[6]

Robeson shared the universal adjustment difficulties of all college freshmen, but compounded and confused by racial factors. With his classmates he went through the traditional initiation rites, but in Robeson's case it was difficult to tell where initiation ended and his special treatment as a black began. A select number of newcomers, arriving with a reputation firmly in hand, would be courted by representatives of school clubs and organizations, ranging from fraternities, the Glee Club, and the *Targum* (the Rutgers newspaper) to the school's debating team. Robeson was not among them. Paul endured with patience and good humor the ritual of upperclassmen critically appraising him, wondering what, if anything, the exclusion meant.

But in the area of athletics, in particular football, the situation was different. Football would provide Robeson his means of winning acceptance at Rutgers. His outstanding play, especially during his junior and senior years, would put Rutgers on the map, transforming the rural cow college into a formidable athletic powerhouse, able to hold its own against the best collegiate teams in the country. Despite the lip service given to education, none of Robeson's academic achievements would even come close to opening the doors that a brilliant college football career opened for him. It would be for his prowess on the gridiron that Robeson would first be recognized and, in many cases, most remembered by sports-infatuated America. Football would introduce Robeson formally to the white world, reinforce for him the importance of modesty and self-effacement as strategies for getting along, and teach him that success—big success—could do much to ameliorate racial prejudices. Playing football would put Robeson's name in the limelight and give him his first real taste of fame. It was an experience he never forgot, and one that changed his life.

Robeson's years at Rutgers coincided with the period during which the game of football, so long denounced for its brutality, would finally come into its own as a sport, commanding attention and respect. The road to such acceptance was long and rocky, and the game as we know it today was still in its infancy in 1915. As late as 1910, deaths and serious injuries in the sport were commonplace. (In 1905 eighteen college and secondary school players died, and another 159 were injured; in 1909 thirty players, eight of them college men, lost their lives to the game.) Public outrage peaked in 1905 and 1906 as journals like *McClure's, Collier's, The Nation,* and *Outlook* published scathing exposés documenting incidents of premeditated violence (teams often planned to "knock out" opposing players early in the game) and the "insidious" role of money in the game. By 1906 Columbia and the Massachusetts Institute of Technology had abolished the sport altogether, while Stanford and California substituted rugby in its place.[7]

Advocates like Coach Walter Camp and "Mr. Athletics" himself, Theodore Roosevelt, ultimately beat down a nationwide crusade to ban the sport. What emerged in the aftermath was essentially a new game, as reforms and rule changes forced the development of new styles of play. Once a simple contest of brute strength, now skill and well-planned maneuvers emerged as equally important considerations in the game. The dramatic upset victory in 1913 of Notre Dame's Fighting Irish over the indomitable West Point eleven heralded the metamorphosis. Brilliant and breathtaking tactical innovations like the Gus Dorais–Knute Rockne forward pass caught the public's eye, and soon colleges and schools throughout the country took a fresh look at the sport.[8] Rutgers was no exception. With increased newspaper coverage and public acceptance of contact sports, football would become by Robeson's junior year the American college sport. And, precisely at the time when the nation was turning itself on to college athletics, Robeson would emerge as one of the game's most gifted players, selected to Walter Camp's elite All-American team to join players of the caliber of Walter Eckersall of the University of Chicago, Carlisle's Jim Thorpe, Eddie Mahan of Harvard, Army's Elmer Oliphant, and Frederick Douglass ("Fritz") Pollard of Brown.

Rutgers had a long football tradition dating back to 1869 when the college hosted Princeton in America's first intercollegiate game. But historically the school's attitude reflected that of the nation as a whole: It tolerated the sport but never promoted it. That picture changed in 1913 when a small but influential group of alumni, led by the head of the Delaware and Hudson Railroad, Lore F. Loree (class of 1877), decided to put its money and business know-how into building an eastern powerhouse competitive with Yale, Brown, Princeton, and Harvard. President Demarest, anxious to secure increased alumni support of school affairs, encouraged the effort.[9] With the newly launched *Alumni Quarterly* fanning school spirit, Loree easily engaged others to support him in the formation of a "syndicate" to underwrite the improvement of Rutgers' athletic facilities, including erecting stands, building a fieldhouse, and grading and surfacing "the old coppermine field littered with gravel and stone" where the team had played prior to 1914.[10]

The syndicate wanted the best possible coach and so set its sights on the successful Columbia, West Point, and Yale veteran, Foster ("Sandy") Sanford, an athlete cut from the mold of football greats Walter Camp, "Pop" Warner, and Amos Alonzo Stagg.[11] Loree convinced Sanford to take the job even though as coach he would receive no compensation. Sanford owned a prosperous insurance business in

New Haven and, according to player Steve White, "rumors of the day" were that "unofficial payment came from the insurance business he [Sanford] got from Loree's railroad."[12]

Although Sanford agreed only to "come for a few years" to develop a "graduate coaching system" of former players who would eventually take his place, he remained at Rutgers for ten years, earning in that time an impressive record of fifty-six wins, thirty-two losses, and five ties. For a full decade, from 1913 to 1923, Foster Sanford's innovations and trick plays—the hurdle play, the Rutgers formation, and the multiple kick—kept opponents guessing, the Rutgers team scoring, and fans sitting on the edge of their seats.[13]

Rutgers had never known such a personality. Articulate, commanding, colorful, and dynamic, he immediately became an idol to his players and to the vast majority of the student body as well. Without exception, players, including Paul, spoke of Sanford in superlatives and looked to him for advice and encouragement both on and off the football field.[14] Sandy insisted the team be provided proper protective equipment, a training table, and a full-time trainer. He demanded amenities such as undershirts and towels, and secured for his men the voluntary services of a team doctor. Fanatic in his devotion to the game, Sandy even had built for himself a high platform from which he could oversee practices and shout orders to players below. "A splendid physical specimen himself, he influenced me more than any man in my life," said player Steve White. "He was like my father. He taught us to achieve beyond our abilities," said All-American Robert ("Nasty") Nash, a veteran senior who later coached at Rutgers and played professionally with Paul in the fledgling National Football League. "Sandy insisted on strict training habits," recalled White. "He did not smoke or drink, nor did he use profanity, but he could talk a very rough English, which everyone understood. He taught us epigrams, written out on posters in the locker room, such as 'When I come out on the field, it's with a stranger's eye' and 'I never judge a man by his yesterday, but always by his tomorrow and his today.'"[15] Many team members, even as old men, could still easily recall the sayings Sanford had drilled into them a lifetime ago.[16]

As Sanford began his third year at Rutgers in 1915, he was well on his way to shaping the "Scarlet Scourge" into a football team to be reckoned with. "Rutgers definitely had its eye on Paul, and the coach knew he was a good player," recalled Somerville High School classmate Douglas Brown.[17] Robeson was not invited to fall camp, and competition to make the team was stiff.[18] Rutgers had earned a fine record the previous year and could afford to overlook even a talented newcomer. Veteran players quickly made their feelings known. "It was hard enough just making the team," said White, "without having some newcomer like Robeson take over your position."[19]

Robeson understood players would fight to defend their spots and anticipated a rough go of it, some mistreatment even, during tryouts. His initiation, however, proved more trying than even his most grim expectations. Race, while not the sole cause of his testing, added fire to the fervor with which upperclassmen put him through the paces. The coincidental and widely publicized exploits of the notorious black prizefighter Jack Johnson, the only black athlete most white Americans had ever heard of, did not make Robeson's task any easier. (Only a very few blacks, a total of fourteen between 1915 and 1919, played on white college teams, and none had the name recognition of Johnson.[20]) Johnson's victories—winning the heavyweight championship in 1908 and successfully defend-

ing his title against Jim Jeffries, the "Great White Hope," in 1910—stunned white Americans. His attitude, both in the ring (he badgered, taunted, and jeered white opponents) and outside of it (he was a big spender and a flashy dresser, with large cars and a white woman always in tow), exacerbated white America's most deeply held racial fears. Most whites were relieved when finally, in 1915, Jess Willard, the giant farm boy from Kansas, "restored the color line" and won back the title, knocking the infamous heavyweight champion out in the twenty-sixth round in Havana, Cuba. Johnson's arrogance and "disrespect" had shaken white America, right down to the small cow college in northern New Jersey. Rutgers players did not want to lose their spots—period. But if they did, they most certainly were not about to be sidelined by a Negro.[21]

Sanford's position was that, as far as making the team was concerned, Robeson was on his own; he would not interfere. As coach he understood that if Robeson could not hold his own against his teammates, he would never be able to withstand the assault from opposing teams in a real game situation.[22] Even as late as 1935 blacks playing on desegregated college teams needed not only outstanding ability but also tremendous self control. Harry Kipke, coach at the University of Michigan, recalled demanding that his veterans pound a black candidate "without mercy" during practice. Said Kipke: "If, at the end of the week he doesn't turn in his uniform then I know I have a great player."[23]

"There's a big darky on the field," Sanford announced to the squad in the dressing room before practice. "If you want him okay, if not okay." "I was 17 years old when that happened," Robeson said later. "Rutgers had a great team that year, but the boys—well—they didn't want a Negro on their team, they just didn't want me on it. On the first day of scrimmage they set about making sure I wouldn't get on their team. One boy slugged me on the face and smashed my nose, just smashed it. That's been trouble to me as a singer every day since. And then when I was down, flat on my back, another boy got me with his knee, just came over and fell on me. He managed to dislocate my right shoulder."[24]

Robeson's injuries were serious enough to have him sidelined for ten days. Discouraged, he wondered whether or not making the team or even continuing at Rutgers was really worth it. His brother Bill visited him while he was recuperating and urged him not to quit: "Kid, I know what it is. I went through it at Pennsylvania. If you want to quit school, go ahead, but I wouldn't like to think, and our father wouldn't like to think, that our family had a quitter in it!"[25] Paul listened. After ten days in bed and a few days at the training table he was out on the field again.

"Oh yes, he took a terrific beating," recalled Nash, "one of the first colored boys, you know. We gave him a tough time … but he took it well."

"Remember, Paul was no little boy," Paul's friend Revels Cayton wryly observed. "He was inexperienced, but he had raw physical strength and knew how to use it. He had spent summers working in a brickyard, loading bricks onto a chute all day. 'Believe me,' he told me, 'that was slave labor! And when I finished the day I knew I was tired, but by the time I got to Rutgers I was already as strong as many of these older white fellows.'"[26]

Although Coach Sanford said he wanted "no more monkey business with Robeson on the field," when Paul returned to practice, veteran players continued to muscle in on him. One incident stood out in Paul's mind for years. He had landed on the ground after making a tackle, flat on his back with his arm stretched out, right palm facing down. One of the regulars spotted him and stomped on his unpro-

tected hand. "He meant to break bones," Paul said. "The bones held, but his cleats took every single one of the fingernails off my right hand." Robeson remained in the scrimmage but made up his mind to get revenge. (There were precious few situations in which a black man could safely express anger toward whites, but football was one of them.) On the next play, "the whole first string backfield came at me. I swept out my arms … and then three men running interference went down. Next came the ball carrier, a back named Kelly, I wanted to kill him, and I meant to kill him. It wasn't a thought, it was just a feeling." Catching up with Kelly, Paul lifted him back up over his own head. "I was going to smash him so hard to the ground that I'd break him in two, and I could have done it, but just then the coach yelled the first thing that came to his mind, he yelled 'Robey you're on varsity!' That brought me around."[27]

Some of Paul's teammates later denied that racial considerations played any part in the abuse. William Feitner, himself a 1915 freshman scrub, went so far as to call Robeson's rendition of his tryouts "slanderous." "No one ever stepped on Paul's hand," Feitner insisted, nor was anyone "out to get him because he was colored. Paul was treated no worse than any of us scrubs. All of us were worked hard to see if we were men enough to make the team. It was something we had to live with until we were accepted."[28] Nasty Nash, while less quick to dismiss the racial factor, also took issue with Robeson's "not exactly true" recollections. "Scrubs got all the poorest equipment — worn pads, shoes two sizes too big, and oversized helmets that spun around your head when you got hit. It was not racial," Nash said, but added with a knowing grin, "Let's just say we didn't exactly greet him with open arms."[29]

All-American Fritz Pollard, a friend of Paul's who had endured similar experiences at Brown University where he was the only black on the football team, insisted Paul's story was true. Although he was a great ballplayer, Pollard was not a scholar and devoted his energies primarily to playing ball and finding new ways to make money. On the campus at Brown and summers at Narragansett Pier he ran successful pressing and tailor shops, the first of many business ventures. His biographer, John Carroll, refers to him as a "tramp athlete," and indeed Pollard attended college specifically for the opportunity it afforded him to play football. He played for Dartmouth and Harvard before even enrolling as a student, played for Brown but never graduated, and then went on to play professionally.

Pollard knew what playing with an all-white team was like, and said Paul did not exaggerate. "I not only had to practice by myself, separated from the rest of the team, but I was segregated in the locker room as well," remembered Pollard. "My brothers had played football. Leslie played at Dartmouth, and he coached me when I was still in high school. They told me the whites would be out to get me, but by the time I left high school in Chicago and went to Brown I was used to that. In scrimmages I was a scrub, and then later in games against opposing teams I had to be especially careful about gang tackles. My brothers taught me to protect myself by keeping my legs and elbows and arms kicking and swinging. That stopped tacklers from piling on. I was a kicking and swinging fool, I'll tell you! At Brown the day the team handed out the uniforms, the athletic department wouldn't give me one. Maybe they thought my color would stain the uniform. That hurt more than any of the other stuff, beatings and all. I went back to my segregated section of the locker room, down in the boiler room — even there they didn't want me — and I hid behind the lockers and cried my eyes out."[30]

Robeson survived his initiation, won a place on the team, and was accepted at the mealtime training table, which, according to Nash, "meant he was really one of us."[31] As a freshman Paul was a solid, rugged ballplayer but still crude and undisciplined. Coach Sanford, who would play such a pivotal role in shaping this raw talent, saw to it that the team helped Robeson improve his play.[32] "Remember, this was long before specialization in football, and you might be called to play a variety of positions — tackle, guard, or end," said Kenneth ("Thug") Rendall. "But Paul was a willing learner. He said very little but listened hard."[33] Player Harry Rockafeller agreed: "Paul's willingness to learn and his desire to be excellent were his major strengths."[34]

Like Pollard, Robeson would be fair game for opposing players out to "kill that nigger," and Coach Sanford personally took charge of teaching him special strategies for protecting himself. At practice Sandy lined up wooden orange crates on each side of Robeson, and then had Paul, from a three-point stance, vault upward on signal, flailing away with his elbows and forearms until he had smashed the crates to pieces. "Sandy taught Paul how to use those elbows and forearms as protective weapons. Extremely powerful in the thighs and legs, Paul would get off the mark, bounding up very quickly. As he did so, those elbows and forearms moved with lightning speed. In a game situation he flattened his rival before the opponents or the official even knew what was happening. By the time the victim realized what had hit him, Paul was usually down the field."[35]

The 1915 season put Rutgers in the national limelight as the Scarlet Scourge posted a record of seven wins and only one loss, and led the nation in scoring, outdistancing its opposition by a staggering margin of 351 to 33. As the wins mounted, Sandy emptied his bench, allowing freshman

Paul Robeson and other members of the Rutgers football team. Courtesy of Special Collections, Rutgers University Library.

Robeson to see action in a number of games. "From the very beginning Paul had a rough defensive assignment," said Steve White. "He was on the left side of the line, opposite the offensive right, and since most of the teams ran right, they came straight at him. You knew he was going to be in on a lot of tackling and it would be rough."[36] Used primarily as left tackle or guard, Robeson, with his enormous hands, demonstrated equal talent on offense as a pass receiver. "I remember him backing up the line," said John Wittpenn, "moving around with that excited nervous energy, calling to the lineman 'Give me light, just let me see 'em.'"[37]

Rutgers' only real challenge that season came from the Princeton University team. The rivalry between the two schools was an old one, dating back to 1869 when Rutgers beat Princeton in that historic first intercollegiate match-up. But in twenty-one games from 1870 to 1912 Rutgers had failed to score a single victory against this formidable opponent. "Oh, how we wanted to beat Princeton," player Steve White reminisced with emotion. "They were elite snobs who looked down their noses at us. Rutgers didn't have any of that recognition. They thought we were a small country cow college and we resented their superior airs." Robeson, who remembered well that in Princeton "smart" Negroes kept their place, had his own reasons for wanting to trounce Rutgers' southern rival. But victory eluded them all as Princeton edged Rutgers out by a score of 10 to 0. "Princeton had to fight like hell to beat us ten to nothing," Steve White remembered. "Still, it was a tough loss."[38]

Robeson did not play in the Princeton match-up. According to several of his teammates, he was benched not because the Princeton team refused to play with a black man in the opposing lineup, but because Sanford did not want to play an inexperienced freshman in such a crucial game. Robeson's lack of experience and control did on occasion cause him problems that year. One reporter described Rutgers' 39 to 3 victory over Stevens Tech as "marred a number of times by the unfair tactics used by Robeson." Specifically, the writer detailed a botched play resulting in a fumble and subsequent scramble for the loose football on the Rutgers 22-yard line. A Rutgers man recovered the pigskin, but when a Stevens player tried to tackle him Robeson "threw his arms around his neck" to prevent him from making the tackle.[39]

Overall, however, Robeson's first season had been a good one. He had listened and learned, and his teammates and Sandy liked him. Often Robeson was seen "walking back to the old gymnasium on Hamilton and George Street after practice on Neilson Field … arm-in-arm with Sanford" as the two "raised their voices in a rendition of 'On the Banks of the Raritan'" or Sandy's favorite, "Goofa Dust."[40]

Off the football field, in other areas of Rutgers life, Robeson followed a similar strategy for getting along: He watched and listened, kept his feelings to himself, and tried to do the "right" thing. At Rutgers Robeson refined the social etiquette he had learned living in white Westfield and Somerville. Trespassing racial lines in social settings inevitably caused embarrassment, and Robeson did everything he could to avoid such incidents. No one told him to monitor his mingling with Rutgers students, to refrain from joining friends for a sandwich and nickel beer at Hennessey's, the local pub, or to decline meeting them at the drugstore on Eastern Avenue for morning coffee and doughnuts. Robeson understood the social etiquette and had no intention of challenging it.

And, indeed, Robeson had read the unspoken rules correctly. No Rutgers fraternity asked him to join. Paul frequently visited Rendall's and Van Fleet's fraternity, "the Queen's," and enjoyed house privileges at several others as well, but because he was not allowed into white fraternities he joined Alpha Phi Alpha, the oldest black fraternity in the country. "I fought in my fraternity, Delta Epsilon, to get Paul in," said Pitt. "But there was a national by-law forbidding the mixture of race. Jews were not allowed in either."[41]

Robeson was never asked to join the school Glee Club either, undoubtedly because of the socializing (with female choruses from other schools, with whom Rutgers would sing in joint concerts) that followed performances. There was no question he was qualified; nor was Rutgers unaware of his musical talent. Robeson used his fine singing voice whenever he had the opportunity: in churches and at informal gatherings on campus (accompanied on the piano by Mal Pitt), with his football teammates in between courses at team suppers, and possibly, on occasion, at local Rutgers Glee Club performances. (Robeson did not consider such occasional participation in the Glee Club as membership, nor did *Targum*, which never listed Glee Club as among Robeson's extracurricular activities.)[42] As classmate Andrew F. Eschenfelder explained, "Social functions were all-white, and Robey never forced himself in. As people used to say in those days, he 'knew his place.'"[43]

For the most part Robeson said nothing about these slights. Every now and then he talked with his friend Fritz Pollard, one of the few people in a position to understand what he was going through, and on a few occasions with family members. But, generally, Paul absorbed the full impact of these experiences himself. Problems that arose traveling with the football team Robeson handled matter-of-factly, as if where he stayed or ate did not matter at all to him. "Never mind making eating arrangements for me. I'll make my own way when I get there," Robeson told the team manager that first year. "The rest of the team didn't want to allow it, but that was the way Paul wanted to approach it," Mal Pitt remembered. "Paul was very sensitive about the race question. Finally, he did agree to eat and stay with the team, but told the manager that if there were any difficulties he would take care of himself."[44]

Often Paul used humor to ease the tension when such incidents occurred. "When he was not allowed into a restaurant with us and had to eat in the kitchen," John Wittpenn remembered, "he kidded us afterwards. 'I feel sorry for you guys. You got such little helpings out there in the restaurant. In the kitchen they fed me royally!'"[45] According to Mal Pitt, on those few occasions when he "did talk about racism he was almost always satiric about it. 'Sure, I can play sports but can't join the Glee Club because that's too *social*! Ha! Ha!'"[46]

Although Paul might have said it was his friends' feelings he wanted to spare, in fact, it was his own sense of self-worth he was trying to maintain in adopting either a humorous or an indifferent attitude toward racial slights. Emotionally, the experience of Jim Crow was so damaging that he would do almost anything to avoid being reminded of the extent to which he was still at the mercy of that social code. Robeson retreated and tried to blend in, but such compliance took its toll on him psychologically. White students saw only a gregarious and easy going Robeson, singing the old favorite "Goofa Dust" with Sandy and the boys, never the isolated and occasionally despairing young Robeson who on more than one occasion wanted to quit Rutgers altogether.[47]

Robeson was treated with far more tolerance, however, than were the Jewish members of the school's student body. As the only black man on campus his first year, and one of three blacks enrolled during his junior and senior years, Robeson's presence constituted no serious threat to the larger student body. The college's Jewish population, however, most the children of recently immigrated eastern European Jews, was substantial; and anti–Semitism at Rutgers, as at other colleges, was not only widespread but tolerated in its most blatant manifestations.[48] A number of Paul's friends recalled jeering the school's "New York Jews," warning them "to go back to CCNY where they belonged."[49] "Thug" Rendall remembered being "made to sit at the back of the classroom with the Jewish students" as punishment from a chemistry teacher who disliked him because he played football and did poorly in academics.[50] When Leo Frank, a successful Atlanta Jewish businessman convicted of raping white employee Mary Phagan, was lynched in 1915 in Marietta, Georgia, a few days after the governor commuted his death sentence, many at Rutgers felt he got exactly what he deserved. None of the school's fraternities would consider accepting Jews; and when Jewish students in 1915 attempted to organize their own fraternity, hostilities flared. Three years later, in 1919, after much controversy, the school finally granted the Jewish Phi Epsilon Pi formal permission to exist. The student body, however, pointedly expressed its disapproval by conspicuously ignoring the new fraternity. Similarly, the formation of another Jewish organization, the Campus Club, met with such opposition that members, conceding defeat, bitterly disbanded in 1918.[51]

One can only speculate on how Robeson reacted to Rutgers' anti–Semitism. One thing is clear: He missed none of it. Paul later told friends that he had always felt "a mystical feeling, an almost unexplainable rapport with Jews."[52] Small wonder. There was the shared experience of bigotry, no doubt, but for Paul the ties ran deeper. As a child he had witnessed the easy friendship between his father and his neighbor, the Russian Jewish immigrant Samuel I. Woldin. Samuel Woldin was the only white person Paul had ever seen treat his father as both an equal and a friend; it was an experience Robeson never forgot.[53]

Paul's personal experience with Jews at Rutgers would only solidify the identification. Like Rutgers' Jewish population, Paul was expected to room with "his own kind" or by himself. During his first two years at Rutgers Robeson roomed alone in room 142 in Rutgers' legendary Winant's Hall. (White classmate Steve White conjectured that Robeson preferred this arrangement. "He was not trying to innovate," White said. "He was not liberal or radical at Rutgers; he was just trying to make his way."[54] Given Paul's temperament, one can safely assume he did not want to make an issue of his rooming arrangements, which is not the same as saying that living alone was what Robeson preferred.) In his junior year Paul was assigned space with two younger black students, Robert Ritter Davenport of Orange, New Jersey (Class of 1920), and Leon Harold Smith of Saugerties, New York (Class of 1921); but as a senior Paul roomed with a white Jewish student, Herbert Miskend (Class of 1922), apparently without incident.[55] Should anxious parents or alumni protest this apparent breach of racial etiquette, Rutgers officials would have an out: Robeson's roommate may have been white, but he was not a Gentile.

Still, Jewish students at Rutgers had each other to lean on, whereas Paul was virtually alone. Rutgers would offer Robeson things he wanted badly — status, achievement, a sense of legitimacy — but his need for community, family, and a social life he would meet elsewhere: in the black communities of Princeton, Somer-

ville, and New Brunswick (all were within fifteen to twenty miles of each other); during summers at Narragansett, Rhode Island; and at gatherings of black college students held periodically throughout the year. During his college years Robeson lived two rich but distinct lives: one in the white world and the other in the black community. So separate were these worlds that most Rutgers students had no idea that Robeson had *any* social life. Some, like track manager Harold Higgins, occasionally wondered where Robeson disappeared to when the team traveled. "We had a meet one time, just outside of Princeton, and Robey was nowhere to be found. I finally tracked him down, but he never said a word about where he had been. I assumed he had sneaked off to visit a girlfriend."[56]

"I don't recall Paul going to any of the social functions—dances, the Military Ball—things like that," said Malcolm Pitt. "He never said anything about it one way or the other. I think his parents were more of the old school, which meant it was kind of wrong to go to such events and stir racial feelings."[57] Most of Robeson's classmates never gave the matter of his social life much thought. They appreciated his "sensitivity" and would later praise him for knowing enough "never to push himself into social situations."[58] Robeson did not attend Rutgers social functions, and there the matter rested.

On occasion, shuttling back and forth between two worlds created conflicts Paul found difficult to resolve. Most Sundays, for example, Paul returned to Somerville to help his father by singing and reading the Gospel at the various churches where he preached, and, during the summer, teaching Sunday school. The emotional, elemental African Methodist Episcopal Zion church services, with their animated preaching, singing, shouting, and receiving of the spirit, were unlike anything Paul saw in the white world of Rutgers. Paul's familial and communal loyalties drew him to church services, but once back at school he felt shame and embarrassment over his participation in what the white world regarded as ignorant emotionalism.[59] More often than not, however, the embarrassment passed. "I'd leave college a little ashamed of my frequent conversions," Robeson later recalled, "but if I went to Church, before the service was over I would be singing with the rest of them."[60] Although Robeson would later describe himself to friends as being not particularly religious, singing spirituals nonetheless evoked in him something very much like a religious experience in its emotional power. Later, it would be Robeson who would himself, singing the spirituals, move his secular, wordly audiences to an experience they would describe as religious in its intensity.

Other times the differences between the two worlds were easier to reconcile. Robeson played basketball for Rutgers, but the college placed little emphasis on the sport and, in 1915, even threatened to cancel the entire season unless alumni contributed funds to defray the season's expenses.[61] But Robeson also played for better, more competitive teams as well, as these games were social as well as athletic events. During his freshman and sophomore years, for example, Paul often combined visiting his father with playing basketball with the "Manhattan Machine," New Brunswick's all-black YMCA team, against other black teams in Freehold, Orange, and Elizabeth. During his junior and senior years Robeson played for the Harlem-based, all-black St. Christopher's "Red and Black Machine," a team that played top-notch, high-powered basketball. Win or lose, Manhattan Machine and St. Christopher games always ended with a dance. When the Manhattan Machine, led by "the Rutgers athlete [Robeson] … high man for the Manhattans," made the

February trek from New Brunswick to Harlem for a match with the Alpha Moguls, the *New York Age*'s Ted Hooks accorded the occasion the attention it deserved and listed by name not only team members ("Lloyd Ivy and C. Ivy, H. Hoagland, Branch, A. Reed, and W. Brokaw") but also the loyal female following and other fans ("Misses Olive Rancher, Isabelle Mason, Estella Stanford, Anna White, Anna Fletcher, Messers Chester and Henry Jennings") who accompanied the team to New York.[62]

Summers at Narragansett put Paul in still another black setting. When he wasn't working, Paul made friends, socialized, gave informal recitals, walked the beaches, and practiced football. Fritz Pollard ("a sort of big brother in a small package," was Pollard's own description of his friendship with Robeson) played baseball with Paul and played piano for him when he sang in a small club organized by the summer work staff. Pollard knew his way around the area. He operated a small pressing and tailoring shop at Narragansett, modeled on the one he ran during the school year on the Dartmouth campus; he introduced Paul to people in Narragansett, and took him by train "up to Providence to introduce him to the black society there."[63] Paul spent time with Joe Nelson, a Princeton friend attending Howard University who worked with him at the Imperial Hotel (Paul got him the job), and "together we socialized with Narragansett Indians and with a few white Jewish girls who lived in the area. We went to the beach just about every day," Nelson remembered. "Paul brought a football with him and practiced while we watched. It was such a sight to see — that enormous person catching passes on the beach. Among all of us there was an ease and friendliness," remembered Nelson. When asked if anyone complained that he and Paul were socializing with young white women, Nelson replied: "It

Paul Robeson and other members of the Rutgers basketball team. Courtesy of Special Collections, Rutgers University Library.

really wasn't dating; we usually did things together, as a group. We didn't pay any mind to it—color, that is. Fannie Chopek (her father was a tailor at Narragansett) was white, we were black, and the Indians were red. We were all having a good time, that's all. But, then again, I suppose it would have been a different story if we had been in Jim Crow Washington, D.C."[64]

Marguerite Upshur, a year-round black Narragansett resident whose parents ran a local laundry business, remembered playing piano for Paul at small, informal recitals held at a little theater hall on Beach Street.[65] "We even sold tickets to make a little extra money. Some of the white help came and went back and told their employers about Paul's voice, and at the next recital some of the employers came. Paul sang some popular songs, standards, but aside from these, the spirituals was what he sang. Whites thought blacks sang naturally, and Paul—so polite and gentlemanly—sang just what they wanted to hear. At our own get-togethers Paul was great fun. He always liked to sing and loved to dance, too, and was good—very easy on his feet. He was so different from his brother Ben; Paul was the life of it."[66]

When the summer ended, Robeson switched gears and returned to life at Rutgers, which meant another season of football and another year of the grind to keep his grades up. (Robeson's much improved grades in the second semester of his freshman year, after the football season had ended — all As, with the exception of one B — suggest the toll football exacted on his studies.)

The 1916 Rutgers football team faced a tougher schedule than in the previous year, but its 1915 showing had been encouraging, and the team was ready for the challenge. The season began magnificently, with the team easily downing Villanova 30 to 0; and Robeson, stronger and more disciplined after a year's experience, started and played a full sixty minutes. Players and fans hoped for an especially good showing on Homecoming Weekend against Virginia's Washington and Lee University. Rutgers was celebrating its 150th anniversary, and Homecoming activities promised to be unusually spirited, "*the* big event of 1916, a gala weekend."[67]

More than 200 delegates, representing over 150 colleges, universities, and learned societies from around the world, and some 900 alumni packed the Alumni House and New Brunswick hotels that beautiful autumn weekend in October. The cow college had come into its own as a reputable academic institution, and the coming year would see that new identity given formal sanction, as the former private Reform Church School was officially designated the State University of New Jersey. That Saturday, after the recognition of delegates and conferring of honorary degrees in Kirkpatrick Chapel, the alumni parade (numbering in its ranks the ten survivors of Rutgers' original 1869 football team) formed on the Queen's Campus and marched through the city and on to Neilson Field for the contest with Washington and Lee.[68] For many, football, now a staple feature of Rutgers life, embodied the school's new winning spirit. Fans expected a good game, and the Scarlet Scourge was determined not to disappoint them.

But in the midst of these happy events Robeson faced a painful and humiliating dilemma. Before the game, Coach Sanford gathered the team in the locker room and informed them that Washington and Lee refused to play with a black man in the lineup. "It's up to you fellows," Sanford said. "Does he [Robeson] play or not?"[69] "Paul understood Rutgers would be in an awkward position if no football game were played after thousands had turned out for the big Homecoming contest," player William Feitner remembered. Finally Robeson broke the silence and "smoothed everything over" by voluntarily benching himself. "'You don't need me,' Paul told the team. 'You can beat them without me.'"[70] Paul's teammates were relieved. As one teammate put it, "The colored boy knew his place and did not butt in or crusade." As they saw it, Paul had done the right thing, apparently taking the incident in stride, and that was the end of it.[71]

Playing without Robeson, Rutgers held Washington and Lee to a 13 to 13 tie and had a great celebration afterward, followed by a Sunday morning of festivities, none of which Paul attended. Instead, he went home to talk with his father. William Robeson understood what being on the team meant to Paul and, despite his insistence that Paul put his studies first, he had been, from Paul's freshman year on, his son's most avid fan. (By Paul's sophomore year, classmates had grown accustomed to seeing his father, an anachronism in his frock coat, "so long it looked like a six footer's cast-off," at what had become *his* place in the stands. Some even looked upon the "grizzled little pastor" as a "sort of good-luck charm.")[72] Paul was upset about the incident, wanted to leave Rutgers, and told his father as much. "But my father told me he hadn't sent me to college to play football and vetoed my plan to switch colleges [from Rutgers to Dartmouth]."[73] Long before Paul even set foot on the Rutgers campus, his father had "drummed it into his head that he would be on display ... and so would have to bend over backwards to be a good sportsman." In William's mind this case was no exception.[74]

Judging from Robeson's performance during the remainder of the season, his absence cost Rutgers a clear victory on Homecoming Day. For Robeson the disappointment ran deeper than chagrin over a lost game. Like his teammates, Paul looked up to Coach Sanford: Although he was white, Paul trusted him and regarded him as a friend and father figure. In several instances he went to him with personal problems, and on those occasions when Paul, afraid of injury or holding back for some other reason, failed to work up to his potential, Sandy would call him "into the office and straighten him out."[75] In this case, Sanford had let Robeson down. His refusal to come to Paul's defense, or to say anything on Paul's behalf, had, by default, placed all the responsibility on Robeson who, as an unheralded sophomore, had little choice but save face as best he could by gracefully backing out.

Neither had Paul's teammates, either individually or as a group, supported him by refusing to play without him.[76] In later years, when he reminisced about his adolescence, it was Somerville classmate J. Douglas Brown and Mal Pitt from Rutgers who Robeson singled out as friends. He rarely mentioned Sanford or any of his Rutgers teammates. Possibly their behavior in the case of Washington and Lee had hurt him deeply, enough so that he would never really consider any of them friends.[77]

Outwardly, however, Paul "took it," and the next week went back to play before a cheering crowd of 5,000 in Providence, Rhode Island, where Rutgers clashed with Fritz Pollard's formidable Brown University team. Pollard, who talked with Robeson about the Washington and Lee incident at the Rutgers-Brown game, said that, "he didn't say much, mostly listened while I talked, but he was still mad as anything about what had happened the week before. The football field was really the only place where you could do some physical beating up on those white boys, and the racial thing sure made you play all the harder. Well, that was it, and Paul played a hell of a game defensively against us that day." Rutgers held onto a slim 3 to 0 lead at half-time and bettered Brown well into the third period before Brown moved into high gear and beat Rutgers 21 to 3. "Paul was mad, but he hadn't lost his sense of humor. We actually had some fun together on the field that day," said Pollard. "With two blacks out there, each on opposing teams, they couldn't very well pick on us as 'niggers' that game. There was big Paul staring me down with that smile of his, and joking as he came at me, 'Now Fritz be careful. Look out! Fritz, I don't want to hurt you.'"[78]

Rutgers went on to play West Virginia University to a hard-fought scoreless tie, then rolled over Dickinson, 34 to 0, and beat Washington and Jefferson 12 to 9. Local newspapers had praised Robeson's play all season, but his role in the Washington and Jefferson victory earned him his highest accolades to date. "The strongest man on the [Rutgers] team.... Robeson tore great holes in the opposing line," wrote Frank Hathorn, covering the game for the *New York World*. "When given the ball [he] plunged ahead with such power that it often required two or three men to bring him down.... His tackling was deadly."[79]

The team was disappointed with its record of three wins, two losses and two ties. But the season had been a good one for Robeson — he had started every contest (with the exception of Washington and Lee), played a full sixty minutes per game, and earned some glowing press coverage.[80] In short, he had demonstrated his ability and set the stage for what would be two years of uncontested greatness on the gridiron.

Academics and a host of new extracurricular activities — the Philoclean Literary Society, the Rutgers debate team, winter and spring sports — filled the gap left when the football season ended. Paul had his father's love of oratory, and at Rutgers demonstrated his prodigious talent by winning every major elocution and debating contest he entered, as well as leading the school's debating team to successive victories.[81] In addition, he played basketball, baseball, and ran track for the school teams, and on weekends at home in Somerville he played more sports and took part in local social activities.

The surface picture — the record of academic achievement and a wide array of extracurricular accomplishments — suggests an energetic, enthusiastic, and socially well-adjusted young man who apparently preferred to do many things well rather than a few things perfectly. (Paul's grades in his sophomore year, although still honors ranking and a solid B average, included three Cs and a D in physics lab, hardly the flawless performance his father wanted.) Robeson's choices for favorite reading matter (on a form filled out for the school yearly), however, hint at a more brooding side to his personality.[82] All of his choices — Tennyson's haunting *Rizpah*, Shakespeare's *Hamlet*, Hardy's *Tess of the D'Urbervilles*, and Kipling's poem "If" — feature isolated and lonely protagonists. Each faces the future grimly, with a certain amount of stoicism, and alone. Selected lines from Kipling's "If" illustrate this well.

If you can wait and not be tired by waiting,
Or being lied about, don't deal in lies,
Or being hated, don't give way to hating,
And yet don't look too good, not talk too wise

… … … … … … … … … … … …

If you can force your heart and nerve and sinew
To serve your turn long after they are gone,

And so hold on when there is nothing in you
Except the Will which says to them: "Hold on!"…

…If neither foes nor loving friends can hurt you,
If all men count with you, but none too much;
If you can fill the unforgiving minute
With sixty seconds' worth of distance run,
Yours is the Earth and everything that's in it,
And — which is more — you'll be a Man, my son!

Mal Pitt, Paul's closest college friend, confirmed what Paul's reading preferences suggest: "I think that for all his gregariousness, Paul was really a solitary and lonesome person. Everyone thought of him as a friend, but with the exception of his brother Ben, he was never really close to anyone. Even though he was a favorite at Rutgers, believe me, Paul was always on guard, always careful about stepping out of line."[83] Robeson's prodigious appetite for activity thus may well have been prompted as much by his need to fill the sense of isolation as ambition to do it all.

His sophomore year Robeson again listed Mal Pitt as his best friend but added Robert "Davvy" Davenport, who, along with Paul, comprised Rutgers' black student body that year. It was at the end of sophomore year, also, that Paul first met Geraldine ("Gerry") Neale, the pretty, intelligent, and ambitious young black woman with whom he would be romantically involved over the next several years. Gerry Neale lived in nearby Freehold and was just beginning her training at Teachers Normal in Trenton. Like Paul, she had been raised a striver, but a considerably more combative striver than Paul. At Trenton Normal, for example, when she heard that Negroes would not be allowed to join the Shakespeare Club, she decided to confront the situation and find out for herself, something Paul would not have done. And, "Of course," she said matter-of-factly, "I was admitted."[84]

At first Gerry Neale and Paul saw each other intermittently, at parties and occasionally when he visited her in Trenton, but then they began spending time together more regularly. "Paul was not one of those fellows who was everywhere — going to this dance and that dance," remembered Gerry. "Most often I saw him at social affairs, in Trenton and other places where we all came together, those of us blacks attending college. Paul came, and fellows from the University of Pennsylvania, New York College, and other schools all over the East Coast came. I met Marion [Paul's sister] at one of these affairs, and we became lifelong friends. We had a wonderful time. Paul was outgoing but still reserved, almost shy. I first heard him sing at one of our small social gatherings, all very informal, of course." Gerry remembered Paul as thoughtful and sensitive, even to small slights, and recalled how wonderful it was when that sensitivity was exercised on her behalf. She cited as an example Paul's habit of altering lyrics (something he would do throughout his performing career), in her case to fit a Negro girl. "He was very fond of 'I Love You Truly' and 'Gray Days Are Your Gray Eyes,' and he used to change the words because, he said, 'Negro girls have brown eyes.' The song went, 'Gray days are your gray eyes/ Gold days are your hair/ Come storm or sun to me/ All days are fair,' and he would sing, 'Gray Days are your *brown* eyes,' and so on. He was thoughtful like that."[85]

Life at Rutgers changed suddenly and dramatically in the spring of 1917: The United States was at war. College sports teams throughout the country were left depleted as older student-athletes enlisted. Harvard, Yale, and Princeton announced they would cancel their football programs entirely and focus instead on military training. Coach Sanford, however, followed a different course: "Heart and soul in back of football as a war preparedness effort." Sanford announced that rather than drop its football program, Rutgers would make it bigger than ever. With administrative backing, large-scale student support (nearly 100 students tried out for the team), and the largest budget ever allocated for the sport, Sanford substantially enlarged the school's football program.[86]

Rutgers had its problems. Only three of the team's starters were veterans: Rendall, Feitner, and Robeson. But in the season's opener the team, still "a bit crude, showed signs of power," beat Ursinus 25 to 0. As the season continued the Scarlet Scourge picked up momentum, mowing down the service team Fort Washington 90 to 0. Its first real test, however, came in the contest against Syracuse, a team with both experience and the home field advantage. Players fumbled and penalties abounded on the muddy field that October afternoon in a game described by the *Times* as "about the most bloody battle ... seen ... in years." What little punch Rutgers could muster came from Robeson, "the giant colored end from New Brunswick [who] stood head and shoulders above his teammates for all around playing. He was a tower of strength on the Scarlet defense.... Practically every forward pass Foster Sanford's men used was built around Robeson. He towered over every man on the field and when he stretched his arms up in the air he pulled down forward passes that an ordinary player would have to use a stepladder to reach."[87] The game ended in a 14 to 0 loss for Rutgers, but not because of any lack in Robeson's play.

Coach Sanford was disappointed. He had hoped for a season with no losses, but he took heart watching Robeson. With Paul on the team Rutgers could still turn the season around. In the weeks that followed, the Scarlet Scourge did just that, pounding in succession Lafayette (33 to 6) and Fordham (28 to 0). Robeson's play again was singled out: "It can hardly be said that one player stood out on the Rutgers aggregation, unless it was Robeson, the giant Negro at left end," wrote the *New York Tribune*'s Charles Taylor. "He was a tower of strength on the offense and defense.... Twice the big Rutgers Negro raced down the field after receiving a perfect toss from Whitehill.... On the other occasion Robeson raced twenty-four yards before being brought to earth again close to the Fordham goal line. Each of these passes gave Rutgers a chance to score, and Rutgers did not throw away the opportunity.... The dark cloud was omnipresent."[88]

Coach Sanford drilled the team relentlessly in preparation for the contest against the formidable Gilmour Dobie, who coached West Virginia Mountaineers, working his men until long after dark on the day before the game. Robeson, touted in the press (albeit, often with coon song euphemisms like "dark cloud") as Rutgers' star player, felt especially pressed to make a good showing. He was good, but he was also black, which meant he would be in the spotlight, watched and singled out by the Southern team. Shortly before the day of the game, the rumor spread that the Mountaineers would refuse to play if Robeson appeared in the lineup. Perhaps if Paul had been the inexperienced sophomore he was when the issue came up with Washington and Lee, Rutgers might have acquiesced. But, with Robeson a prospective All-American and the team's most valuable player, Rutgers flatly refused, and as the team's student manager put it, "told them [the West Virginia team] to get lost."[89]

With Robeson definitely in the lineup, word spread that the Mountaineers "were out to get that nigger," and according to Pare Lorentz, then a young West Virginia

fan attending the game, play had barely begun when "a number of Mountaineer fans began hollering 'Kill that nigger! Kill that nigger!' If Paul heard it, and it was certainly loud enough to be heard, he didn't look in the direction of the jeers and didn't appear fazed by them."[90] However, before the game had ended, Robeson vented his anger on at least one of his West Virginia opponents. Years later Paul described the incident to theater critic Heywood Broun: "When we lined up for the first play, the man playing opposite me leaned forward and said, 'Don't you so much as touch me, you black dog, or I'll cut your heart out.' Can you imagine? I'm playing opposite him in a football game and he says I'm not to touch him. When the whistle blew I dove in, and he didn't see me coming. I clipped him sidewise and nearly busted him in two and as we were lying under the pile I leaned forward and whispered, 'I touched you that time. How did you like it?'"[91]

The contest ended in a 7 to 7 draw. Rutgers continued its winning spree, leveling Springfield College (61 to 0) and Philadelphia's United States Marine team (27 to 0). On November 24, at Ebbets Field in Brooklyn, the Scarlet Scourge faced its stiffest challenge of the season: the all-powerful Newport, Rhode Island, Naval Reserve team. Dubbed "invincible," and star-studded with All-Americans, this team of seasoned veterans was unbeaten and unscored upon, downing easily the likes of Brown, Colgate, and Dartmouth. And facing them was "little" Rutgers, its eleven men averaging just slightly over nineteen years in age and outweighed by their Reserve opposition by at least ten pounds per man. "The Naval team had eighteen All-Americans," recalled Rutgers' Thug Rendall, "and when we met in the locker room those Navy guys were riding us, calling us tiny high school boys. I got nervous and wanted Paul to stand up and shut them up with his size. But Paul shrugged his shoulders and said he hadn't heard them talking. Whatever Paul had to say, he'd say it on the field that day."[92]

Although the Naval Reserve team had the advantage, it was Rutgers' finest hour that afternoon, as before an estimated crowd of 15,000 the Scarlet Scourge trounced their opposition in a stunning 14 to 0 upset. Between the halves, stunned and jubilant Rutgers students snake-danced around the gridiron, shouting school cheers and singing rousing choruses of "On the Banks of the Raritan," while alumni in the stands threw their hats and scarves deliriously into the air. The final victory came quickly and easily, as the Naval Reserve team had never really been in the game, managing only two first downs. Frost-bitten fans rocked the stands, cheering themselves hoarse: The Scarlet Scourge had buried the noses of Cupid Black and his other All-Americans. It was Rutgers and Robeson all the way, the *New York Times* reported: "The work of Robeson, Rollins and Whitehill on the defense was so brilliant that they broke up the Naval Reserve's plays in the making."[93]

Robeson's pivotal role in Rutgers' surprise defeat of the Naval Reserve team provided a tailor-made occasion for the larger-than-life, lavish sports reportage so popular in those days, and sportswriters made the most of it. "A tall, tapering Negro in a faded crimson sweater, moleskins and a pair of maroon socks ranged hither and yon on a wind-whipped Flatbush field yesterday afternoon," wrote an enamored Louis Lee Arms of the *Sunday Tribune.* "He rode on the wings of the frigid breezes: a grim, silent, and compelling figure. Whether it was Charlie Barrett, of old Cornell and All-American glory, or Gerrish or Gardner who tried to hurl himself through a moving gauntlet, he was met and stopped by this blaze of black and red. The Negro was Paul Robeson of Rutgers College, and

he is a minister's son. He is also nineteen years of age and weighs two hundred pounds. Of his football capacity you are duly referred to 'Cupid' Black of Newport and Yale. He can tell you. It was Robeson, a veritable Othello of Battle, who led the dashing little Rutgers Eleven to a 14–0 victory over the widely heralded Newport Naval Reserves."[94]

It was a great win for Rutgers, and the team easily maintained its dominance for the remainder of the season, scoring an average of thirty points per game. Of the season's nine contests, Rutgers won seven, lost one, and tied the other. Six of the team's victories were shutouts, with Rutgers totaling a whopping 295 points against their opposition's paltry 28. Walter Camp, Yale legend and the architect of the All-American football team, speculated on the possibility of a national championship match between Rutgers and the Georgia Tech Yellow Jackets, a team boasting a perfect record of nine wins and no losses; and the New York *Sun* placed seven of the Rutgers Eleven on the All-East team, led by Paul Robeson. More than anything Paul would accomplish at Rutgers, this single event, the surprise drubbing of the Naval Reserve team, skyrocketed him into the national limelight, as sports writers across the country dubbed him the best of the best. Walter Camp perhaps most succinctly summed up the acclaim when he called Robeson "the greatest defensive end ever to trod the gridiron," and officially acknowledged his outstanding performance by naming him All-American, thus selecting him to join the ranks of football's all-time greats for all-around ability and performance in football.

Like Fritz Pollard the year before, Paul had earned fame for himself and recognition for his race. The black community, justifiably proud, crowned Robeson with its own laurels. Few things did more to fire hope for the future than publicizing the accomplishments of gifted young blacks like Robeson. Black weeklies like the *New York Age*, the *Chicago Defender*, and *Philadelphia Tribune* eagerly sought out such information as it documented, individual by individual, racial progress. "Last Fall it was Frederick Douglass Pollard of Brown who shone forth as the most brilliant of the football stars," wrote Lester Walton of the *New York Age*. "I now take pleasure in introducing to you Mr. Paul Robeson of Rutgers College, New Jersey, another gentleman of color, who has become the sensation of the present football season. For two successive years the Negro has carried off the highest honors on the gridiron, which in the vernacular of the turf, 'is going some.'"[95]

That year Paul returned "home" to the black communities of Somerville, Princeton, and New Brunswick a hero, not only for his dazzling feats on the gridiron but equally so for his less heralded academic achievements. Robeson had made national sports headlines and been selected for membership to the Phi Beta Kappa honor society, and this while still in his junior year. "I knew of Paul many years before I met him," said one black northern New Jersey friend. "As young kids we were in grammar school and he was in college, but we all knew his activities. We all wanted to be like Paul who had proven himself both as a student and as an athlete. We thought that anybody in college was the greatest thing. We thought of him as a giant."[96]

Robeson was a giant, the fulfillment of the black community's fondest hopes. Carlton Moss, whose family had been one of those to migrate north in the 1890s, explained: "I was from Essex County, which includes Newark, Montclair, and the Oranges. You had after the turn of the century a small black community, some of the extremely courageous blacks who left the rural South and started branching out. My dad was one of them. He didn't want New York because it was already becoming a crowded center. So he and other blacks like him went into these very small New Jersey communities. Scattered up the East Coast from Trenton on up all the way to Jersey City were pockets of black families, and they were all striving families. They came at a time when 95 percent of the black population lived in the South. These were pioneer people, and their whole emphasis was on finding a solution to the problem of getting an education. They felt that the further North they came, the better opportunity their kids would have. You had this tremendous drive on the part of parents to work so that their kids would have an opportunity to go to high school and then to college."[97]

By the time Paul began his college education he was already well known in these northern New Jersey black communities. His high school successes marked him as one of the community's promising prospects, and, as Moss put it, "to top it all, Paul was going to a white college and a good one. There was great status attached to attending a white college. Most of us who went to college attended black schools like Morgan, Howard, and Virginia State. We always thought of going to a white school like City College. At that time, when you were growing into adulthood, you talked about those things. For some reason we all went to black schools. But Paul was out of the ordinary. He competed with whites and was head and shoulders better than them."[98]

While the press of both races heaped accolades on him, at white Rutgers Robeson maintained the unassuming manner he had always presented. His "Review of the 1917 Football Season" (*Rutgers Alumni Quarterly*) eulogized Coach Sanford and praised individually every team member, from veteran seniors and underclassmen who would lead the team the following year to the scrubs and assistant coaches, Wittpenn and Nash. But about himself and his own accomplishments Paul wrote nothing.[99] Any acknowledgment of his own contribution, however slight, might have been interpreted as boasting and thus link him with "uppity niggers" like Jack Johnson rather than with fellow athlete Fritz Pollard, described by the white press as a "modest ... gentleman of color ... [who] always shrinks from the spotlight of all athletic demonstrations."[100]

That summer, in fact, a white guest at Narragansett would chastise Robeson for what the guest viewed as just that kind of unseemly "boasting." "I was waiting on a table in a very swank hotel," Robeson recalled. "The other waiters were very proud of me. We were all Negroes. One elderly waiter, a roly-poly, good-natured fellow ... was so proud, he'd tell everyone, 'that waiter there is Paul Robeson of Rutgers, All-American end.' Some guests decided that I must be an uppity kind of guy, so they proceeded to insult me at every turn. Nothing was right, and the scorn on the man's face — his insistence upon my being a 'servant,' not an All-American — was ugly. Finally, in order not to throw the tray in his face, I quietly left my tray on the stand, and went to the waiters' room, took off my waiter's jacket and started toward the waiters' quarters. Someone ran after me. I refused to answer. They said, 'You'll lose your job.' And I answered nothing.

"The guests stayed for days. I stayed in the quarters and played baseball. The headwaiter — I shall never forget him — came over to me that first evening. Patted me on the shoulder, and said 'I understand. Take it easy until these folks leave, then come back.'"[101]

Robeson had learned that if one wanted to get along in the white world, modesty was a required trait. Thus it should come as no surprise that Paul said nothing when he was overlooked as the logical choice for

captain of the next year's team. Robeson as team captain would have presented one problem after another: a black man doing the coin toss before games, speaking at pep rallies, meeting alumni, shaking hands with opponents — all almost impossible to imagine. It would take Robeson years to get over the practice of discounting (and later embellishing) his achievements according to what made whites comfortable. It would prove a psychologically costly habit, one that interfered with his ability to assess himself and heightened his sense of inferiority in that it inextricably linked his sense of self-worth to what whites thought of him.[102]

In the spring of a year that should have been among Robeson's happiest, Paul suffered a crushing loss. During the early part of the year his father, now seventy-three years old, had begun to fail noticeably. Paul always visited his father regularly — there was no one he loved and respected more — but while he was sick Paul pushed himself to the limit to keep up with his studies while traveling back and forth from Rutgers to care for William. Gerry Neale spoke with great feeling as she remembered how wrenching and difficult this period was for Paul. "He and his father were all alone. There was just the two of them — no one else. Paul went back and forth from Rutgers to Somerville, nursing his father while he was going to school. By the spring Paul was really exhausted." On Friday morning, May 12, 1918, William Robeson died.[103] Again, Paul's extraordinary devotion to his father moved Gerry Neale: "Rutgers had an oratorical contest for every class level. Paul had won in his freshman and sophomore year, and had another contest coming up in the middle of May. His father, sick as he was, remembered this and had told Paul, 'Whatever happens to me ... I don't care what happens to me ... I want you to go and give your speech and I want you to win.' And really, before the contest came off his father died. Actually, on the day of the contest his father was lying in state before the funeral.[104]

"I went with a couple of friends to the contest. What we saw was this giant, fatigued-looking human being. The subject of his speech was the Negro and the Constitution. He won … but I think the remarkable thing was the high standard his father had always set for them all. Imagine winning an oratorical contest while his father was lying in state. But that was his father's philosophy for all his children: Whatever you do, do it best, don't take anything that's second best."[105]

Right up until the very end, William Robeson goaded Paul to achieve, demanding in this case that his son put aside even grief, at least long enough to win first prize.[106] That the ties between this father and son were unusually strong was obvious; even casual observers noted it.[107] Paul worshiped his father and would have done anything for him.[108] Indeed, as Paul writes in his autobiography, the desire to please his father would persist long after William Robeson's death. As late as 1958 Robeson, reflecting on his own life, still wondered, "'What would Pop think?' … Often I stretch out my arms as I used to, to put it around Pop's shoulder and ask, 'How'm doin' Pop?' My Pop's influence is still present in the struggles I face today."[109]

Robeson's loyalty to his father became all the more resolute in the wake of his passing. Shortly after William Robeson's death, the Bustills decided to reestablish contact with the Robesons, specifically with Paul, whose accomplishments had not escaped their notice. After years of silence, in the summer of 1918 his mother's relatives invited Paul to their famed annual family reunion held at a private picnic grounds (Maple Grove) in Philadelphia. According to one member of the Bustill clan allied by marriage but not by blood,

"Paul was not at the Bustill picnics until 1918, but don't mention my name when you write that or I'll be thrown out of the family." The annual Bustill picnic drew not only nearby family but people from all over the East Coast. It was an elaborate all-day event, including a huge feast, entertainment, and the traditional celebration of the Bustill family genealogy, complete with a reading of the family history by Robeson's cousin, Annie Bustill Smith, and orations by various family members, including that year, Paul.[110]

The Bustills had apparently decided to bestow on Paul the legitimacy they had denied his father. It was a victory of sorts, but coming as it did so close to his father's death it was a bittersweet triumph at best. It is unclear what motivated Paul to accept the invitation or how he felt once he was actually among his mother's relatives. Did, for example, the misspelling of his name on the program — "Roberson" instead of "Robeson" — add salt to old wounds?[111] Robeson chose as the subject of his speech "Loyalty to Convictions" because, as he later explained, "it was the text of my father's life." Whatever else he did that day, Robeson took pains to make it clear that he credited his own success not to his mother's elite progenitors but to the ambition and striving for excellence he had learned from his father.[112]

Forty years later, recalling that day in his autobiography, Robeson makes little attempt to hide the old anger and bitterness. He treats the occasion with calculated indifference, informing readers that he would have forgotten about the event entirely had he not come across a copy of the program in a college scrapbook. Robeson does mention the misspelling of his name, noting with amusement that the error highlighted the one aspect of William Robeson's life the Bustills would have most preferred to forget: his slave heritage. "It is likely," Robeson writes, "that 'Roberson' was [in fact] the ancestral name of the slave-holding Robesons from whom my father got his name."[113]

With his father gone, Paul felt not only loss but an anguished sense of rootlessness. His older brothers had lived away from home for years and were now fairly well settled. Not so for Paul. For so long his father had been his only anchor: Without him there was no place that felt like home.

In between the time his Rutgers classes ended and his work at Narragansett began, Paul worked briefly at a shipbuilding plant in Newark, New Jersey, doing his "bit for Uncle Sam."[114] At Narragansett, by 1918, he knew his way around and was among old friends. "Everyone knew him, black and white," remembered Joe Nelson. "All you had to do was be around him and you could see why he was so admired. He was so big and in such good shape physically. Then, on top of it all, he was so modest, even a bit embarrassed about his own accomplishments. Everywhere he went people wanted him to sing. Even then his voice was magnificent. Any time a group got together it was almost a given that we would ask Paul to sing."[115]

On their way back to college, waiting at the train station in Providence, Paul and Joe Nelson talked about the coming year. "While we were talking we saw soldiers' coffins being sent home for burial. The soldiers who died — most of them — had not been killed in battle but died from influenza. There was an awful influenza attack in the country then, but it seemed to kill men in the army more than anyone else. It was frightening. We both were afraid of being drafted. We were the same age and eligible, but neither of us had registered yet. So we decided the first thing both would do when we got back to college was volunteer and sign up right away for SATC [the Student Army Training Corps] just to be on the safe side."[116]

Patriotic fervor ran high at Rutgers that fall, fired by President Demarest's "high noon" speech to the student body, urging a wholehearted backing of the war abroad. Occasionally, this enthusiasm assumed a sinister tone. When a naive freshman publicly denounced the sale of Liberty Bonds, for example, irate students seized him, held him for several hours in a room in Ford Hall, and then turned him over to a mob to be stripped, covered with molasses and feathers, and paraded through the town.[117] Rutgers students exhibited ardent devotion to the ideal of democracy abroad but, like the nation as a whole, showed little concern over its uneven application at home. Few whites saw the irony of American blacks volunteering to "keep the world safe for democracy" and then being confined to segregated units.

By the time classes began in the fall, the SATC had all but taken over the college, converting fraternity and other buildings into military housing facilities so that the school looked more like a military camp than an educational institution. Robeson, along with 450 Rutgers men, joined the SATC that fall and was inducted in a formal ceremony held on the campus on October 1, 1918.[118] Rutgers' new "soldiers" were paid thirty dollars a month by the government for their services and followed a rigid schedule that began with a 6:00 A.M. reveille, followed by room inspection, rifle drills, and kitchen police duty.[119] Robeson, unlike most black servicemen, underwent his SATC training alongside his white classmates, predating President Truman's executive order integrating the armed forces by some thirty years. First appointed squad leader and later assigned the rank of corporal, he became one of the few blacks not required to undergo his officer's training at a segregated center.[120]

The issue of blacks fighting in the war for "democracy" was hotly contested among black leaders of the period. Dating back to the American Revolution, blacks, segregated and the victims of gross discrimination in the military — most recently, the excessively harsh treatment black soldiers received in the aftermath of the 1908 Brownsville, Texas, riot, and the 1917 Houston altercation — were used as soldiers only when absolutely necessary. Nonetheless, time and time again they stepped forward — during the Civil War, as Buffalo Soldiers in the West, in the Spanish-American War, and with Theodore Roosevelt in Cuba — willing to spill their blood in the hope that whites might once and for all accept them as full citizens. When W. E. B. Du Bois (according to biographer David Levering Lewis, after much soul-searching and the offer of a commission in the Army Military Intelligence) in July of 1918 publicly announced his support of the war effort in what would be perhaps his most famous and eloquent *Crisis* editorial, entitled "Close Ranks," other black leaders, including William Monroe Trotter (editor of the *Boston Guardian*), Archibald Grimke, and A. Philip Randolph, were outraged. But neither Paul nor his brother Ben, who served as a chaplain for a segregated unit, were among those objecting.[121]

The new SATC-enforced military schedule forced the cancellation of many of Rutgers' extracurricular activities. Football, however, was not among them.[122] Team members, taking their lead from Coach Sanford, and backed by school officials and the military men on campus, went through the paces of their training with an energy quickened by patriotism. Like Walter Camp himself, Sanford believed that football developed character and experience: Players would demonstrate on the battlefield the same courage they exhibited on the gridiron. "The men who had gone into the opposing football line when their signal came went 'over the top' with the same abandon," Camp wrote

in 1919. "Those who had made a stand on the last five-yard line in the grim determination of the gridiron field faced the scrimmage of war with the same do-or-die fortitude."[123] As Sanford saw it, winning would be Rutgers' contribution to the war effort. And with Robeson on the team the Scarlet Scourge would be unbeatable.

Beginning the season three weeks late due to a severe influenza epidemic, Rutgers won against Pelham Bay's Naval Reserves, but by a disturbingly narrow margin of 7 to 0. Coach Sanford worked the team relentlessly for its next game, and his efforts paid off. Rutgers mauled Lehigh 30 to 0, with Robeson leading the way. Gathering still more momentum, Rutgers crushed the Naval Transport Unit of Hoboken 40 to 0. By midseason not one of Rutgers' opponents had yet succeeded in gaining a first down. Statistically, if all the plays scored by Rutgers' opposition had been made consecutively, the total would have amounted to a mere eighteen yards. Rutgers' defense, led by the invincible Robeson, was superb. Undefeated in its first five games, Rutgers fully expected to surpass its spectacular 1917 record.

But the Scarlet Scourge was stopped, dramatically and decisively, in the final two games of the season. Playing on Brooklyn's Ebbets Field, where only a year before they had routed the invincible Naval Reserve team, the Scarlet Scourge suffered a crushing loss, 54 to 14, its first in two years, at the hands of the Great Lakes Naval Station. With that its championship climb was halted in what the *Alumni Quarterly* described as the "greatest upset of the decade."[124]

In the season's final game against Syracuse, played two weeks later, the team's superb defense once again shone as Rutgers limited Syracuse to only three first downs from scrimmage against Rutgers' own thirteen. Outplayed, Syracuse still managed to blank Rutgers 21 to 0. The surprise collapse of the team disappointed fans and alumni. Some have conjectured, and Paul himself on occasion admitted, that at the time when both his prowess and national recognition peaked, Robeson stopped enjoying the game. "When you had it hammered into you ... that you must beat such and such a team, the emphasis was too great. Instead of playing for the love of it, you then were playing only to win," Robeson said years later.

"Nothing was quite the same for Paul after his father's death," Art Van Fleet remembered. "I just don't think his heart was in football. Besides missing his father, the game had lost some of its glow. Let's face it, playing under Sandy was tough. And then, too, Sandy expected more of Paul than of the others: He was an All-American and had better play up to that standard. Opponents really wanted to get him and, big as he was, Paul got pretty beat up his senior year."[125] Robeson's performance, if not his personal best, was still top-notch, and for the second year in a row Rutgers' star player was named to Walter Camp's All-American team. In other school sports he had amassed an enviable record as well, earning an unprecedented twelve varsity letters, four in football, three in basketball, three in baseball, and two in track.

Of Paul as a track man, teammate Feitner reminisced: "Paul may not have had correct form or technique for a weight man in track, but his natural athletic ability and raw strength made up for that and enabled him to achieve anyway. Paul and I both threw the javelin. Neither of us were that good, but we held our own and the team managed to go undefeated senior year and against some pretty stiff competition."[126] In his junior and senior years Robeson sandwiched track in between baseball practice and games. He was the team's third top scorer for the 1919 season, with one of his most memorable feats the javelin throw in Rutgers 1919 match with

Swarthmore, when he "hurled the javelin 137 feet, 5 inches [five inches better than his nearest competitor], and this against a fairly strong wind."[127] Teammate Wittpenn remembered, "He [Robeson] just picked up the javelin, heaved it against the wind, and off it went. That was sheer strength."[128] In April of his senior year Paul traveled alone to Philadelphia to represent Rutgers in the Penn relays, and went the next day to Schenectady where he was catcher for the Rutgers baseball team. In Philadelphia, facing some of the toughest track competition in the nation, Robeson finished tenth in the running broad jump (18', 5.5" against the winning 20', 3.5") and fifth in the javelin throw (127', 10" to the winning throw of 147', 05").[129]

In baseball the story was much the same. Paul played catcher's position for three years, occasionally filling in as an outfielder. "He certainly made a big target behind the plate," said teammate A. F. Eschenfelder. "The pitcher really had someone to throw to. And he talked it up behind the plate, too; that voice was that powerful even then. Paul was not the greatest hitter to come down the line, but you knew he was there when he was catching."[130]

In basketball ("Rutgers wasn't much beyond the peach basket stage in those days," said one player, "a little running, no fast breaks, two-handed sets—not much action") Robeson filled any position, as needed, and his play figured fairly consistently in Rutgers' victories.[131] "Paul was not one of the quickest men on the court, although he was fast for his size," remembered three-year basketball teammate Calvin Meury. "He was used mainly at center and forward, acting as muscleman under the boards. He stood out like a sore thumb ... one of the few big men in the game, then. Most were five feet ten, or so."[132]

Robeson's desire to "do it all" athlet-

Paul Robeson, catcher, Rutgers baseball team. Courtesy of Special Collections, Rutgers University Library.

ically was not without its humorous moments. In May of 1918, for example, he competed in a Rutgers track event against New York University while playing catcher for Rutgers' baseball team on an adjoining field. In both events Robeson performed well, placing second in the shot put and the hammer throw, and holding his own on the diamond as well. Art Van Fleet said that his most vivid memories of Paul in sports were "not of Robey on the gridiron" but of having the baseball game held up while "Robey sauntered across Neilson Field over to the track meet for the javelin or hammer or shot event and then sauntered back to continue the baseball game."[133]

By the time Robeson was ready to graduate, he had changed since that warm September day in 1915 when a nonentity, an ambitious black youngster from rural New Jersey, first made his way across the Rutgers campus. Four years later, "Robey of Rutgers" was the pride of both the black community and the class of 1919. The black press across the country sang his praises while, locally, the New Brunswick YMCA presented him with a purse as a gesture of the local black community's respect and admiration.[134] Among his graduating class at Rutgers no one could compete with Robeson for all-round achievement — academic honors; athletic excellence and versatility (Robeson had earned an unprecedented 12 letters in Rutgers athletics); membership in Phi Beta Kappa; the coveted Skull and Cap award (an honor given to the four seniors who best represented the ideals and traditions of Rutgers); and yearly oratorical prizes.[135] A front-page eulogistic com-

Paul Robeson, about the time of his graduation from Rutgers, with Phi Beta Kappa key and football on chain. Courtesy of Paul Robeson, Jr.

mentary in the June issue of *Targum* said it all: "May Rutgers never forget this noble son and may he always remember his Alma Mater."[136] The student yearbook likewise crowned Paul a Rutgers great:

All hats off to "Robey"
All honor to his name
On the diamond, the court or football field
He brought old Rutgers fame.

To those looking on, it appeared there was nothing that Robeson could not do. His astounding versatility helped to create the larger than life image many of his classmates remember: Paul Robeson was a phenomenon. Perhaps his friend Earl Schenck Miers best expressed the sentiments of the class of 1919 when he wrote many years later: "The hero of the campus was Paul Robeson ... in my generation Rutgers men said proudly, 'I go to Paul Robeson's school.'"[137]

Classmates would remember Robey as never having earned less than an A. He was "the most brilliant student at the college," said one classmate; and another, "He led his class. None of us could hold a candle to him. He was pure black and proved beyond any doubt that a black man can have the highest intelligence."[138] But, contrary to the legend, Robeson did not earn perfect grades. He did receive both the Ann Van Nest Bussing Prize and the Monsignor O'Grady Prize for oratory and extempore speaking, but he did not win any of the academic "Special Subject" prizes, and earned third rather than first or second academic honors, graduating with a solid B average.[139] Although he was one of several commencement speakers, Robeson was not among those first selected for the honor; rather, he was asked at the last minute to take the place of a student suddenly taken ill. And finally, his senior thesis, "The Fourteenth Amendment: The Sleeping Giant of the American Constitution," submitted on May 29, two weeks before graduation, while creditable, was far from brilliant.[140] A straightforward account of the history of the Fourteenth Amendment, with special stress given to Article I (how citizenship is defined, the privileges and immunities of U.S. citizens, due process of law, and equal protection of the law), the essay was what one might expect from an undergraduate but not particularly profound or exceptional. That Robeson chose the Fourteenth Amendment as his subject matter (he was one of a handful of students who chose a sociopolitical subject) indicates he was think-

ing about his own and his people's status as citizens. But, while he might well have criticized white America for its failure to enforce the amendment, he chose instead to cite numerous legal cases that proved that properly enforcing the amendment provided protection from the changing tides of state legal codes. His approach was logical, reasoned, moderate, and conciliatory. He meticulously avoided editorializing in the essay, enough so that one must read carefully between the lines to sense the plea made on behalf of himself and his people for enforcement of the amendment.[141] In short, Robeson was not a flawless student. But his overall performance at Rutgers—in terms of both breadth and quality—was indeed remarkable, a testament not only to his many and wide-ranging talents but equally so to his dogged pursuit of success.

Commencement services for the class of 1919 began on the morning of June 9 with Class Day Exercises: the reading of the class poem, prophecy, and history, which predicted Robeson would one day become Governor of New Jersey, dimming even "the fame of Booker T. Washington" as a "leader of the colored race in America."[142] The high point of the first day of festivities, however, took place in the afternoon, with the Rutgers-Princeton baseball matchup. Alumni and students—a total of over 1000 fans—hoping yet again to rout the Tigers (Rutgers had failed to beat Princeton at any major varsity sport since 1869), paraded over to Neilson Field led by Angus Fraser and his Scotch Kiltie Band. Finally Rutgers got its win, and fans and alumni went wild. On the heels of a poor season, the Rutgers team pounded out thirteen hits (one of which was a single by catcher Robeson) and downed Princeton 5 to 1. The fifty-year jinx had at last been broken, and no one was happier with the win than Paul. For the team, it meant the defeat of a powerful rival; for

Robeson, "the defeat of a long-hated institution."[143] Robeson reaped well-deserved praise in the *Targum* for his performance, which proclaimed Rutgers' "overwhelming victory over Princeton ... a fitting climax to [his] great career."

June 10 was a warm, sunny day. The academic procession for the 153rd Rutgers commencement formed on the Queen's Campus at 11:15 A.M. From there the sixty-nine graduating seniors proceeded to the Second Reformed Church for the 11:30 graduation exercises. Class of 1918 graduates who had missed their own commencement because they had enlisted had returned and were seated with Paul's class, eagerly awaiting formal reception of their diplomas. The mood was optimistic and upbeat: The war was over, democracy had triumphed, theirs would be a better world. Robeson, along with the two classmates also scheduled to speak, waited his turn and then walked slowly to the podium. He looked out at a sea of white faces— faculty, parents, alumni, and friends— and, in that rich, sonorous voice that had won him one oratorical prize after another, began.

In his speech, "The New Idealism," Robeson outlined the process by which he and other blacks would achieve their rightful place in American society. As in his senior thesis, his approach to his topic was measured, gently admonishing but never directly criticizing the "favored race." Robeson predicted that the same spirit that had won the war would lead to a "reconstructing of American life" at home. This "new spirit" would create a sense of national unity and a renewed determination to make freedom and equality realities for all Americans, including the "less favored race." Having proved their allegiance in the war, American blacks were now ready to take their place among other full-fledged American citizens.

"We of the less-favored race realize that our future lies chiefly in our own hands," Robeson assured his audience. "On ourselves alone will depend the preservation of our liberties and the transmission of them in their integrity to those who will come after us." Negroes, Robeson predicted, would raise themselves up by practicing those virtues most typically American: "self-reliance, self-respect, industry, perseverance, and economy." Exhorting white America to live this "new spirit," Robeson stressed the importance of practicing Christian principles and cooperation between the races. Only when "black and white shall clasp friendly hands in the consciousness of the fact that we are brethren and that God is the father of us all" would this new idealism be achieved.[144]

In his speech Robeson exhibited those qualities whites not only admired but expected from exceptional blacks: dignity, decency, and, above all, modesty. His racial philosophy, as articulated in this commencement address, had changed little since high school. Had he been less successful at Rutgers, had the racial etiquette he learned growing up not worked for him, Robeson might have been forced to move beyond the strategy of patience, self-effacement, and hard work. But the etiquette had worked — and worked spectacularly — for Robeson. Ironically, then, it was success that retarded (and would continue to retard) Robeson's personal and political growth and kept him bound to a racial etiquette that couldn't help but reinforce his sense of racial inferiority.

Robeson returned to his seat amid thunderous applause. According to the *Sunday Times*, "Some declared that no commencement orator in all the tradition of old Queens had ever received such applause for an oration."[145] Robeson's was a message of hope, with none of the admonishments of the first speaker, classmate John W. Armstrong, who warned radicals and others enamored with Russian socialism about presuming to criticize the

American way of life. "We have no room for idle dreamers, for scheming demagogues or for rabid Bolsheviks ... the Trotskys and Leninists must seek a more congenial clime. Other nations may succumb to their influences, but in America they will have no effect."

Of all those gathered for the 1919 graduation ceremonies there was no one to whom this remonstration would one day more aptly apply than Paul Robeson. But on this, the eve of the Red Summer of 1919 and the subsequent Palmer raids, Robeson was far removed from the political awareness that would in later years so alter the course of his life. Robeson in 1919 applauded, enthusiastically and loudly, along with other members of his graduating class, Armstrong's patriotic sentiments.

Notes

1. William H. Demarest, *A History of Rutgers College, 1766–1924* (New Brunswick, NJ, 1924), 501–550.
2. See Chapter 2 of Boyle and Bunie, *Paul Robeson.*
3. PR [Paul Robeson] interviewed by *News Review,* June 1, 1939; John M. Carroll, *Fritz Pollard: Pioneer in Racial Advancement* (Chicago: University of Illinois Press, 1992), 59; *Daily Home News* (New Brunswick) Sept. 2, 3, 7, 1919. In 1919 approximately twenty-five race riots broke out in cities across the country. New Brunswick papers chronicled the mistreatment of blacks locally.
4. Patricia Sullivan interviews with Malcolm Pitt, May 30, 1975, and Dec. 6, 1976 (telephone). During his freshman year Paul filled out a form (filled out yearly, presumably for yearbook purposes) on which he listed Malcolm Pitt as one of his best friends. Like J. Douglas Brown (Somerville High School classmate), Pitt was a scholar, not an athlete. Pitt later became head of Hartford Seminary, and Brown was Dean of Princeton University.
5. Interview with Steve White, Sept. 15, 1975.
6. Robeson transcript, Rutgers University. Concerning the C in English composition,

Malcolm Pitt and others explained that Paul could write well but lacked the patience to edit and polish his work.
7. Benjamin G. Rader, *American Sports* (Englewood Cliffs, NJ: Prentice Hall, 1983), 140–41. See also John Richards Betts, *America's Sporting Heritage: 1850–1950* (Reading, MA: Addison Wesley, 1974).
8. *Ibid.* By 1914, over 450 colleges and 6,000 secondary schools were playing the sport.
9. Richard P. McCormick, *Rutgers: A Bicentennial History* (New Brunswick, NJ: Rutgers University Press, 1966), 163. By 1910 Rutgers alumni had formed fourteen clubs in localities across the country, from Boston to southern California.
10. Pat Julin interview with Kenneth Rendall (Rutgers football teammate), Oct. 2, 1975; McCormick, *Rutgers,* 163. The Rutgers *Alumni Quarterly* began publication in October of 1914.
11. McCormick, *Rutgers,* 161.
12. White interview, Sept. 15, 1975. See also Harry J. Rockafeller, "Foster Sanford" in George Lukac, *Aloud to Alma Mater* (New Brunswick, NJ: Rutgers University Press, 1966), 107–108.
13. Larry Pitt, *Football at Rutgers: A History, 1869–1969* (New Brunswick, NJ: Rutgers University Press, 1972), 27–50; Rockafeller, "Foster Sanford," 107–112.
14. White interview, Sept. 15, 1975; Pat Julin interview with John Wittpenn, Aug. 28, 1975.
15. White interview, Sept. 15, 1975; interview with Robert Nash, Oct. 12, 1975.
16. White interview, Sept. 15, 1975; Nash interview, Oct. 12, 1975; Julin-Wittpenn interview, Aug. 28, 1975.
17. Interview with J. Douglas Brown, Mar. 29, 1975.
18. Earl Schenck Miers, "Paul Robeson — Made in America," *Nation,* May 27, 1950, 523. See also Miers's fictionalized version of Robeson's life, *Big Ben: A Novel* (Philadelphia: Westminster, 1942), xii, 17–18. Miers, a Rutgers graduate, interviewed Robeson as part of his research for the novel.
19. Steve White interview, Sept. 15, 1975.
20. Arthur Ashe, Jr., *A Hard Road to Glory: A History of the African-American Athlete 1619–1981* (New York: Warner, 1988), 90–94, 173–74. According to Ashe, there was no quota system per se, but it was seldom that more than one black played for the same team.

When they did, both players were starters. In 1915 six black athletes played on white college teams: Frederick Pollard, Brown; Gideon Smith, Michigan State; Joseph Trigg, Syracuse; Edwin Morrison and William F. Brown, Tufts; and Paul Robeson, Rutgers. From 1889 to 1920 the total number of blacks playing collegiate football was sixty-six. See also Robert A. Bellinger, "African Americans in White Colleges and Universities, 1890–1919," Ph.D. dissertation in progress, Boston College, Chestnut Hill, MA.

21. See Randy Roberts, *Papa Jack: Jack Johnson and the Era of White Hopes* (New York: Free Press, 1983); Essie Robeson, *Paul Robeson, Negro* (New York: Hayes and Brothers, 1930), 30 (hereafter ER, *PR, Negro*).

22. White interview, Sept. 15, 1975.

23. Kipke quoted in *Baltimore American*, Nov. 16, 1935. See also Thomas G. Smith, "Outside the Pale: The Exclusion of Blacks from the National Football League, 1934–1946," in *Journal of Sport History*, vol. 15, no. 3 (Winter 1988), 255–281.

24. White interview, Sept. 15, 1975; Robert Van Gelder, "Robeson Remembers, 'An Interview with the Star of *Othello*,' Partly About His Past," *New York Times*, Jan. 16, 1944, sec. 2, p. 1; also ER, *PR, Negro*, 31–2 and *Rutgers Alumni Monthly*, Nov. 1930, 44.

25. Van Gelder, "Robeson Remembers," 1.

26. Interview with Revels Cayton, July 16, 1980, and Jan. 16, 1981; see also M.H. Halton, "Negro Free When All Men Emancipated," unnamed newspaper, 1938, Robeson Collections, Moorland-Spingarn Library, New York City, PR, Jr. (hereafter Robeson Collections, PR, Jr.); and Miers, *Big Ben*, 93–106. Miers devotes a number of pages to Paul's summer job working at the brickyard and erroneously portrays the teenage Robeson as a union crusader fighting injustice, in this case an unfair foreman.

27. Van Gelder, "Robeson Remembers," 7; ER, *PR, Negro*, 32.

28. Pat Julin interview with William Feitner, Aug. 27, 1975.

29. Nash interview, Oct. 12, 1975.

30. Interview with Frederick Douglass Pollard, Sept. 16, 1974. See also John M. Carroll, *Fritz Pollard: Pioneer in Racial Advancement* (Urbana: University of Illinois Press, 1992), 41–56, 61–62; "Fritz," *Brown Alumni Quarterly*, Oct. 1970, 31; Carlo Nesfield, "Pride Against Prejudice," *Black Sports*, Nov. 1971, 30.

31. Nash interview, Oct. 12, 1975.

32. *Ibid.*

33. Julin-Rendall interview, Oct. 2, 1975.

34. Harry Rockafeller letter to Andrew Bunie, Mar. 1975.

35. Nash interview, Oct. 12, 1975.

36. White interview, Sept. 15, 1975; Julin-Wittpenn interview, Aug. 28, 1975.

37. Julin-Wittpenn interview, Aug. 28, 1975.

38. White interview, Sept. 15, 1975.

39. *New York Times*, Nov. 1915.

40. Ronald Dean Brown interview with Harry Rockafeller, *Rutgers Daily Targum*, Apr. 10, 1973; Julin-Feitner interview, Aug. 27, 1975.

41. Sullivan-Pitt interview, May 30, 1975.

42. Lawson, "Robey Comes Home," 22–23; Rendall interview, Oct. 2, 1975; Sullivan-Pitt interview, May 30, 1975; Paul Robeson, *Here I Stand* (Boston: Beacon Press, 1959), 19. Miers claims that because of the dance that followed Glee Club performances, Robeson never asked to be admitted to Rutgers Glee Club.

43. Andrew F. Eschenfelder letter to Bunie, Mar. 24, 1975, and telephone interview, Apr. 6, 1975.

44. Sullivan-Pitt interview, May 30, 1975.

45. Julin-Wittpenn interview, Aug. 28, 1975.

46. Telephone interview with Mal Pitt, May 14, 1975; Sullivan-Pitt interview, May 30, 1975.

47. Ronald D. Brown interview with Harry Rockafeller, *Rutgers Daily Targum*, Apr. 10, 1973.

48. Marcia Graham Synnot, *The Half-Open Door: Discrimination and Admissions at Harvard, Yale and Princeton, 1900–1960* (Westport CT: Greenwood Press, 1979); also Steven Steinberg, *The Academic Melting Pot: Catholics and Jews in American Higher Education* (New York: McGraw-Hill, 1974).

49. Telephone interview with Rendall, Oct. 2, 1975.

50. *Ibid.*

51. Leo Frank: John Hingham, *Strangers in a Strange Land: Patterns in American Nativism, 1860–1925* (1955), 66–67; Leonard Dinnerstein, *The Leo Frank Case* (Athens: University of Georgia Press, 1987), 134; Lucy Dawidowicz, *The Jewish Presence: Essays on Identity and History* (New York: Holt, Rinehardt and Winston, 1960), 127; McCormick, *Rutgers: A Bicentennial History*, 160–1.

52. Interview with Miki Fisher, Sept. 13, 1978.

53. Woldin: see Chapter 2 of Boyle and Bunie, *Paul Robeson*.

54. White interview, Sept. 15, 1975.

55. Lawrence W. Pitt (professor of Educational Policy Sciences, Dean of the College of N.J., Union, New Jersey) to Bunie, June 22, 1977. Pitt obtained the information from Bill Miller and Harmony Coppola of the Rutgers Archives.

56. Julin interview with M. Harold Higgins, Aug. 27, 1975.

57. Sullivan-Pitt interview, May 30, 1975.

58. White interview, Sept. 15, 1975.

59. *New York Age*, Feb. 25, Mar. 11, 1915; Feb. 12, Sept. 28, Oct. 12, Nov. 9, 1916. By 1915 the *New York Age* featured news of the Robeson family, Paul in particular, on an average of once a month. Much of the material was gathered by an itinerant "reporter" in the area, quite possibly William Robeson himself.

60. PR interview with Percy N. Stone, *New York Herald Tribune*, Oct. 17, 1926; also ER, *PR*, *Negro*, 23.

61. *New York Times*, Oct. 28, 1915.

62. *New York Age*, Feb. 17, 1916.

63. Interview with Bertha (Reckling) Blunt, Dec. 6, 1978; Pollard interview, Sept. 16, 1974. See also Carroll, *Fritz Pollard*, 58. Reckling's family lived year-round in Narragansett. Reckling recalls Paul singing and visiting with her family.

64. Interview with Joe Nelson, Jan. 15, 1983.

65. According to Carroll (*Fritz Pollard*, 58), Fritz Pollard accompanied Paul on the piano as well.

66. Interview with Marguerite Kennerly Upshur Creed, Oct. 18, 1975.

67. Nash interview, Oct. 12, 1975.

68. Demarest, *History of Rutgers*, 531–532.

69. White interview, Sept. 15, 1975; Julin-Feitner interview, Aug. 27, 1975. Player Kenneth Rendall, however, in a telephone interview (Oct. 2, 1978) claimed most of the negotiating had taken place beforehand and that everyone knew well in advance Robeson would not be in the lineup.

70. Julin-Feitner interview, Aug. 27, 1975. See also Miers, *Big Ben*, 126–127.

71. White interview, Sept. 15, 1975.

72. Julin-Wittpenn interview, Aug. 28, 1975; ER, *PR*, *Negro*, 34; Edward Lawson, "Robey Comes Home," *Anthologist* (Rutgers University), Jan. 1932, 22.

73. PR interviewed by George C. Carens, *Boston Traveler*, Aug. 14, 1942.

74. Interview with Angus Cameron, Feb. 10, 1977.

75. White interview, Sept. 15, 1975. According to Kingsley Martin, Paul, reminiscing about his football days, described himself as "naturally lazy and difficult to arouse." He said that on occasion "one of the other men on his own team would give him a sly kick to engage him. 'Of course, he's yellow, you know.' They would make sure that he [Paul] had heard them talking about him." That kind of comment usually got Paul going. (Kingsley Martin, ed., *New Statesman Years, 1931–1945*, London, 1968.)

76. In 1919 Rutgers alumnus James Carr, a Phi Beta Kappa and Rutgers' first black graduate (1892), at the time district attorney and assistant corporate counsel in New York City, irate over a similar incident that occurred in June of 1919 when Penn State bowed to pressure from the Naval Academy and benched its black athlete, wrote to Rutgers College president William Demarest to voice the first formal opposition to the now three-year-old Washington and Lee incident. "I am deeply moved at the injustice done a student of Rutgers ... one of the best athletes ever developed at Rutgers— who, because guilty of a skin not colored as their own, was excluded from the honorable field of athletic encounter, as one inferior," Carr wrote. "Can you imagine his [Robeson's] thoughts and feelings when, in contemplative mood, he reflects in the years to come that his Alma Mater faltered and quailed when the test came, and that she preferred the holding of an athletic game to the maintenance of honor and principle?" Carr concluded: "The Trustees and Faculty of Rutgers College should disavow the action of the athletic manager who dishonored her ancient traditions by denying to one of her students ... equality of opportunity and privilege." (Carr to Demarest, June 6, 1919, Special Collections, Rutgers University Library, New Brunswick, New Jersey).

77. Robeson may simply have had more in common with someone like Mal Pitt, whose father was also a Methodist preacher and whose academic and artistic interests more closely matched his own. In his autobiography (*Stand*, 27–28) Robeson says nothing about his football career at Rutgers.

78. Pollard interview, Sept. 16, 1974; also

telephone interview with Wallace Wade, Dec. 3, 1964, and Frederick William Marvel Scrapbook, Brown University Athletic Scrapbooks, vol. 8, Brown University.

79. Frank Hathorn, *New York World*, Dec. 28, 1919.

80. The *New York Times* post-season survey did not rank Rutgers in its roster of top fifteen teams in the East but did include Brown University (3rd) and Washington and Lee (14th); Fritz Pollard won first team selection in the all–Eastern pollings, but no one from Rutgers was chosen (*New York Times* Apr. 19, 28, 1919).

81. *Targum*, Apr. 30, 1918.

82. Yearbook form, Rutgers University.

83. Telephone interview with Pitt, May 14, 1974.

84. Kathy Kelly interview with Geraldine Neale Bledsoe, May 1975. Robeson biographer Lloyd Brown (*The Young Paul Robeson*; Boulder, Colorado: Westview Press, 1997, 67) claims that Robeson first met Neale in the spring of 1916 in Freehold while he was visiting a local Sunday school,

85. *Ibid.*

86. *New York Times*, Aug. 25, 1917.

87. *Ibid.*, Oct. 14, 1917.

88. Charles Taylor, *New York Tribune*, Oct. 28, 1917.

89. Interview with Roland Tailby, June 11, 1978. On coon song euphemisms see William H. Wiggins, Jr., "Boxing Sambo Twins: Racial Stereotypes in Jack Johnson and Joe Louis Newspaper Cartoons, 1908 to 1938," *Journal of Sport History*, vol. 15, no. 3 (Winter 1988), 246.

90. Interview with Pare Lorentz, Dec. 27, 1974.

91. Heywood Broun, "It Seems to Me," *Cincinnati Post*, Oct. 2, 1929. This was one of the few times Robeson openly discussed foul play on the part of whites.

92. Rendall interview, Oct. 2, 1975.

93. *New York Times*, Nov. 25, 1917.

94. Louis Lee Arms, *New York Sunday Tribune*, Nov. 25, 1917.

95. Lester Walton, *New York Age*, Nov. 29, 1917.

96. Valerie Oblath interview with Carlton Moss, July 16, 1981; Robert Macieski telephone interview with Moss, July 16, 1980.

97. Oblath-Moss interview, July 16, 1981.

98. *Ibid.*

99. "Review of the 1917 Football Season,"

Rutgers Alumni Quarterly, January 1918, reprinted in Lukac, *Aloud to Alma Mater*, 120–127. *Quarterly* editors prefaced Robeson's article with a note that filled in the gap.

100. Unnamed newspaper, Providence, RI, 23, Robeson Collections, PR, Jr.

101. Marie Seton, *Paul Robeson* (London: Dennis Dobson, 1958), 23.

102. Edwin R. Embree, *Thirteen Against the Odds* (New York: Viking, 1944), 253.

103. William Robeson's obituary in the *Somerset Messenger* included a large photo, taking up about a third of the page (May 22, 1918).

104. *Daily Home News* (Somerville), May 21, 22, 1918. The funeral was delayed until May 26 to allow Ben time to return home from Camp Taylor (army training), Louisville, Kentucky.

105. Kelly-Bledsoe interview, May 1975; *Daily Home News* (Somerville), May 21, 1918.

106. Interview with Helen Rosen, Feb. 9, 1981. Rosen, a close friend of Paul's in later years, repeatedly used the word "goaded" to describe William's dealings with Paul.

107. PR, *Stand*, 1; "I have often remarked on the happy relationship between you two," wrote an acquaintance to Paul shortly after the death of William Robeson ("Lawrence" to PR, May 20, 1918, PR Collections, PR, Jr.).

108. Helen Rosen (interview Feb. 9, 1981) described William Robeson as "not only an itinerant preacher but, at times, an itinerant parent as well."

109. PR quoted in Seton, *Paul Robeson*, 18–19.

110. Interview with unnamed Bustill relative, April 1975; interview with Charles Blockson, Aug. 30, 1991; interview with Julia Porter, Sept. 2, 1991.

111. PR, *Stand*, 8.

112. *Ibid.*, 8–9.

113. *Ibid.*, 8.

114. *Daily Home News* (New Brunswick), June 13, 1918; also Shirley Graham, *Paul Robeson, Citizen of the World* (New York: Julian Messner, 1946), 93; Seton, *Paul Robeson*, 22.

115. Nelson interview, Jan. 15, 1983.

116. *Ibid.*

117. McCormick, *Rutgers: A Bicentennial History*, 165.

118. *Ibid.*, 166; *Targum*, Oct. 13, 1918.

119. McCormick, *Rutgers: A Bicentennial History*, 166.

120. *Targum*, October 13, 1918.

121. *Somerset Messenger*, Apr. 17, 1918.

122. McCormick, *Rutgers: A Bicentennial History*, 166.

123. Walter Camp, "Industrial Athletics: How the Sports for Sailors and Soldiers Are Developing into Civilian Athletics," *Outlook* 122 (1919), 253, in S. W. Pope, *Patriotic Games: Sporting Traditions in American Imagination, 1876–1926* (New York: 1997), 150. Walter Chauncy Camp, author of nearly thirty books and more than 200 magazine and newspaper articles, personally helped put order into a game formerly known only for its brute physicality. Camp shaped modern football's rules and introduced the concepts of the eleven-man side, downs and yards gained, and a new points-scoring system.

124. Rutgers *Alumni Quarterly*, 1918.

125. Pat Julin interview with Arthur Van Fleet, May 8, 1975.

126. Julin-Feitner interview, Aug. 27, 1975.

127. *Targum* 50 (June 1919), 537.

128. Wittpenn interview, Aug. 28, 1975; *Targum* 30 (June 1919), 572–573.

129. *Targum* 50 (June 1919), 547.

130. Eschenfelder interview, Mar. 24, 1975.

131. Interview with the Rev. Calvin G. Meury (class of 1920), May 14, 1975; *New York Times*, Jan. 8, 20, 1918. In the 1916-1917 season Rutgers was beaten twice by Princeton in two close games (28 to 21, and 22 to 20). In the 1917-1918 season Rutgers posted five wins and three losses.

132. Meury interview, May 14, 1975.

133. Julin-Van Fleet interview, May 8, 1975.

134. *Daily Home News*, June 5, 1919.

135. *Ibid.*, June 15, 1919.

136. Robeson earned four letters in football, three in baseball, three in basketball, and two in track. The Skull and Cap award was, according to one classmate, "the most important of all honors, as it was given only to those seniors exemplifying excellence in all facets of Rutgers life." During his four years at Rutgers Robeson won every oratory contest he entered (*Targum*, Apr. 30, 1919, 515).

137. Earl Schenck Miers, *The Trouble Bush* (Chicago: Rand McNally, 1966), 148–149.

138. *Targum*, Apr. 30, 1919, 515; David Kelly (Class of 1920) to Bunie, May 30, 1975; Anton Ward to Bunie, May 17, 1975.

139. *Targum*, Apr. 30, 1919, 515; Robeson Transcript, Rutgers University.

140. Edward Lawson, "Robey Comes Home," *The Anthologist* (Rutgers University), Jan. 1932, 23. Robeson's Senior Thesis is reprinted in Philip S. Foner, ed., *Paul Robeson Speaks* (Secaucus, NJ: Citadel, 1978), 53–65.

141. Robeson refers to civil rights cases involving blacks that occurred in the 1870s and 1880s, but he makes no mention of the Supreme Court's 1896 upholding of the "separate but equal" doctrine set forth in *Plessy v. Ferguson*. Similarly, while he cites cases involving prejudicial treatment of Chinese and Japanese (*Yick Wo v. Hopkins* [1886] and *U.S. v. Wong Kim Ark* [1898]), he is silent about the Chinese Exclusion Acts (beginning in 1882) and the anti-Japanese sentiment in California that culminated with the "Gentlemen's Agreement" in San Francisco's schools. (Japanese: see Peter Irons, *Justice at War: The Story of the Japanese American Internment Cases* [University of California Press, Berkeley, 1983], 125).

142. Francis E. Lyons, "Prophecy of the Class of 1919," *Targum* 50 (June 1919), 563.

143. ER, PR, Negro, 36–7.

144. "The New Idealism," *Targum*, June 1919, 570–1, reprinted in Foner, *Paul Robeson Speaks*, 62–65. The speech was delivered on June 10, 1919.

145. *Sunday [New York] Times*, June 8, 1930, 12.

Something to Cheer About: Paul Robeson, Athlete

JOSEPH DORINSON
Long Island University

The turn of the millennium is the best of times for sports heroes. The field of dreams lures all-star athletes with astronomical sums for their specialized talents. Money, however, measures only one dimension of the good life. When death summoned Joe DiMaggio and Florence Griffith Joyner, the media encouraged a soul-searching analysis of their impact on us. With A. E. Housman, we offer lamentation when athletes die young. Watching the once magnificent Muhammad Ali light the Olympic torch with unsteady hands filled viewers with pity and sadness. Excessive blows to the head and the ravages of Parkinson's on the body of "the greatest" boxer compels us to compare now and then. Confronting the final curtain with Frank Sinatra, therefore, we grapple with the meaning of life.

As a callow youth, I was intrigued with sports heroes. Only as I grew older and looked through a glass darkly did I begin to ruminate on the impact of heroes. Because of my "Red Diaper" origins, I was particularly fascinated with Paul Robeson and other Negro (the preferred designation then) sports stars. The arrival of Jackie Robinson in 1947 alerted me to the importance of athletes as agents of social change. Twenty years later, academic necessity propelled me into African-American History, and my research shifted to the study of black leaders. Weaving various strands of social history, I discerned a pattern. Exemplary figures from the arenas of sports, politics, and society seemed to manifest certain paradigmatic behaviors. To simplify and to prune the jargon, my subjects faced three modalities of action: aggression, avoidance, and acceptance.[1] Obviously, these responses often overlap; but for reasons of clarity they invite isolation.

Concentrating on sports, I was drawn to those athletes who mirrored a Du Boisian doubleness. With clinical precision, Dr. W.E.B. Du Bois cut to the heart of the American dilemma when he dissected the black soul as "two souls, two thoughts, two unreconciled strivings, two warring ideals in one dark body whose dogged strength alone keeps it from being torn asunder."[2] Blacks wanted to be accepted as equal Americans, yet because of discrimination also felt alienated from American society. Because he embodied this dualism, my childhood icon, Paul Robeson, invited further study. Although athleticism was only part of his heroic lifestyle, which crossed so many different pursuits, I reasoned that since sports brought Paul his first national acclaim, it would provide a touchstone to the larger story.

To understand the athletic years of the great Robeson, a brief discussion of the heroic life is in order. Historically, the image of a hero changes, like a chrysalis, to meet the special, often psychic, needs of society. According to Joseph Campbell, the great writer on mythology, heroes project a thousand faces. Thus, in classical Greece, they appeared as God-men. In medieval Europe they reemerged as God's men while some women also vaulted to the pedestal with the adoration of Mary as the "eternal female." During the Renaissance, women were toppled from their perch while the heroic courtiers described by Castiglione regained center stage as well-rounded virtuosi or "Renaissance men." They evolved as gentlemen in the eighteenth century, self-made men in the nineteenth, and common men in the twentieth century.[3]

Basically aristocrats by nature if not nurture, heroes experience mercurial careers in democratic societies. They flash into fame and fade into obscurity in a single generation. One day they are the people's choice; the next, society's discard. In 1999 sports authorities were bent on naming names. No, not in the shameful wake of Senator Joe McCarthy, but in the equally foolish pursuit of identifying the greatest athletes in the last century. They came up short. Most of my students failed to recognize anyone prior to the Michael Jordan

era. Their apparent amnesia signifies a deeper malaise. The glaring indifference to history, coupled with a minuscule span of attention, issues no doubt from excessive exposure to television. It is therefore categorically imperative to recapture figures like Robeson whose political persuasion pushed him into purgatory. Lest we forget, this brilliant scholar/athlete blazed a path to glory for many black athletes who excelled in football, baseball, basketball, track, tennis, and golf.

"A life is not important except in the impact it has on other lives," wrote Jackie Robinson before his untimely death in 1972. African-American athletes have put their stamp on other people's lives to be sure; but a debate rages on whether this influence is salutary or not. Black athletes are clearly superior. This superiority is manifest in the following statistics: 80 percent of the NBA and 65 percent of the NFL consist of African-American players. Is this dominance rooted in genes or beans, nature or nurture, heredity or environment? This volatile issue, which refuses to vanish, is the subject of a new book, *Taboo: Why Black Athletes Dominate Sports and Why We Are Afraid to Talk About It* by Jon Entine.[4] White supremacists cling to their spurious sense of physical and mental superiority. Black social critics view athletes as modern gladiators who entertain white affluent spectators for the benefit of corporate giants. Some fear that a dichotomy between brawn and brain will work to the disadvantage of blacks. Whatever one's take, African-American sports heroes continue to generate controversy.

Add author John Hoberman to the mix and the conclusions are explosive. His *Darwin's Athletes: How Sport Has Damaged Black America and Preserved the Myth of Race* argues that success in sports precludes advancement in other, more intellectual, pursuits. Popular perceptions pit physical supremacy (blacks) against intellectual superiority (whites). Thus, the emphasis on the sporting life contributes to racism. In fact, Hoberman argues that the sports arena is actually a metaphorical prison, which denies access to middle class avenues of success by funneling African Americans into a narrow channel. By confining blacks to athletic prowess, the establishment propels them into a state of perpetual subordination. He even argues that Jackie Robinson's achievements have been overplayed.[5]

Though well researched and forcefully written, Hoberman's book is off-base. What this Texas scholar fails to appreciate, I believe, is the vital, indeed pivotal, role black athletes have played in shoring up ethnic identity and penetrating the barriers of a once unyielding caste system — as illustrated in the early life of Paul Robeson. Before Robeson entered the mainstream, prominent blacks were typed as the inversion of America's "Protestant Ethic." They appeared as either docile or savage, faithful or tricky, pathetic or comical, childish or oversexed. This public perception perverted the black persona and reinforced segregation in sports as well as in society.[6] In order to survive, black athletes had to conform. This meant submission to white coaches, coupled with a display of moral respectability. They had to fuse individual ambition and collective action.[7]

For blacks the sports opportunity structure in the nineteenth century was limited to horse racing, boxing and baseball (briefly). Success not only bolstered race pride, it also led to wealth. Three-time Kentucky Derby winner jockey Isaac Murphy purchased large tracts of land. The first black to enter major league baseball, Moses "Fleet" Walker (prior to Jackie Robinson), owned a hotel, several movie houses in Steubenville, Ohio, and an opera house.[8] His career also saved his life. In a street brawl, Fleet Walker beat a white man to death. Although he was booted out of

baseball by Cap Anson, an all-white jury acquitted him, probably on account of his athletic renown. Ultimately, however, Walker concluded that blacks could only survive separate from whites. In his book *Our Home Colony*, he warned that integration might lead to a societal volcano in which whites would turn ferociously on blacks who sought to better their lot.[9]

Explosive or not, black athletes carved out a distinctive niche in American society. Boxer Jack Johnson, the subject of a prior study by this author, challenged white supremacy. He appeared "ill-mannered, defiant and absolutely incorrigible." He consorted with white women, married three, and bested the "white hope" on merit. For Johnson, sports may have mirrored life. He developed a distinctive style. Defensively, he feinted, countered, and tricked his opponents. Then he lowered the boom. A knockout followed. If not, Johnson retreated into a defensive pose. This served as a strategy for survival. He beat white fighters methodically and disdainfully.[10]

On the gridiron, blacks had more margin for maneuver. Earning distinction as the first national football figure, Bill Lewis entered Amherst College in 1888. He played center for a fine team. After graduation, Lewis studied law at Harvard where — unfettered by current NCAA rules — he continued his outstanding football play. One hundred and seventy-five pounds of tempered steel, Lewis, agile and fast, played both defense and offense. Walter Camp dubbed him an All-American, the first black to be so honored. As a great student of the game, he subsequently became a coach. Success went beyond the football arena. Bill Lewis rose to prominence in the field of legal battle. He became the first black to serve as United States Assistant Attorney General.

The next star that elicited national attention, Fritz Pollard, played for Brown. A halfback with blazing speed, Pollard preferred sports to study. In 1916 he led Brown to victories over favored Yale and Harvard in successive weeks. Before graduating, he turned pro, earning admiration from opponents as well as from teammates.[11] One was Paul Robeson.

If any single scholar-athlete dispelled the racist stereotypes that dominated nineteenth century thought, it was Paul Robeson. April 9, 1998, marked the hundredth birthday of this complex, brilliant Renaissance man. Athlete, singer, actor, activist, Robeson's talents transcended his first national arena, the football field. Growing up in a segregated society, Robeson enjoyed a spectacular career as an athlete. Most studies of this genius pay tribute to his sporting life and then quickly move to other facets of his career. Nevertheless, it is important to remember that Paul Robeson became a national figure through his athletic prowess. Clearly, events in the sporting arena mirror American society. And it was through sports that African-Americans entered the mainstream of our culture.

According to biographer Lloyd Brown, sports came naturally to young Paul. Born in Princeton, New Jersey, the youngest of four surviving children, Robeson was orphaned in 1904 when his mother Maria Louisa died as a result of an accidental fire. Robeson rarely referred to his mother. Perhaps he repressed painful memories. Yet one of his favorite spirituals spoke to this loss: "Sometimes, I Feel Like a Motherless Child."

The family moved to Somerville, New Jersey, in 1910. Attending the town's "colored school," Paul attracted attention on the baseball field. While still in grade school, he was drafted as a "ringer" to play shortstop for the integrated high school. When Robeson entered Somerville High School legally, he was one of 250 students, and only one of eight enrolled in college preparatory work. At Somerville, Robe-

son — encouraged by his venerable father, William Drew Robeson, a runaway slave whom he affectionately called "Pops" — excelled. His model for athletic performance was older brother Ben, "who most inspired," he recalled, "my interest in sports." Ben had the ability to make it as an All-American in football or as a professional baseball player, although he ultimately became the pastor of the Zion African Methodist Episcopal Church in Harlem, New York.[12]

The younger Robeson played forward on the basketball team, and hurled the javelin and threw the discus in track and field. In baseball he played shortstop and catcher. During inter-city games Paul experienced racism. In one encounter Paul whacked a tremendous triple. The High Bridge principal stormed out on the field and thundered: "That coon did not touch second!" A major rhubarb, to echo the signature phrase of broadcaster Walter "Red" Barber, was prevented when Robeson's teammates protected him from a possible physical confrontation instigated by the incendiary principal.[13]

In high school football Paul played fullback. On this field, too, he became the target of opposing players. In battling Somerville's archrival Bound Brook, Paul broke his collarbone. But he held his ground, winning approval from all with his courage, tenacity, and talent. His teammate, Doug Brown, later dean and provost at Princeton University, remembered Paul as the heart — at least nine-tenths of it — of the football squad. Although sports brought young Robeson his public acclaim, he also excelled in debating, singing, and scholarship.[14]

As a result of a statewide exam, Rutgers opened its doors to this highly qualified scholar-athlete in the autumn of 1915. A private school then, Rutgers had only 500 students. Paul was only the third black to attend Rutgers since its inception in 1766. While trying out for the football team, this 6'2", 190-lb. marvel incurred injury and endured pain. In the very first scrimmage he sustained a broken nose, a smashed hand, and a dislocated shoulder. Robeson's father William and brother Ben did not let him quit, and after ten days of recuperation Robeson was back on the field. Robeson recalled his ordeal by fire in an interview with *New York Times* critic Robert Van Gelder.[15] He admitted to rage — a rage to kill. Lifting a tough running back named Kelly above his head for a bone-crushing tackle, he was deterred by Coach Sanford who blew the whistle to prevent serious injury. Robeson had made the team.

Former teammates differ on whether Paul was deliberately subjected to a brutal hazing during scrimmages. Biographer Martin Duberman, in an effort at objectivity, presents both sides. I tend to believe that Paul's reconstruction of this traumatic event gets closer to what actually happened. One mate, Robert Nash, recalled that Robeson "took a terrific beating."[16] Perhaps the Rashomonic truth is no less elusive today than it was eighty-five years ago.

Robeson's skill as a football player, however, brooks no doubt. Contemporary reporters, cited by Lloyd Brown, extolled Paul's versatility and excellence. He played many positions on both offense and defense — all brilliantly. Paul Robeson, Jr., informed me that his famous dad established a pattern for contemporary players on offense as well as on defense. He developed into the prototypical tight end who could block proficiently and turn short passes into long yardage while bowling over would-be tacklers. As a roving defender, Paul Sr. inaugurated the role of middle linebacker. Contemporary observers marveled at Robeson's brilliance. But although the young athlete affected an insouciant manner while engaged in a myriad of activities, he harbored resentment against the town of Princeton for the treatment accorded his father, brother, and fellow blacks. He wanted to meet and beat Princeton on the playing fields as a channel for his pent-up anger.

Coach George Foster Sanford, who Robeson adored, taught him how to protect himself with a well-placed elbow, and how to play offense.[17] As a freshman, Robeson remained a substitute tackle until November 20 when he earned a start against Stevens Tech. Rutgers won 39 to 3. Stardom loomed in 1916 as Robeson played in six of seven games at guard and tackle. The only game that Robeson missed resulted from a demand issued by Washington and Lee to bench the n----r. Shamefully, Rutgers capitulated. Coach Sanford rationalized this as a move to protect Robeson from the hostile Southerners. It was not the finest hour for the Scarlet Knights. Without their star player, they could only manage a 13–13 tie.[18] When Robeson returned to his tackle position, *The Newark Evening News* reported, the whole line improved.[19]

In 1917 Paul gained fame as an offensive end, and defensive end, and tackle. Robeson wrote about this year in detail. Reprinted in Philip Foner's excellent collection, *Paul Robeson Speaks*, the retrospective offers a solid analysis of Rutgers' banner year. More importantly, it provides a clue to his character. Published in the *Rutgers Alumni Quarterly*, January 1918, it begins with a bang:

> The season of 1917 is over, but the memories thereof will fire the hearts of Rutgers men as long as football is football. For the team fighting as only a Rutgers team can fight, and inspired by the indomitable spirit of that greatest of football mentors, George Foster Sanford, rose to the greatest heights, and stands not only as one of the best teams of the year but as one of the greatest of all times.[20]

Robeson on the football field. Courtesy of Special Collections, Rutgers University Libraries.

Robeson mentions that only three veterans returned to the team: Rendell, Feitner, and himself, to whom he refers in the third person. In the first game the Scarlet Knights defeated Ursinus 25–0. The next game was a rout of Fort Wadsworth: 90–0. The third game was played in Syracuse. The home team capitalized on miscues to beat Rutgers 14–10. Shouldering the blame for the defeat, Robeson exonerated Coach Sanford.[21]

Redemption came against Lafayette one week later as the Scarlet Knights whipped the men of Easton 33–6. In the big game against a highly touted Fordham team led by future baseball star Frankie Frisch, the Scarlet Knights crested and Robeson excelled. You would not know this from Robeson's narrative, but the *New York Times* (October 28) provided ample evidence. In the 28–0 romp, the paper reported that Robeson made two important catches of 35 and 24 yards to set up two

touchdowns. As a blocker at left end, he knocked three Rams out of the game. No less graphically, Charles A. Taylor wrote (*New York Tribune*, October 28, 1917): "A dark cloud upset the hopes of the Fordham eleven yesterday." No silver lining appeared as Paul Robeson (evidently the "dark cloud") was all over the field.[22]

Threats against Robeson sullied the next game opposite Greasy Neale's team from West Virginia University. Crudely, Coach Neale warned that his Southern boys would try to murder Paul. To his credit, Coach Sanford refused to knuckle under to racist blackmail. Entering the contest, West Virginia was heavily favored. On the first play from scrimmage, an opposing player threatened Robeson: "If you touch me, you black dog, I'll cut your heart out." Roused to fury, Robeson clipped him and "nearly busted him in two," Paul remembered. He taunted the redneck: "I touched you that time. How did you like it?"[23] The target of enemy cleats and forearms, Robeson absorbed tremendous punishment. Nevertheless, he made a game-saving tackle on the two-yard line during the final period. Even the biased coach had to concede that Robeson showed a lot of "guts" (like a white man?). Rutgers dominated the first half; but their opponents recovered a blocked punt on the twelve-yard line from where they punched in a touchdown in two plays. The game ended in a 7–7 tie.[24]

Disappointed, the Scarlet Knights vented against Springfield College with a 61–0 drubbing. They bested the United States Marines from Philadelphia 27–0, despite a lackluster performance. The season's climax occurred at Brooklyn's Ebbets Field on November 24. A team of Naval Reserves composed of All-Americans under coach Cupid Rogers invaded Brooklyn. Robeson enumerates the opponents: Barrett of Cornell, Black and Callahan of Yale, Schlacter of Syracuse, Gerrish of Dartmouth. Having trounced Colgate and Dartmouth, these gridiron Goliaths faced the Davids of Rutgers. Led by Robeson, the underdogs triumphed 14–0. The young star conferred praise on Coach Sanford. Again the press pointed in another direction — his. For example, sports reporter Louis Lee Arms, of the *New York Sunday Tribune* (Nov. 25, 1917), wrote: "A tall tapering Negro ... dominated Ebbets Field." He cited the gaping holes that Robeson opened in enemy lines, lifting little Rutgers to victory.[25] Writing for *The New York World*, November 28, 1917, George Daley called the Negro star "a football genius." Significantly, Robeson earned kudos for brains as well as brawn. The young Knight scored one touchdown and starred on defense. The victory brought a season's best record: 7–1–1.[26]

How did the one loss occur? Robeson, as writer rather than player, explained. Football, he argued, "is method and not men.... Rutgers has the best methods taught by the greatest of football coaches, George Foster Sanford." He goes on to sing the praise of this marvelous coach, as an "advocate of clean play in life as on the field." He lauds the man as an adviser, guardian, and molder of character. Above all, Robeson pinpoints teamwork and team spirit as the stuff of greatness. He analyzes every player's contribution but his own. Foreshadowing his evolving political philosophy, young Paul Robeson put the group — an all-white group except for himself — above the self. This uncommon man celebrated the common cause. Such selflessness is unusual among athletes of today.[27]

In a questionable expression of patriotism during wartime, in 1917 Walter Camp and other sports authorities refused to name an official All-American team. Evidently, the war to make the world safe for democracy, not to mention communism, precluded football honors. Camp hailed Robeson, however, as worthy of that temporarily suspended honor. The same applied to the 1918 season, which resulted in a 5–2 record for the Scarlet Knights of the Raritan.[28] Strangely, there is far less coverage of Robeson at Rutgers during the final year of World War I. As his illustrious collegiate career drew to a close, more attention was paid to his intellectual prowess, including the coveted Phi Beta Kappa key and prizes for oratory.[29]

Nevertheless, Robeson continued to excel in the sports arena. In June 1919 a campus paper reported that Robeson hurled the javelin 137'5" against Swarthmore College, twelve feet better than his nearest competitor.[30] He also finally led Rutgers' lion to a victory over the hated Princeton tiger in baseball. On June 10, 1919, after delivering the valedictory address at his graduation ceremony (in which he exhorted his classmates to achieve justice, democracy, and equality for all in "The New Idealism"), he donned "the tools of ignorance" (his catcher's gear) and boosted his baseball team to victory over Princeton, 5–1. By his own admission, observes biographer Lloyd Brown, this last game for Robeson at Rutgers, in which the long-time nemesis was defeated for the first time, represented, arguably, his finest hour.[31]

A final chapter in the Robeson at Rutgers saga can be found in *The Scarlet Letter* (the college yearbook, not Hawthorne's novel). Describing Paul's spectacular performance against Navy, the author writes[32]:

> And as a thorn in her flesh, the tall towering Robeson commanded Rutgers' secondary, dived under and spilled her wide oblique angle runs, turned back line plunges and carried the burden of defense so splendidly that in 44 minutes those Ex–All American backs ... made precisely two first downs.

After college, Robeson entered Columbia Law School. To pay his tuition, Paul assisted Fritz Pollard as football coach at Lincoln University. He also joined Alpha Phi Alpha, the first black fraternity in America. While studying law, he played professional football with both Pollard and Conzelman before a ban was imposed on blacks in 1934. His first professional venue was Hammond, Indiana, in 1920. He switched to the Akron Pros that year and stayed until 1921. He finished his football career with the Milwaukee Badgers in 1922. He earned anywhere from $50 to $200 per game.[33]

Largely ignored, professional football did not keep records, so it is difficult at best to judge Robeson's postgraduate performance. We do know, however, that Paul Robeson and Fritz Pollard led an all-black team to victory over an all-white all-star team 6–0 at Schoolings Park on December 10, 1922. You can look it up.[34] And by 1922, Albert Britt observed that this "Dusky Rover" and "Football Othello"

towered above his contemporaries in the sports pantheon.[35]

Did Paul Robeson make a difference as a sports hero? In assessing his athletic career, sociologist and baseball administrator Harry Edwards observed that Paul won respect from opposing coaches with his fierce play. His coach called him "the greatest player of all time." One coach, oblivious to the explicit racism in his praise, dubbed him "a white man in black skin." Yet, on road trips, Robeson had to sleep in segregated facilities and often took meals on the team bus. There is no evidence that Paul protested publicly. In short, he was compelled to adapt a posture of either acceptance or avoidance. On the field, however, he could — and did — act aggressively. Thus, Robeson developed a bipolar stance against a bipolar world.

Author Murray Kempton, in a less than generous appraisal, invidiously compared Paul Robeson to Blues singer Bessie Smith and union leaders Thomas Patterson and A. Philip Randolph.[36] Kempton claimed that the great baritone escaped from the horrors of racism inflicted upon American blacks. An expatriate's life in Europe constituted an "avoidance" adaptation. Lionized in London, Robeson did not shoulder the awful burden of race as in America. Yet even Kempton had to concede that the young Robeson was also victimized on the gridiron, as

> Rival football players were accustomed to remind him that he was a Negro with concentrated violence. But his conduct on these occasions was a model for any sportsman. It was generally agreed that he knew his place. Only in 1950, so much later, would Paul Robeson remember his football days and report with dreadful satisfaction that there had been moments when he used his fist in the pile-ups.[37]

Kempton is wrong on at least one count. Robeson mentioned his aggressive behavior on the football field earlier than

1950. Moreover, his point about gentlemanly conduct articulates a superficial truth. Indeed, football was, and is, a sport of sanctioned violence. Robeson's game, unlike that of his brilliant black contemporary, Fritz Pollard, relied on awesome power and keen intellect rather than blinding speed. But Kempton deserves credit for describing the ambivalence that marked Robeson's persona.

If ambivalence represented one "mark of oppression," athletic achievement served as a counter. In persistence and perseverance, Paul became a forerunner, as he acknowledged: "Sports was an important part of my life in those days."[38] Professor Lamont Yeakey forcefully argues that Paul Robeson, as athlete and scholar, smashed the myth of white supremacy.[39] In his graduate thesis, Professor Yeakey made a powerful case for reexamining the early life of Paul Robeson. This innovative study sheds new light on "The Great Forerunner" and his subsequent career.[40]

It is imperative to recall the historical context during Robeson's collegiate years. The *Crisis* reported that 224 people were lynched in 1917. One Rutgers' student, a white male, was in fact stripped, dipped (in molasses), feathered, and thrust out of town by classmates. Samuel Chovenson, the victim, had refused to give a speech in support of Liberty Loans in class. In this hate-filled era, Robeson demonstrated grace under pressure, the hallmark of a Hemingway hero. He also displayed a marked superiority to white players. Moreover, he did not fear whites.[41] In his successful pursuit of athletic glory, Robeson debunked the widely held belief that blacks were inferior. In the process, Yeakey contends, Paul broadened the humanity of whites.[42]

Professor Yeakey takes many eminent historians to task for omitting Robeson from their tomes or neglecting his impact. He chides John Hope Franklin for ignoring this African-American hero. A quick glance at the latest edition of his highly regarded *From Slavery to Freedom* confirms this critique first offered in 1971. The Cold War campaign to destroy Paul Robeson, waged primarily through the media, permeated the historian's craft, lamentably. Public figures also attacked Robeson. He slipped into obscurity.

Unintentionally, the Scarlet Knight may have contributed to this underestimation. When the press lauded his talents and rued his graduation, Paul responded curiously. "Negro prejudice has two sides. When people hate you they go a little crazy. But when they like you they go a little crazy too. In football days, I got more praise than I deserved."[43] Although he was offered thousands of dollars to engage in professional sports, boxing as well as football, Robeson spurned both as corrupting and alien.[44]

In 1954 Rutgers University published a list of its 65 greatest football players. Conspicuously and absurdly absent: Paul Bustill Robeson. Sports Information Director William McKenzie called it "a conspiracy of silence." Because his alma mater refused to sponsor him, the rejection of Robeson spilled over to the National Football Hall of Fame housed at Rutgers.[45] A reversal of fortune began in 1970 when a committee of sports cognoscenti and Rutgers' personnel, including Coach John Bateman, put his name in nomination. Rejected until August 25, 1995, the great athlete at long last entered his alma mater's Hall of Fame.[46] For Robeson the union with football's elite came too little, too late. For the faithful, however, this delayed honor proved author Leo Tolstoy correct in his profound observation that "God sees the truth — but waits."

In the final analysis, when football functioned as the moral equivalent of war, what did this noble warrior accomplish along the banks of the Raritan River? True, segregation did not vanish during his glory years. Nor could Robeson strike a fatal blow against segregation away from the battlefields of sports. Thanks to his presence, however, black participation in a once totally white intercollegiate environment measurably improved. And public appreciation of black talent also increased, markedly.

As Professor Jeffrey Stewart astutely observes, Robeson's body became the subject of riveting attention, his intellectual accomplishments, the object of awe. In a cache of photographs recently discovered, the portrayal of Robeson in the nude may have contributed to a profound insight issuing from the Harlem Renaissance in which Paul Robeson played an integral part — namely, that black is beautiful. This extraordinary athletic Apollo was the epitome of black beauty.[47]

There is, alas, also one disturbing afterthought. Robeson's account of his football experience is almost too sweet in self-denial. He must have harbored deep rage within, which, when unleashed, caused the fire in his soul to burn incessantly. The oxygen of other atmospheres— such as the Soviet Union and Eastern Europe, where he was lionized, admired, and loved — fed his anger at America. But despite his support of Communism, we must not extenuate or distort the injustice visited on this great man. We must also remember that Paul Robeson's heroic entry into the deep river of American life coincided with his immersion — let's call it baptism — in sports.

Notes

1. C. Eric Lincoln, *The Black Muslims*, third edition (Grand Rapids, MI: William B. Eerdmans Publishing Co., 1994), 32–34, employed these useful behavioral archetypes.

2. W. E. B. Du Bois, *The Souls of Black Folk* (New York: Fawcett, 1961), 17.

3. Marshall Fishwick, "The Hero in Transition" in Ray Browne and Marshall Fishwick, eds., *The Hero in Transition* (Bowling Green, OH: Bowling Green State University Popular Press, 1983), 5–14, 60–61.

4. Jim Holt, "Taboo," review of *Taboo: Why Black Athletes Dominate Sports and Why We Are Afraid to Talk About It* by John Entwine, *New York Times Book Review*, April 16, 2000, 11.

5. John Hoberman, *Darwin's Athletes: How Sport Has Damaged Black America and Preserved the Myth of Race* (Boston: Houghton Mifflin Mariner Books, 1997), 3–51. For a balanced critique of this controversial work, see Christopher Shea, "'Darwin's Athletes,' A Professor Explores Americans' Reverence for Black Sports Stars," *The Chronicle of Higher Education* (March 7, 1997), A15–16.

6. David K. Wiggins, "The Notion of Double-Consciousness and the Involvement of Black Athletes in American Sport" in George Eisen and David K. Wiggins, eds., *Ethnicity and Sport in North American History and Culture* (Westport, CT: Greenwood Press, 1994), 133.

7. *Ibid.*, 134.

8. *Ibid.*, 134–135.

9. *Ibid.*, 137–138. Athletic prominence may have saved Walker from the noose, argues Sidney Gendin, "Moses Fleetwood Walker: Jackie Robinson's Accidental Predecessor" in Joseph Dorinson and Joram Warmund, eds., *Jackie Robinson: Race, Sports and the American Dream* (Armonk, NY: M. E. Sharpe, 1999), 27.

10. *Ibid.*, 140; also see Joseph Dorinson, "Black Heroes in Sport: From Jack Johnson to Muhammad Ali," *Journal of Popular Culture*, 31:3 (Winter 1997), 116–117.

11. Stephen Fox, *Big Leagues: Professional Baseball, Football, and Basketball in National Memory* (New York: William Morrow, 1994), 317–321.

12. Paul Robeson, *Here I Stand* (New York: Othello Associates, 1958), 22.

13. Lloyd L. Brown, *The Young Paul Robeson: "On My Journey Now"* (Boulder, CO: Westview Press, 1997), 46.

14. *Ibid.*, 46–47; Francis C. Harris, "Paul Robeson" in Jeffrey Stewart, ed., *Paul Robeson: Artist and Citizen* (New Brunswick, NJ: Rutgers University Press, 1998), 36, quotes Doug Brown as quantifying Robeson's as three-quarters of the team's heart. Whatever the true fraction, Paul played a central role.

15. *Ibid.*, 61–62. Robert Van Gelder, *New York Times* (June 16, 1944), Sec. 2, 7.

16. Martin B. Duberman, *Paul Robeson* (New York: Knopf, 1988), 21. Also see L. Brown, 62.

17. M. Duberman, 21–22.

18. *Ibid.*

19. As quoted in *A Paul Robeson Research Guide: A Selective Annotated Bibliography*, hereafter *RG*, Lenwood G. Davis, compiler (Westport, CT: Greenwood Press, 1982), #699, 308.

20. Philip S. Foner, ed., *Paul Robeson Speaks: Writings, Speeches, Interviews 1918–1974* (New York: Brunner/Mazel Publishers, 1978), 49–53.

21. *Ibid.*

22. As quoted in *RG*, #700, 309.

23. As quoted in M. Duberman, 23.

24. *Ibid.*

25. As quoted in *RG*, #702, 310.

26. *Ibid.*, #704, 311.

27. P. Foner, 51–53; *RG*, #102, 66–67.

28. L. Brown, 81–82.

29. F. Harris, 41–44.

30. *RG*, #711, 313.

31. L. Brown, 95–96.

32. "Paul Robeson," *The Scarlet Letter* (Rutgers University Yearbook, 1919), 167 as cited in *RG*, #714, 314.

33. F. Harris, 44–45.

34. Joe Powers, Sr., and Mark Rogovin, *Paul Robeson Rediscovered: An Annotated Listing of His Chicago History from 1921 to 1958* (Chicago: Columbia College Paul Robeson 100th Birthday Committee, 2000), 7.

35. Albert Britt, "The Dusky Rover," *Outing* (January 1918), as cited in *RG*, #711, 313.

36. Murray Kempton, *Part of Our Time: Some Ruins and Monuments of the Thirties* (New York: Simon & Schuster, 1955), 233–260.

37. *Ibid.*, 238.

38. Paul Robeson, "Here's My Story, Sports Was an Important Part of My Life," *Freedom* (November 1951), 1, 7, as cited in *RG*, #193, 67.

39. Lamont H. Yeakey, *Journal of Negro Education*, 42:4 (Fall 1973), 489–503.

40. Lamont H. Yeakey, "The Early Years of Paul Robeson: Prelude to the Making of a Revolutionary," Master's thesis, Columbia University, 1971.

41. *Ibid.*, 28, 49.

42. *Ibid.*, 53.

43. *Ibid.*, 39–40.

44. *Ibid.*, 56–57.

45. M. Duberman, 760, n8, 763, n21.

46. F. Harris, 45–47.

47. Jeffrey C. Stewart, "The Black Body: Paul Robeson as a Work of Art and Politics," in J. Stewart, *Robeson: Artist...*, 135–155.

Robeson the Athlete: A Remembrance

LESTER RODNEY
The Daily Worker

How good an athlete was Paul Robeson? Well, at Rutgers University from 1915 to 1919 he won 15 letters in four sports: football, baseball, basketball, and track and field. Almost 30 years later, another young athlete named Jackie Robinson had the college sports world buzzing when *he* became the first four-sport athlete (the same sports) in the history of UCLA.

How good an athlete was Paul Robeson? Lou Little, long-time renowned football coach at Columbia, said, "I think there has never been a greater player in the history of football than the Robeson who was named an All-American end by Walter Camp." It should be explained that when Robeson played college football, there was just one All-American team. Eleven players, period. No competing AP, UPI, Sports Illustrated All-Americans. Robeson made that solely recognized team twice. In commenting on his selections, Camp called Robeson "the greatest end that ever trod the gridiron."

Robeson's formal sports career began as a 13-year-old student at Somerville High School in New Jersey. He was one of only two African Americans at the school. Not many details survive on his sports life at Somerville, but we do know that he played both football and catcher on the baseball team.

In 1915 Robeson entered Rutgers as the winner of a statewide competition for a four-year scholarship. When he went out for the varsity football team, on the first day a couple of thugs who didn't want a black on the team slugged him during scrimmage, breaking his nose and dislocating his shoulder. He bounced back after a few days. Robeson of Rutgers was a stellar blocking and pass catching end on the offense, and an all-around dynamo on the defense.

Here are some game story quotes from sportswriters of the time:

New York Times, Oct. 28, 1917:

> Fordham Crushed by Rutgers Power.... Robeson, the Sturdy Negro End, Plays a Stellar Role in the Aerial Attack.... He

was a tower of strength both on the offense and defense and it was his receiving of forward passes which shattered the hopes of Fordham.... Robeson invariably spilled two men and several times three and four were dropped to the ground, even before the play was well under way.

New York Tribune, same game, by Charles A. Taylor:

Robeson, the giant Negro, appeared in the lineup at left end, but he did not confine himself to this particular post. He played in turn practically every position on the Rutgers team before the battle was ended.... With his team on the offensive, Robeson was wont to leap high into the air to grab forward passes wherever he saw that the man they were intended for was in another sector of the field. On the defense he was kept busy on the few occasions when Fordham appeared likely to make a score.... Robeson was supposed to play fullback on the defense, and he did, but never did a fullback range so widely as he. If there was a gap in the line Robeson filled it. If the Rutgers ends were the least bit remiss in stopping the ashes of Erwig and Frankie Frisch, Robeson was on hand to prevent any substantial progress.

This was the same Frankie Frisch, "The Fordham Flash," who went on to the Baseball Hall of Fame as the New York Giants' second baseman. He was considered equally good at both sports. Robeson, of course, did not have the option of playing big league baseball. He did play three season of pro football in the loose-knit American Professional Football Leagues, today's NFL. The early league apparently did not discriminate against African Americans, but the NFL did.

The early pro league gave Robeson the opportunity to pick up some sorely needed money as he pursued his law and acting careers. He played for the Akron Pros and the Milwaukee Badgers. The Professional Football Hall of Fame, in Canton, Ohio,

now notes: "When he could clear his schedule, Paul Robeson also joined the lineup. One of the best players of his time and the most famous black player in the land, Rutgers grad Robeson was studying law at Columbia University while pursuing a career as a singer and actor. Understandably, his time for pro football was limited but he made it to eight of the Pro's twelve games in 1921 and starred each time while playing several different positions."

In December of 1922 Robeson took time off for one more football game, with the all–African American Fritz Pollard All-Stars, who defeated an all-white pro team 6–0 at Schorlings Park in Chicago. That marked the end of his formal sports career.

Robeson's most dramatic football performance was undoubtedly with the Rutgers team of 1918 against the famed Newport Naval team at Ebbets Field in Brooklyn on November 17. The Naval team was made up of the cream of the land's college players, and was an overwhelming favorite over the Rutgers undergraduates. Here is how the writer Louis Lee Arms of the *New York Tribune* described what happened:

A tall, tapering Negro in a faded crimson sweater, moleskins and a pair of maroon socks ranged hither and yon on a wind-whipped Flatbush field yesterday afternoon. He rode on the wings of the frigid breezes, a grim, silent, and compelling figure. Whether it was Charley Barrett of old Cornell and all–American glory, or Gerrish or Gardner who tried to hurl himself through the gauntlet, he was met and stopped by this blaze of red and black.

The Negro was Paul Robeson, of Rutgers College, and he is a minister's son.... It was Robeson, a veritable Othello of battle, who led the dashing little Rutgers eleven to a 14–0 victory over the widely heralded Newport Naval Reserves. The Naval warriors came down from Newport upon victory and added glory bent. They had trimmed Brown and Harvard, and that the smooth-skinned youths from the banks of the Raritan could stop them — well, it was beyond belief.

But it wasn't. As a thorn in her flesh, Robeson, commanding Rutgers' secondary, dived under and spilled her wide, oblique angled runs, turned back her line plunges, and carried the burden of defense so splendidly that in exactly forty-four minutes these ex–all American backs, who are fixed luminaries in the mythology of the gridiron, made precisely two first downs.

Among the original tactical maneuvers in Rutgers' attack is the calling in of Robeson to open holes for the backfield. He is shifted by signal from left end to whatever spot along the line has been pre-selected. Thus considerable of Rutgers' line drives were put upon the basis of Robeson's superiority over Black, Schlachter, Callahan or whomever he faced.

Even allowing for the more lush sportswriting style of the time, these are remarkable, unprecedented tributes. Here is one more, by the noted George Daley of the *New York World*, which stresses the cerebral part of Robeson's football prowess:

> Paul Robeson is a football genius…. It is seldom indeed that a lineman can develop such a versatility. Here are some of the duties: opening up holes for his backs on line plays; providing remarkable interference for his backs on end runs; going downfield under punts; taking forward passes, in which, by the way, he handles the pigskin with almost the same sureness as a baseball; supporting the center of the line on defense, or, as some have it, of playing defensive quarterback; plugging up holes from one end of the line to the other; tackling here and there and everywhere; kicking off and diagnosing.

> And the greatest of his accomplishments is accurate diagnosis. His ability to size up plays and quickly get to the point of danger is almost uncanny. He is so rarely at fault that he is at the center of practically every play, and therein lies his greatest value, and therein the truest measure of his all-around ability.

Thirty-five years later, this sportswriter, covering a baseball game at Ebbets Field between the Brooklyn Dodgers and the St. Louis Cardinals, ran into the Newport Naval quarterback of that 1918 football game. He was Jimmy Conzelman, who had gone on to play pro football and then to coach the Chicago Cardinals to a championship. He was now an advertising executive with the baseball Cardinals. I asked him about his memories of Paul Robeson, the athlete, and wrote in the *Daily Worker* on May 8, 1953:

> Jimmy's eyes lit up. "Yes, I played against Robeson right out on this field," he said. "How good was he?" "Great, that's how good, one of the greatest ever. Yeah, we played Rutgers that day. I was quarterback for the great Naval team, we figured to win it, but that Robeson … he beat us…."

> "He was a tremendous offensive end," he enthused. "Did everything, blocked, caught passes, on defense he was a line backer up, tremendous. They'd move him around to tackle to clear the way for the ball-carrier sometimes…. A fine fellow, too," he added. "We played together later as pros at Milwaukee. And a wonderful singer, a real artist, and you know he was Phi Beta Kappa, you know how smart you had to be to be Phi Beta Kappa?"

> "I was sorry to see him take the political tack he decided to take," he put in at this point, and then his eyes lit up again. "Yes, right out here at Ebbets Field. One of the truly great players! Truly great!"

The Political Struggle

A Man of His Times:
Paul Robeson and the Press,
1924–1976

MARY E. CYGAN
University of Connecticut

"The majority of the negroes in Washington before the great war were well behaved.... Most of them admitted the superiority of the white race, and troubles between the two races were undreamed of. Now and then a negro intent on enforcing a civil rights law would force his way into a saloon or a theatre and demand to be treated the same as whites were, but if the manager objected he usually gave in without more than a protest."

The *New York Times* printed the editorial from which these sentences are taken on July 23, 1919, a few weeks after Paul Robeson graduated from Rutgers University, and only five years before the reviews of his early performances appeared.

The white mainstream press covered Paul Robeson's career from his acting debut in 1924 until his death in 1976. The story of how Robeson was silenced at the height of his career, how the federal government hounded him, how contracts were canceled, how halls were closed to him, how his films were withdrawn from circulation, and how he was denied the right to travel even to Canada and Mexico has been told elsewhere.[1] W.E.B. Du Bois believed that in the 1950s and 1960s Robeson was "the best known American on earth, to the largest number of human beings. His voice [was] known in Europe, Asia and Africa, in the West Indies and South America and in the islands of the seas.... Only in his native land [was] he without honor and rights."[2] The press played a key role in the process of making Robeson disappear from public view in the United States. The white mainstream press moved from reporting on anti–Communist attacks on Robeson in the early 1940s to participating in the demonization of Robeson in its massive coverage of his activities in 1949, including his remarks before the Paris Peace Conference and his attempt to give a concert at picnic grounds outside Peekskill, New York. The following year Robeson became a non-person in his homeland.

This article examines what was said about Robeson in the press before and after 1949, seeking in those reports a clue about how an artist and political figure of Robeson's stature could be so completely erased in the 1950s. It demonstrates that tension and limits to the coverage could already be seen before 1949, and that the way the image of Robeson was manipulated in the late 1960s and 1970s, when he was "rehabilitated," parallels the way other controversial African Americans have been treated by the press. Robeson's career, as filtered in the American press, can be seen to fall into five main periods: 1) The New Negro, 1924–1939; 2) *Othello* and Civil Rights, 1939–1949; 3) Turning Point, 1949–1950; 4) Silence, 1950–1958; and 5) The Tragic Figure, 1958–1976.

The New Negro, 1924–1939

In the first years of Robeson's public career, the white press portrayed him as a figure who entertained, and also reassured, white audiences. We can see in the press coverage of this period the positive influence of the Harlem Renaissance, but also tendencies from 1920s nativism. The exotic cultural artifact or performance, whether from Black Harlem or a European peasant past, was welcome, but only as a "contribution" to the dominant Anglo-Saxon culture. Robeson appeared as a romantic figure who stirred the imagination but never threatened prevailing presumptions.

Interviews and personal profiles portrayed Robeson not only as "the greatest actor of his race,"[3] but as a model African American. His opinions were characterized as those of "the intelligent Negro," "the educated Negro," or "the New Negro." (In the *New York Times*, he was "Paul Robeson, negro actor"—and, at least once, "giant negro actor"—until April 1930 when he became the "Negro singer and actor."[4]) A

AMBASSADORS THEATRE
West St., Shaftesbury Avenue, W.C.2
(Near Leicester Square Tube Station)

Nightly at **8.40.**   Matinees Tuesday and Friday at **2.30**

PAUL ROBESON
as
THE EMPEROR JONES

EUGENE O'NEILL'S PLAYS
The Emperor Jones
AND
THE LONG VOYAGE HOME

Program from Ambassadors Theatre, London, 1925. Courtesy of Paul Robeson, Jr.

reviewer of Robeson's pathbreaking 1925 concert devoted entirely to African-American spirituals and secular songs concluded that "the voice of Paul Robeson is the embodiment of the aspirations of the New Negro who pleads best the race's progress by adhering strictly to the true endowment of his ancestors."[5] When reports circulated after Robeson's successful performance as *Othello* in London that an American production casting Robeson opposite Lillian Gish might be in the works, a reviewer announced that the production would be a "milestone in the struggle of a race."[6] According to the press, Robeson and his wife, Eslanda, were "in a position to help tremendously the cause of their people in the United States."[7]

Robeson was not seen so much as a token but as a trailblazer, a successful phenomenon who presaged a new era of understanding and optimistic accommodation. Interviews focused on his accomplishments as well as his wife's. A report on Robeson's acting debut in *All God's Chillun'* in 1924 noted that Eslanda Goode Robeson held an unprecedented position as a technologist in a New York hospital, and that the young couple had "friends of both races," demonstrating "hope for the younger generation."[8]

In this period, the press was surprisingly ready to acknowledge that Robeson faced racial discrimination, though in the 1950s it would deny that race played any role in attacks on Robeson. The *New York World* noted public criticism by members of the Dutch Treat Club when, after Robeson sang there, the officers declined to confer an honorary membership as was customary.[9] Similarly, when the Philadelphia Art Alliance refused to allow the display of Antonio Salemme's celebrated statue of Robeson, newspaper coverage was generally sympathetic to Robeson and implied that the art organization offered only weak excuses for its position.[10]

In reporting the outrage over these insults, reporters and columnists implied that racists were a dying breed, that thanks to African Americans like Robeson, racism was in decline. All that was required was more people like Robeson who could put white people at ease and who, with his charm and outstanding talent, could dissolve barriers painlessly (for both blacks and whites).

A review of Eslanda Goode Robeson's 1930 biography of her husband appeared under the headline: "Up From Slavery Indeed! Paul Robeson's Life Written by Wife Is Glowing Record of What Talented Negro May Accomplish." The review concluded that though Robeson was a "northern Negro … his wife takes pains to show that he was never 'uppity.' He simply moved along on his tremendous natural momentum, finding white friends aplenty who were glad to call him Paul … he was not the King of Harlem, he was free all over town."[11]

Press coverage of this period portrayed Robeson's growing interest in African-American and African cultures, and the connections between them, as a curious hobby — a sort of dabbling in a "noble savage" mystique.

Robeson reassured some people in the press when he wore a tuxedo in performance of his debut concert of spirituals, which one critic pointed out was presented "without deference or apology."[12] But Robeson initially alarmed reporters when he spoke before the League of Colored People in London and said that the "Negro race should redeem its African heritage." The *Associated Press* pressed for a clarification and finally reported that Robeson had "no intention of quitting civilization for a leopard-skin life in the interior of Africa — or somewhere."[13] He could present folkloric gifts, so long as he accommodated the values and assumptions of the white world.

Othello *and Civil Rights,* *1939–1949*

In 1939 Robeson returned to the United States after nearly a decade abroad, more visible thanks to his European success, and more vocal. He now protested segregation and strained the image of someone effortlessly "breaking barriers." A more threatening figure, Robeson no longer fit the model of the New Negro as fashioned by the white press. During this period, while his image was in flux between the old Robeson as the press had filtered him and the new, politically active Robeson, the *New York Times* printed no editorials about him — though editorials had appeared in the earlier period and many would appear in the following period, when a new, negative image emerged.

Robeson's performances received enthusiastic coverage. Reports of his concerts consistently noted the warm ovations he received from his audiences. The 1943 New York production of *Othello* enjoyed wide and serious discussion. Despite criticism for some details of Margaret Webster's production, New York critics were as impressed by Robeson's new performance as Othello as London critics had been thirteen years earlier. But an unease with his stronger political voice crept into the personal profiles. A backstage interview included the observation that Robeson's manner was "normally friendly but can grow coldly stern in defense of his race."[14]

The *New York Times* did not cover Robeson's first major protest of segregated seating at a Kansas City concert in February of 1942, though other newspapers, like the *New York World-Telegram* did.[15] But by April 1942 the *New York Times* acknowledged Robeson's growing activism, running an article describing Robeson as a politically involved artist, a universal humanist:

Experience in other movements, he feels, far from damaging him as a musician, has enriched him both as a human being and as an artist.... Finding something bigger than himself and linking himself to the whole progressive movement ... has also made him more serious about his work ... he feels ... he represents the forces of freedom.[16]

In a few years the *New York Times* would claim Robeson represented very different forces. Several headlines on Robeson's views as chair of the Council on African Affairs reveal the direction of the trend:

> WOULD HELP COLONIES (April 25, 1944)
> SINGER PLEADS FOR AFRICA (May 15, 1946)
> ROBESON ACCUSES THE U.S. OF EXPLOITING AFRICA (April 7, 1948)

Robeson had decried colonialism in Africa and the United States support of European imperialism since the 1930s, but the press did not begin to characterize his criticisms as attacks on the United States until the late 1940s.

Anti-Communist politicians began investigating Robeson as early as 1942 when Martin Dies, Chairman of the House Un-American Activities Committee (HUAC), included Paul Robeson's name on a list of alleged Communists. In 1946 Robeson was called before the Tenney Committee of the California state legislature where he publicly denied that he was a member of the Communist Party. By 1947 Senator J. Parnell Thomas was taking testimony against Robeson before HUAC, and some reporters began asking Robeson if he were a Communist.[17] But in this period, Robeson was still identified as a representative of African American opinion — as "Negro actor" or "Negro singer." For example:

Paul Robeson as Othello and Peggy Ashcroft as Desdemona, London, 1930. Courtesy of Paul Robeson, Jr.

Paul Robeson, Negro actor and singer, declared yesterday afternoon in an interview that the temper of the American Negro had changed during the war and that the Negro now "wants his freedom."[18]

In 1944, when Robeson was denied the use of a Baltimore theater, the *New York Times* noted that the same theater had refused a joint request by Eleanor Roosevelt and the NAACP for a meeting place. By 1947, when Robeson was refused a hall for a scheduled concert in Peoria, and was forced to get a court writ to sing in an Albany high school, his political views were seen as a major cause of the opposition to him, but racism was also identified as a contributing factor. In reporting on the Albany incident, the *New York Times* quoted Robeson's lawyer that the ban was a "slur on the Negro people as a whole," sought a quote from the pastor of the A.M.E. Church, and covered a protest of the ban by thirteen clergymen. After 1949 the *New York Times* would ignore similar protests by African Americans, though they would appear in African-American newspapers. Until 1949 the *New York Times* reported on the red-baiting of Paul Robeson but refrained from actively developing the image of Paul Robeson as "un–American."

Turning Point, 1949–1950

In 1949 and 1950, as the press worked through and settled on a new interpretation of Robeson, the amount of space devoted to him increased significantly. From 1940 to 1948 an average of 12.6 articles a year in the *New York Times* mentioned Robeson. The peak year in that period was 1947, the year in which Robeson announced he was giving up singing to devote himself to civil rights work, when 22 articles about him appeared. In 1949 the *New York Times* ran 159 articles (77 of them on the Peekskill affair) mentioning Robeson. In 1950 another 37 articles appeared. After this period, coverage would drop significantly to less than eight or nine brief notices, a few sentences each, per year until the 1960s when Robeson disappeared altogether from the press.

Once the new interpretation of Robeson as a Communist sympathizer appeared in 1949–50, the *New York Times* separated him from the African-American community. Attacks on him which the press previously interpreted as racially motivated, now were alleged to be reactions to Robeson's politics pure and simple. The African-American press, in contrast, occasionally disavowed specific political positions taken by Robeson, but insisted that the racial dimension of the attacks on him should be acknowledged.

The Baltimore *Afro-American* summed up its view during the anti–Communist witch hunts of the 1950s:

> The word "COMMUNIST" has developed into the nation's No. 1 "curse-word." If a person wants to "put you in the dozens," compare your forefathers with lower animals, use God's name in vain when describing you, he does it all simply by calling you a "d__n COMMUNIST." You are deep-red if you stand against racial segregation. You can kiss the feet of Stalin, wear a red rag around your head, have a sickle and hammer engraved on your teeth, oppose the Marshall Plan, take trips to Moscow — and you will only be a "suspected Communist." You will be investigated before you are condemned.

> But the moment you reveal that you hate Jim Crow, that you really stand for the equality of all mankind before the face of God, that the color of a man's skin has nothing to do with the quality of his mind or the goodness of his heart, you immediately become a "d__n RED."[19]

Robeson's appearance at the Paris Peace Conference protesting the formation of the North Atlantic Treaty Organization in April 1949 would precipitate the thoroughgoing re-interpretation of his person in 1949–1950. Delivering a speech at the conference on behalf of the London Coordinating Committee of Colonial Peoples, he warned against pressuring Third World countries into taking sides in the increasingly tense stand-off between the United States and the Soviet Union. According to his memories, Robeson added the remark that it was "unthinkable" that African Americans would take up arms to fight for the United States in an imperialist war — "In the name of an Eastland [Senator from Mississippi]."[20] He said later that, "I thought it was healthy for Americans to consider whether or not Negroes should fight for people who kick them around."[21]

Robeson's comments were met with an agitated response. The *New York Times* printed three editorials about Robeson in the three months following the Paris Peace Conference and gave extensive coverage to African Americans appearing before HUAC to refute Robeson's comments.[22] A July 15, 1949, *New York Times* article on testimony about Robeson's Communist affiliation, as alleged by Manning Johnson before HUAC, bore the inflammatory headline: "Black Stalin Aim Laid to Robeson."[23] And in 1949 and 1950 a special category appeared in the *New York Times* index exclusively for articles about Robeson's comments at the Paris conference: "international relations/big powers/Negroes (American) stand in case of war."

The three editorials took Paul Robeson

to task for stepping outside of the image created for him. Whereas Robeson had been the pre-eminent African American, now he was disassociated from the black community altogether, and the editors promoted other persons who could be interpreted as figures vanquishing (still) disappearing racism. Though the term "New Negro" no longer appeared in the *New York Times*, the role still remained to be cast by new candidates.

> We do not believe that making speeches of any sort can do as much for the American Negro as is being done by great American Negroes who in their own personalities demonstrate how hollow is prejudice and how ill-grounded is discrimination. Nothing that Mr. Robeson can say will be half as important as the fact of the existence of Roland Hayes and Ralph Bunche, of Joe Louis and Jackie Robinson, of Marian Anderson and Dorothy Maynard and yes, of Paul Robeson.[24]

The editors gave Robeson one last chance to reassume the old role.

> He is mistaken and misled, as many other persons are and have been. We hope profoundly, that his passion for a good cause will not lead him permanently into support for a bad one. We want him to sing and to go on being Paul Robeson.[25]

The other two editorials recommended Ralph Bunche and Jackie Robinson as praiseworthy African Americans in contrast to Robeson, whom they further discredited. "Jackie Robinson's statement [repudiating Robeson's comments] is impressive testimony to the vitality of American democracy, to the determination to keep on 'fighting race discrimination until we've got it licked.'"[26]

Throughout the late spring and early summer of 1949, the *New York Times* ran a series of articles showcasing African Amer-

icans who denied that Paul Robeson could speak for the African-American community (including two front page articles in July). Among those cited as disavowing Robeson was Adam Clayton Powell, Jr. (a member of Congress from the twenty-second district and pastor of the Abyssinian Baptist church in Harlem), whose statement ran under the headline, "Robeson as Speaker for Negroes Denied."[27] The same day, a different article reported that "Walter White [executive secretary of the National Association for the Advancement of Colored People] ... said that Mr. Robeson's remarks in Paris did not represent the views of the majority of American Negroes."[28] In an article headlined "Red Failures Here Told by Minorities," a rabbi claimed that Jews were anti–Communist and "another Negro, Thomas W. Young of Norfolk, a publisher, declared that Robeson has broken the bond he once had with the Negro mind."[29] A few days later a front page headline, spanning two columns, announced, "Jackie Robinson Terms Stand of Robeson on Negroes False."[30]

The *New York Times* gave the impression that the African-American community unanimously and unequivocally condemned Robeson. In so doing, it ignored African-American newspapers that saw a much more complex picture, often distancing themselves from Robeson's left-wing affiliations but affirming his importance as a critic of segregation. During the same summer that the three *New York Times* editorials appeared denying Robeson could speak for African Americans, the Baltimore *Afro-American* printed an editorial that decried the tendency to discredit Robeson's civil rights activism. The real issue, it claimed, was:

> What will happen when there are 10,000 Robesons or 2,000,000 or 10,000,000? All any oppressed masses need is leadership and the House Un-American Activities Committee is simply fearful that Mr.

Paul Robeson addresses a rally in Madison Square Garden, 1949. Photograph by Julius Lazarus. Courtesy of Paul Robeson, Jr.

Robeson represents that type of leadership.[31]

In its reporting on the spring 1949 Paris Peace Conference and its aftermath, the *New York Times* consistently selected and highlighted quotations from the African-American community that conformed to its own interpretation of the affair and ignored or downplayed those which did not. We can see the same pattern in reporting on events surrounding an outdoor concert near Peekskill, New York, in late summer 1949.

Robeson had agreed to sing at an August 27 benefit for the Harlem Chapter of the Civil Rights Congress. The day before the scheduled concert, eleven Westchester residents asked for police protection for concert-goers and Robeson, citing "inflammatory statements" in local newspapers about the concert and publicity for a demonstration planned by the Joint Veterans Council of Westchester County.[32] However, only four deputy sheriffs were on hand as concert-goers arrived. The violence which ensued as the demonstrating veterans blocked the entrance to the concert grounds—trapping a handful inside and preventing any additional persons from entering—lasted two and a half hours. Robeson, whose car was turned away before it reached the concert grounds, never sang. Soon after, the Civil Rights Congress announced plans to reschedule the concert.[33]

On September 4 chartered buses, private cars, and trains brought a crowd of

15,000 to hear Robeson sing at a Westchester County picnic ground near Peekskill, while several thousand veterans sympathetic to Robeson formed a defense perimeter around the concert area. According to the *New York Times*, the veterans supporting the concert organizers "were strictly disciplined and obeyed almost without exception the orders of their committeemen who ran the encampment as if they were setting up a headquarters post in an enemy area."[34] Approximately 1,000 protesting veterans paraded at the entrance to the concert grounds but were separated from concert-goers by hundreds of state troopers and local law enforcement officers. By late afternoon, unruly crowds assembled and attacked the concert-goers as they left the grounds. The attacks continued until late at night and, according to state police, ranged over ten square miles.

New York Times reports published on September 5 and 6,[35] in the immediate aftermath of the concert, included many telling details that would drop out of summaries of the incidents in later reports and be ignored or contradicted in three editorials. On-the-scene reporting described a diverse crowd of rioters, including "men and women who looked normally like law-abiding citizens," "housewives [who] were seen walking along the roads batting at passing cars with sticks," and youths "who [in the presence of police] started casually flipping pebbles [and] stepped up their missiles to boulders before the police intervened." Though spokespersons for the Joint Veterans Council alleged that the veterans had no connection to the violence because they ended their protest and left the area before the attacks began, *New York Times* reporters described youths with the word "vet" chalked on their shirts, and quoted a local man in a bar saying, "Why should we get sweated up? The kids can do a better job and the cops don't run them in."

Stories on September 5 and 6 covered numerous independent yet consistent accounts by those who arrived in Manhattan late on the evening of the 4th describing stoning (broken bus windows corroborated the stories) and complaining of police who made little effort to rein in the attacks. Accounts from passengers and the drivers of the chartered buses coincided. (Some drivers, frightened by the stone-throwing crowds, abandoned their buses in Westchester County, leaving passengers to drive the buses themselves or seek other transportation.)[36] Two buses with African-American passengers returning from an afternoon excursion to Hyde Park, New York, and not connected to the concert had also been stoned. At least sixteen cars were overturned, and authorities verified nearly 150 injuries requiring medical treatment. Reporters covered a press conference held the day after the concert in which Robeson charged not only that state troopers had allowed attacks to occur in the hope of provoking a reaction from concert-goers, but that a state trooper had clubbed Robeson's own car while shouting an epithet. Robeson praised the concert-goers and the veterans protecting them for their self-discipline and restraint.

Despite detailed coverage, which included ample evidence that a racial element characterized the attacks and that authorities did not act to prevent the violence,[37] editorials and later coverage show how the editors reinterpreted the events to support a different conclusion, backing away from troubling information in the *New York Times'* own on-the-scene reports. A headline of September 8 already indicated the direction of this reinterpretation: "Police Commended in Peekskill Fray."

As early as August 29, in the wake of the first attempt to hold the concert, the *New York Times* printed an editorial that was mildly supportive of Robeson but already noted the limits of the editors' sympathy. It concluded that the audience of August 27 "went there to hear Mr. Robeson sing, not to get into a fight." The editorial upheld Robeson's right to sing, regardless of the "twisted thinking" on the Soviet Union "that is ruining Robeson's great career." But an editorial on September 6 described the audience at the second concert in different terms: "a crowd of 15,000 persons, many of them Communists ... [assembled] more or less as a gesture of defiance against those who had forcibly prevented a similar concert from being held eight days previously." This editorial outlined the three main themes that would characterize *New York Times* coverage of two official inquiries into the violence at Peekskill: a report by the Westchester County District Attorney sent to the governor on September 7, 1949, and the report of a grand jury filed in June 1950.

The first theme was that Robeson's supporters sought the mantle of martyrdom and provoked the violence by displaying their strength. On September 6 the editors wrote: "Obviously the persons who promoted this concert knew that there might be trouble, and it is more than likely that a good many of them hoped there would be. Any form of extremism thrives on martyrdom." An editorial of June 18, 1950, echoed this view: "The one thing the Communists can use now most effectively is the role of martyr. It should not be given to them." Though the editors were willing to concede to Robeson the abstract right to hold the concert, they condemned him for rescheduling it. No one alleged that Robeson's supporters had taken part in the violence, but this fact was portrayed as part of a plan to appear to be victims as well as, simultaneously, to appear strong. The editors scoffed at the guards' attempts to prevent violence: "The Communists had at their disposal a well-trained and closely knit quasi-military 'defense' organization

... its discipline was good. This makes it all the more alarming.... It was a calculated display of Communist organizational strength."[38]

The second theme was that the demonstrating veterans were innocent of the violence that followed the demonstrations. The September 6 editorial argued that, "Little groups—mostly youths too young ever to have been war veterans—hurled insults and ... rocks." Not only did on-the-scene reporters describe a more diverse crowd attacking concert-goers, but an article in the same issue of the *New York Times* reported that among the eleven arrested on various charges, including malicious violence, were the son of the Peekskill police chief and the son of an American Legion official.

The third theme was that racism played no part in the attack on Robeson. The June 18, 1950, editorial put it most succinctly: "in the resistance to the Communist display of strength the motives were anti–Communist and not anti–Negro or anti–Semitic. It is a good thing to recognize the Communist tactic of trying to play upon presumptive race prejudice and to create its shadow even if its substance is absent." This position ignored much evidence that racism played a large role in the attacks, including a dramatic detail first reported in the *New York Times* on August 28 (and repeated in three later reports): During the attacks on the first night that Robeson attempted to sing, "someone turned off the flood-lights in the park. A few moments later, several fiery crosses, emblematic of the Ku Klux Klan, blazed on the field."[39]

The editors chose to ignore statements by African Americans about the racial dimension of the violence, even those which appeared in earlier reports published in the *New York Times*. Thus a statement by the NAACP that "anti–Negro sentiment was clearly discernible" at Peekskill was buried in a long article on September 7, 1949; but when A. Philip Randolph wrote a letter a few weeks later, which said that the demonstrators were anti–Communist more than anti–Negro and praised the police, the editors ran the letter under the headline: "The Peekskill Concert/Robeson Fracas Is Discussed from Negro Standpoint."[40] In other words, the official "Negro standpoint," exactly matched the views expressed in *New York Times* editorials.

The *New York Amsterdam News* provided a very different "Negro Standpoint." While the editors agreed with the first of the three *New York Times*' points (predicting that "the Communist Party will certainly make shrewd use of the issue"[41]), it resoundingly rejected the remaining two points. The *Amsterdam News* headlined its coverage of the September 4 events with, "Blame Cops in Riot," and printed a front-page photograph of police striking Eugene Bullard, identified in the caption as the "first Negro WWI pilot." The front page also carried an eyewitness account of the violence that charged that the police attempted "to provoke the husky-looking Negroes" and beat others. An editorial the following week argued that officers were "sympathetic to the veterans' plans and publicly encouraged them," and called for the governor to discipline the Westchester District Attorney and sheriff (rather than put them in charge of an official state report).[42] And the *Amsterdam News* clearly and repeatedly portrayed the Peekskill violence as racially inspired. Accounts on September 10 referred several times to "racial insults" and "racial slurs" hurled at concert-goers, and the editorial of September 17 concluded that the "mob at Peekskill was a close blood relation to the lynch mobs of Georgia and Florida." The editors called on the NAACP to play a leading role in "securing corrective action."

Though the *New York Times* implied that it was reporting on African-American opinion, none of the complexity in the contemporary views of a popular African-American newspaper like the *Amsterdam News* or the *Afro-American* appeared in the *New York Times*.[43] By the end of the Peekskill reports, the *New York Times* editors consistently portrayed Robeson as a maverick, someone on the fringe of the black community. No reader of the *New York Times* would know that many African Americans, even those strongly opposed to Robeson's views on the Soviet Union, believed that Robeson still represented the community in his outspoken criticism of segregation, and had concluded that racism accounted for many of the attacks on Robeson.

By 1950 the editors of the *New York Times* stopped using the prefix "Negro" to describe Robeson. During the Peekskill events he became "the baritone and Communist Singer," "the left-wing singer," the "pro–Communist singer," and, once, the "political storm center." Concert-goers became "left-wing followers of Paul Robeson." The *New York Times* so thoroughly recast Robeson as a left-wing figure that an article on September 9, 1950, could claim that, "Mr. Robeson echoed the Communist party belief that all the world's trouble could be settled in peace."

Silence, 1950–1958

With the June 18, 1950, editorial, the *New York Times* editors closed the book on Paul Robeson. Coverage shrank to a few articles a year, mostly brief reports, a few sentences in length, about legal appeals Robeson filed for return of his passport (revoked in 1950), or mention of awards he received from socialist countries.[44] There were no interviews and no editorials until his death in 1976. The *New York Times* covered Robeson's stormy appearance before HUAC in 1956 in a brief article that also discussed contempt citations for two other witnesses who refused to surrender passports to the committee.[45] In contrast, African-American papers were much more impressed with Robeson's combative statements before the committee. Robeson quoted, in his autobiography, positive coverage in the Baltimore *Afro-American*, the San Francisco *Sun-Reporter,* the *Charlottesville-Albemarle Tribune,* the *Pittsburgh Courier*, and the Oakland *California Voice.* The *Afro-American* said, "We agree with Mr. Robeson that its [HUAC's] members could more profitably spend their time ... bringing in for questioning such un–American elements as ... white supremacists."[46]

Though Robeson's career was seriously curtailed, he continued to sing and speak in African-American churches and union halls (no small accomplishment, since the church or union could endure intimidating queries by the Federal Bureau of Investigation or other forms of pressure).[47] These appearances were not covered by the white, mainstream press. Even larger events failed to pierce the shroud of silence. For example, the British National Paul Robeson Committee (including twenty-seven members of Parliament among its supporters) arranged for Robeson to give a "live" concert in London via trans–Atlantic hook-up in May 1957. Though representatives of all American newspapers with London offices were invited to witness this defiance of the travel ban placed on Robeson by the State Department, no American papers carried news of the concert.[48]

When Robeson's autobiography *Here I Stand* was published in 1958, it received no reviews in the white mainstream press, and was not even listed in the *New York Times* "Books Out Today" section. The silence was unique to the white American press. The book was enthusiastically reviewed by African-American newspapers and by the foreign press, including the *Times* of London.[49] However, in 1967 a biography by Edwin P. Hoyt which presented Robeson as a tragic figure, politically inexperienced, and duped by Communists, was reviewed twice in the *New York Times.*[50]

The Tragic Figure, 1958–1976

Hoyt's biography captured the view of Robeson that had gradually replaced the image of the "pro–Communist singer." Robeson was now seen as politically gullible, as a victim of his own misjudgment, as a talented but tragic figure. Robeson's supporters, as well, were viewed as naive or unaware of his politics. The shift began around 1958 when the State Department received renewed international pressure to restore Robeson's right to travel. Early in the year the silence still held as birthday greetings on the occasion of his sixtieth birthday poured in from around the world. All were ignored by the press except for a proclamation by Jawaharlal Nehru. In reporting on the proclamation and a planned celebratory program in New Delhi, the *New York Times* explained:

> The case of Mr. Robeson is used frequently ... by Indian Communists in efforts to sustain their allegations that the United States suppresses civil liberties and mistreats Negroes.... The planned celebrations ... have attracted some Indians who would be astonished at any idea that they were helping the Communists.[51]

By May 1958 a recital Robeson gave at Carnegie Hall (his first in New York in eleven years) received a favorable review confined to artistic matters. Later that year Robeson received a passport and left the United States for a long series of performances in Europe. When he returned to the United States in 1963, the term "self-imposed exile" was used routinely to describe his five years abroad, as though some hatred that he carried within himself had brought him to leave the United States. The reports did not mention that when he left, there were few places in the country where he could perform, or that the press had helped to create atmosphere which denied him a venue.

Three years before Robeson's death, on the occasion of his seventy-fifth birthday, friends and supporters staged a tribute at Carnegie Hall. Among the celebrants were Harry Belafonte, Roscoe Lee Brown, Ramsey Clark, Angela Davis, Ruby Dee, Dizzy Gillespie, Mayor Richard Hatcher, James Earl Jones, Zero Mostel, Odetta, and Pete Seeger. While the organizers of the tribute celebrated both Robeson's artistic career and his political activity, a review of the event quoted only two persons from the audience: a black professional who said that he was "not interested in politics" and a corporate lawyer who said he had only recently heard of Robeson. The review downplayed the political sympathies of the audience, which gave a standing ovation to Angela Davis, inexplicably reporting only "light applause" for her remarks.[52]

The *Amsterdam News* reported the tribute in more triumphant terms and reprinted the full text of Richard Hatcher's speech. Alongside the speech ran an editorial which asserted,

> To us the issue is not whether you agreed or disagreed, or now agree, or disagree, with the political views of Paul Robeson. The fundamental issue is whether or not the Black community will define its own heroes on its terms, or whether the white print and electronic media and our government will determine who is, and who is not, an "acceptable Black."[53]

When Robeson died in January 1976, the *New York Times* ran articles covering his wake and funeral, a lengthy obituary, and an editorial. In an echo of Peekskill, deadline reporting gave a fuller, more complex picture than the editorial. According to the reports, the wake attracted a steady stream of "mourners, mostly ordinary workers, retired and church-going, [who] ... praised the man who made them feel that there was no distance between them." The funeral was "attended by more than 5,000 people — most of whom were simply dressed and not well-known."[54] The editorial, on the other hand, referred again to Robeson's "self-imposed exile" and recapitulated old themes with the mellowed tone introduced in the last years of his life. Robeson, though gifted, was his own worst enemy.

> The tragedy of Paul Robeson, like that of Othello, was stark: virtue and misjudgment were sharply juxtaposed.... Ultimately he chose politics over art, and the world lost a source of inspiration.... For reasons of politics, his native country had abruptly and callously turned its back on him long ago.[55]

Though not necessarily acting with a conscious policy, the white mainstream press handled Robeson essentially as would the press in George Orwell's Oceania. After a period of silence, during which a troublesome figure is made invisible, the person is rehabilitated and a sanitized version of the career and its significance replaces the older one. Thomas J. Kelly, in a study of four Chicago downtown dailies from 1954 to 1968, discovered that such a pattern held for press coverage of other African-American figures. He concluded that when prominent African Americans directly challenged American racial conditions, "the papers denounced the dissent, not the racism."[56]

For example, Kelly found that the Chicago papers supported Martin Luther King, Jr.'s 1955–56 Montgomery bus boycott, but condemned him when he brought

Paul Robeson's final home. 4951 Walnut Street, Philadephia. Photograph taken and copyrighted (1998) by Martin Desht.

concept of Christian brother-hood."[57]

Kelly showed that the motives of other dissenting African Americans were similarly questioned,[58] while, at the same time, all of the dailies spotlighted success stories, suggesting that racial strife was all in the past. Discussing various awards, promotions, and government appointments, the papers used such telling phrases as, "a wonderful example of the American success story," "just one more example of how Negro citizens have raced upward in their progress toward equality with other Americans," and, "his life story should be known around the world as an example of the opportunities in today's America for its Negro citizens."[59]

We see in such reporting themes, which appeared in the first period of Robeson's career, the optimistic and superficial assumptions that the white press attached to the idea of the "New Negro," the notion that full racial equality had been nearly achieved, and that leaders who appeared friendly and reassuring to white Americans would be most effective in fulfilling the promise of America.

Though much had changed since the *New York Times* editorial of 1919, the press still preferred to write of African Americans who were "well-behaved" and to dwell on instances when "troubles between the two races were undreamed of." By the early 1970s the line had shifted, the nomenclature was revised, but the pattern remained the same.

his struggle to the North. In the 1960s the Chicago *Sun-Times* criticized King in every editorial discussing his northern open-housing demonstrations, asking, "Is his goal decent housing for Negroes or keeping himself and his movement in the headlines and on the TV screens?" The Chicago *Tribune* denounced the open-housing marches as a "deliberate campaign of sabotage."

King was accused by all four Chicago dailies of inciting violence and seeking the role of a martyr by generating hostility. After King's death silenced him, all of the papers agreed on a softer image: a "man of goodwill and great heart" who "sought to lead black and white Americans to a new

Notes

I would like to thank Lawrence Grisham and Sterling Stuckey for helpful comments on earlier drafts of this article.

1. Paul Robeson, *Here I Stand* (Boston: Beacon Press, 1971); Sterling Stuckey, *Slave Culture: Nationalist Theory and the Foundations of Black America* (New York: Oxford University Press, 1987); Martin Bauml Duberman, *Paul Robeson* (New York: Alfred A. Knopf, 1988).

2. Robeson, p. x.

3. *New York Times*, April 30, 1925.

4. *New York Times*, September 12, 1925. As late as February 17, 1930 (well after other newspapers had begun to capitalize "Negro"), the *New York Times* referred to Robeson as the "American negro tenor."

5. Paul Robeson clippings, Manuscript, Archives and Rare Book Division, Schomberg Center for Research in Black Culture, New York Public Library, *New York Daily News*, April 25, 1925. All citations for the 1920s and 1930s, except for the *New York Times*, are taken from the clipping file in the Schomberg collection. Five years after this phenomenally successful debut concert devoted exclusively to African American song, a *New York Times* reviewer in London was still not convinced. "Negro spirituals are, as a form of art, of so little value that it is hard to make them sustain an evening in the sophisticated circumstances of a theatre. They need a special emotional impetus, for they make little appeal to the mind, and emotion of the quality appropriate to them can scarcely be communicated by one singer and his accompanist to a skeptical audience," *New York Times*, September 14, 1930. A reviewer in 1925, however, said of the first series of Robeson's recitals of this type (in New York's Greenwich Village Theatre) that the performance was "a remarkable demonstration of dramatic power which the negro actor has brought to the singing both of the 'spirituals' and secular songs of his race," *New York Times*, May 4, 1925.

6. Unidentified newspaper, Schomberg collection clipping, dated May 21, 1930.

7. *New York World*, June 29, 1930.

8. *New Brunswick Sunday Times*, June 15, 1924.

9. *New York World*, May 22, 1930.

10. *New York World*, May 22, 1930. The *New York Times* did not comment on the Philadelphia incident but covered a similar incident later that year. When the New York Union League club borrowed the Salemme statue but then failed to display it as expected in a special show, the *New York Times* reported without comment, on November 18, 1930, the League's explanation that the statue was intended for another show in the vague future.

11. Review by George Britt, unidentified newspaper, July 1, 1930.

12. *New York Daily News*, April 25, 1925.

13. *New York Sun*, Dec. (n.d.) 1934.

14. *New York Times*, Oct. 24, 1943.

15. *New York World-Telegram*, Feb. 19, 1942.

16. *New York Times*, April 19, 1942.

17. *Boston PM* (Associated Press), May 11, 1947.

18. *New York Times*, April 12, 1944.

19. Baltimore *Afro-American*, Oct. 2, 1958.

20. The *New York Times* reported his comments as, "It is unthinkable ... [that American Negroes] would go to war on behalf of those who have oppressed us for generations ... [against a country] which in one generation has raised our people to the full dignity of mankind," April 21, 1949.

21. Robeson, pp. 41–42.

22. *New York Times*, April 25, 1949 ("The Case of Paul Robeson"), July 19, 1949 ("Dr. Bunche and Mr. Robeson"), July 20, 1949 ("Communist Shut-Out"). The third editorial did not mention Robeson by name, but commended Jackie Robinson's remarks before HUAC (featured in two lengthy articles the previous day) which denied Robeson could be a legitimate spokesperson for the African-American community.

23. The article, about 1,000 words, did quote Lester B. Granger, executive director of the National Urban League, as saying that, "Authentic Negro leadership in this country finds itself confronted by two enemies on opposite sides. One enemy is the Communist who seeks to destroy the democratic ideal and practice which constitute the Negro's sole hope of eventual victory in this fight for equal citizenship. The other enemy is that American racist who perverts and corrupts the democratic concept into a debased philosophy of life." The headline and the tone of this article, like other articles in the *New York Times* during this period, downplayed the careful distinction that many African Americans made between rejecting Robeson's political affiliation and supporting his criticism of racism.

24. *New York Times*, April 25, 1949.

25. *New York Times*, April 25, 1949.

26. *New York Times*, July 20, 1949.

27. *New York Times*, April 24, 1949.

28. *New York Times*, April 24, 1949.

29. *New York Times*, July 14, 1949.

30. *New York Times*, July 19, 1949.

31. Baltimore *Afro-American*, August 6, 1949.

32. *New York Times*, August 27, 1949. The *Times* also reported that the Civil Rights Congress was on Attorney General Tom Clark's list of subversive organizations.

33. *New York Times*, August 28, 1949. A book-length account published by the organization holding the concert agrees on these details: Howard Fast, *Peekskill, USA* (New York: Civil Rights Congress, 1951).

34. *New York Times*, Sept. 5, 1949.

35. Nine separate articles appeared on September 5 and 6, 1949. On September 8, 1949, a long article covered the Westchester County District Attorney's report to the governor and was accompanied by the 2500 word report reprinted in full.

36. New York City police halted buses driven by passengers at 218th and Broadway, refusing to allow drivers lacking chauffeur licenses to proceed further. One hundred passengers had to arrange private transportation from the police station to their homes. *New York Times*, Sept. 5, 1949.

37. Martin Duberman cites eye-witnesses who saw police participate in the attacks, clubbing and dragging concert-goers. Duberman, pp. 369, 695, note 17.

38. *New York Times*, editorial, June 18, 1950.

39. In addition to the report on August 28, 1949, burning crosses were mentioned in reports on August 29, 30, and 31.

40. A. Philip Randolph's letter appeared on October 9, 1949.

41. *New York Amsterdam News*, September 17, 1949. The *Amsterdam News* was one of the more conservative African-American newspapers, in that it gave extensive coverage to African Americans who criticized Robeson's comments at the Paris Peace Council, *New York Amsterdam News*, April 30, 1949. Yet, even though the editors objected to Robeson's political ties, they argued that many attacks on him, as well as the violence at Peekskill, were due to racism. And columnists were not as quick to criticize Robeson's political ties as the editors: On September 17, columnist Earl Brown argued that Robeson's insight into racism was "the reason he is ... doing the things he does."

42. *Amsterdam News*, September 10, 17, 1949.

43. *Amsterdam News* coverage of the Harlem rally preceding the September 4 Peekskill concert also differed substantially from *New York Times* coverage. The *Amsterdam News* stressed Robeson's proposed boycott of Peekskill merchants and his recommendation that African Americans in the South use boycotts to protest racist violence. The paper quoted one Harlem woman who remarked after a protest march that ended the rally, "See what he meant. If we were to spend our money like we march, we wouldn't be worrying about where we're going to find jobs." The *New York Times* did not mention the boycott issue.

44. From 1951 to 1958, on average, 8.7 articles a year mentioned Robeson, but most of these articles were only a few sentences on the mentioned topics. A brief upsurge in coverage with the reinstatement of Robeson's passport raised the number of articles in 1958 and 1959 (27 and 17 respectively). By the 1960s he was mentioned once or twice a year or not at all.

45. *New York Times*, June 13, 1956.

46. Robeson, pp. 42–44. In May 1956, just before Robeson's HUAC testimony, Langston Hughes in the *Chicago Defender* devoted a column to William Faulkner's statement regarding the integration of the University of Alabama: "If it came to fighting I'd fight for Mississippi against the United States even if it meant going out into the street and shooting Negroes." Hughes asked why this remark did not create the same furor as Robeson's statement to the Paris Peace Conference. Christopher C. DeSantis, ed., *Langston Hughes and the Chicago Defender* (Urbana: University of Illinois Press, 1995), pp. 91–2, 247, n7.

47. Marie Seton, *Paul Robeson* (London: Dennis Dobson, 1958), p. 231.

48. Duberman, pp. 449–450. In June 1952 Robeson sang to thousands in Washington Park on Chicago's southside without an echo in the New York press, something which would have been noticed a few years before, Seton, p. 234.

49. The lack of American reviews also meant that the book did not appear in *Book Review* by *Digest*. Duberman quotes from the Baltimore *Afro-American*, the *Chicago Crusader*,

and from an extended interview by Carl T. Rowan in *Ebony*: Duberman, pp. 459–460; other quotes from the foreign press and the African-American press appear in Lloyd L. Brown's introduction to *Here I Stand*, pp. xi–xvi. The book was initially published by a group of supporters, the Othello Associates. It was republished by Beacon Press in 1971. Two years later the *New York Times Book Review* printed an essay by Sterling Stuckey about Robeson that discussed *Here I Stand*, NYTBR, October 21, 1973, p. 40.

50. Edwin P. Hoyt, *Paul Robeson: American Othello* (World, 1967); *New York Times*, Nov. 12, 1967, December 21, 1967.

51. *New York Times*, March 22, 1958. On other congratulatory programs and messages see Duberman, pp. 460–62.

52. *New York Times*, April 16, 1973. The author was present at the event.

53. *Amsterdam News*, April 21, 1973.

54. *New York Times*, January 27, 28, 1976.

55. *New York Times*, January 24, 1976.

56. Thomas J. Kelly, "Editorials on Race," *The Chicago Journalism Review*, vol. 5, no. 8 (August 1972).

57. Kelly, p. 22.

58. For example, when Dick Gregory became active in the civil rights movement, the Chicago *Daily News* labeled his activities "plain press-agentry with no visible benefit to anyone except for the headlines it grabbed for Gregory." Kelly, p. 4.

59. Kelly, p. 4.

Out of the Shadows:
The Political Writings
of Eslanda Goode Robeson

ROBERT SHAFFER
Shippensburg University

Generally overshadowed by the celebrity and controversy of her more famous husband, Eslanda Goode Robeson nevertheless made significant contributions of her own to the field of Americans' understanding of Africa and to race relations in general. A consideration of Eslanda's three books (one of which was co-authored with Pearl S. Buck, the Nobel Prize–winning novelist), and a look especially at the reception of these books by reviewers at the time, provides an opportunity to survey these contributions.

Eslanda's impact as an author, of course, was inseparable from her status as the wife of the well-known singer, actor, and political activist. Indeed, all of her books included discussion of her husband. But Eslanda—called Essie by her friends, and often by the press as well — used these writings to go beyond simply providing readers a vicarious proximity to celebrity, as she probed the intersections between race, class, and gender in the United States, Europe, Africa, and elsewhere.

In the larger scheme of African-American history, looking at Eslanda Robeson's role gives greater depth to recent studies by such scholars as Brenda Gayle Plummer and Penn Von Eschen on the internationalist activities of African Americans. In particular, Eslanda's work illuminates what Von Eschen has called "the politics of the African diaspora," the mutual encouragement of freedom struggles in the United States, Africa, and the Caribbean generated by interconnections between black activists from these varied societies.[1] On a more personal level, this attention to Eslanda's writings and activities corrects the tendency in Martin Duberman's enormously influential biography of Paul Robeson to be overly critical of Eslanda's writings and politics, especially in the period before 1950. Taking Eslanda's writings and activism seriously also emphasizes the collaboration more than the friction between Eslanda and Paul — although it must be noted that Eslanda herself did not ignore the friction, even in her published writings.[2]

Eslanda was born in Washington, D.C., in 1896, her father a clerk in the War Department. Her mother was from the light-skinned Negro elite, whose own father, Francis Lewis Cardozo, had been a prominent South Carolina elected official during Reconstruction.[3] Eslanda attended the University of Illinois, but graduated from Columbia University in New York City with a degree in chemistry. She became the first African American to work at New York City's Presbyterian Hospital. She married Paul in 1921.

Eslanda's first book was a biography of her husband, published in 1930 and written while the couple and their son "Pauli" lived in England.[4] Duberman emphasizes weaknesses in the book, highlighting a handful of negative reviews.[5] In fact, it received quite positive reviews overall, and was received as more than simply an adoring portrait by a wife. Beginning with the title of the book, *Paul Robeson, Negro*, Eslanda clearly intended it as an affirmation of pride for African Americans in the success of one of their number, and an illustration for whites of the capabilities of the "Negro" people. Paul was only 32 at the time, and while several reviews noted the incongruity of a biography of such a young man, most agreed that he merited the attention, having already gained international acclaim as a singer and actor.

Indeed, reviewers picked up on Eslanda's political goal of profiling this example of African-American success. The *Times Literary Supplement* of London, which said the book "leaves a very pleasant impression of both the subject and the writer of the book," noted that Paul's accomplishments demonstrated what many more Negroes could do were it not for the "restrictions and handicaps" they faced due to race.[6] Harry Hansen, the prominent New York book critic, called the book "inspiring," and believed that Eslanda's depiction not only of her husband but of "Negro family life, of Negro traditions and accomplishments," all written with "rich understanding" and "deep pride," was of great importance for white Americans to read.[7]

African-American reviewers as well made clear that profiling Paul's success would, indeed, make Blacks proud, and that they would want to read about it as much as whites. Langston Hughes, whose review was featured on page one of the *New York Herald-Tribune* book section, said that ordinary workers and servants in the black community considered Paul to be "their ambassador to the world," and that with his success, "his old friends who still walk humble are mighty glad."[8] W.E.B. Du Bois, writing in *The Crisis*, the NAACP magazine, placed the biography in the "must read" category, and commented, significantly:

> The hero is made a little too perfect, but with all that, the evident triumph of a fine black man makes fascinating reading and something unusual in these days when everything black in literature has to come from the slums, wallow in Harlem, and go to Hell.[9]

Eslanda supplemented her account of her husband's life with an almost sociological description of the importance of the church in African-American life, and a chapter on the development and significance of Harlem to African Americans. Eslanda considered Harlem a place blacks "can call home; it is a place where they belong," a place where, being in the majority, they no longer have to be on their guard as representing their race to others.[10] She discussed the long history of interracial

Eslanda Robeson took this photograph in 1937 of her husband with members of the International Brigade that fought Franco's fascist regime in Spain. Courtesy of Paul Robeson, Jr.

sexual relations in the U.S. which resulted in distinctions based on color among "Negroes," and the phenomenon of "passing." "Passing" was very relevant to Eslanda's own life with her mixed ancestry and her ability at times to "pass" for white.[11] Eslanda contrasted the racial discrimination even in Northern hotels, restaurants, and housing with the lack of such discrimination in England: "So here in England, where everyone was kind and cordial and reasonable, Paul was happy."[12]

Several reviewers, including Langston Hughes, pointed to these sections on the black community and on race relations as especially noteworthy. Rose Feld in the *New York Times* called the chapter on Harlem "penetrating and thought-provoking," and said Eslanda presented "frankly and interestingly the psychology of the Negro in his relationship to white people and the expressions of escape which his race consciousness gives him." Feld and Harry

Hansen both viewed with alarm the black preference for life in Europe over life in America. Hansen observed with great prescience that "Expatriation is merely an evasion," and that all the Robesons—Paul, Pauli, and Eslanda—"will be in a position to help tremendously the cause of their people in the United States."[13]

There were some negative reviews, mostly charging, with much justice, that Eslanda portrayed Paul as a paragon of "Sunday-school piety." William Soskin in the *New York Evening Post* rightly criticized the book for downplaying any sense of Paul's bitterness at personal encounters with racism. But his review, anti-racist in intent, had more than a trace of the desire for the exotic, and even the voyeuristic, as Soskin wanted to know how Paul felt being surrounded by admiring white women after a successful concert.[14] Most critical was Stark Young, in *The New Republic*, who called the book the "worst type of biographical rubbish," and who objected that the book was framed around Paul as a "Negro" rather than simply as a "remarkable man." One may simply note without comment that Young, in establishing his "credentials" for criticizing Eslanda's portrayal of the black church and life, mentioned that his father owned 350 slaves.[15] Among the few criticisms of Paul that Eslanda raised in the book, which several reviews noted, was what she called his "Laziness, with a capital L." But none of the commentators took Eslanda to task for referring to this laziness as one of Paul's "typically Negro qualities," a stereotype which would unleash a firestorm of criticism today.[16]

Eslanda's next book would not appear for another fifteen years, in 1945, but it would be very influential.[17] Based on her diary of her 1936 trip through southern, central, and eastern Africa with eight-year-old Pauli, the book reflected both the training towards a Ph.D. in anthropology that Eslanda had begun in London and completed at the Hartford Seminary, and her growing concern with the political aspects of colonialism. Describing her encounters with everyone from black South African miners to sympathetic and unsympathetic white colonial officials, and from herdswomen in Uganda and pygmies in the Congo to Edinburgh-trained African doctors, Eslanda focused on the varied people of Africa and the experience of traveling through Africa. She took particular care to detail women's roles and gender relations in the various African cultures she described, according respect for women's labor and knowledge, but noting as well the exclusion of women from certain activities.[18] Her strong and convincing critique of colonialism and racism emerged from her vignettes rather than overpowering them.

Part of the book's appeal, too, consisted of young Paul's "mature observations and reactions," as the *Literary Guild Review* put it, to immersion in very different cultures and to issues of racial discrimination. (For example, about South Africa's Orange Free State, Pauli asked, "What's free about it?")[19] Although "Big Paul" did not accompany Eslanda on the trip, he, too, was a constant presence in the book. After all, the white press in South Africa and colonial officials in East Africa regarded her nervously because she was "Mrs. Paul Robeson." Meanwhile, African — and some European — fans, from the Cape Colony to Egypt, gave her special treatment for precisely the same reason.[20] And with Paul at "the apex of fame" in 1945, to use Duberman's phrase,[21] a book in which he is just off-stage, as it were, but nonetheless central to the plot, would certainly be noticed by the American press and the reading public.

Duberman rightly but briefly notes the favorable reviews that *African Journey* received upon publication, and the personal lift that it gave Eslanda during another strained period in her relationship with Paul.[22] But the book's political significance, too, was enormous, as one of the first published portraits of Africa for an American audience by an African American who had traveled in Africa, combining a first-hand critique of European colonialism and racism with a human portrait of the African people and an appreciation of the cultural achievements of African peoples. To appreciate the importance of such a work, one might note that the fairly thorough *Book Review Digest* listed only five books on Africa published in the U.S. in 1945, and only 30 in the period from 1942 to 1946, with most of those being geared mainly to scholars or foreign policy experts, and several sponsored by European colonial powers. By contrast, there were well over 100 books on China, and over 75 on India, published in this five-year period in the U.S.[23]

African Journey was published by the John Day Company, headed by Richard Walsh but with great input by his wife, Pearl Buck. Buck was among the most prominent Americans who believed that World War II needed to be transformed into an anti-racist and anti-imperialist war—W.E.B. Du Bois wrote that among whites Buck represented "the strongest and clearest elucidation of this point of view."[24] She began corresponding with Paul Robeson after they shared the platform at an April 1942 rally on behalf of allowing black Americans and black Africans to participate in the war without racist restrictions in the army or any other area.[25] This association undoubtedly led to Buck's association with Eslanda as well, and in the fall of 1943 Buck provided a detailed but favorable critique of Eslanda's manuscript, which led to its acceptance at the John Day Company.[26] A lengthy revision process ensued, which nevertheless had the salutary effect of allowing Richard Walsh to publish, in the highly-regarded magazine that he also edited, *Asia and the Americas,* two articles by Eslanda, one which he adapted from a speech she had given, and one excerpted almost directly from the book. Both of these articles, in turn, were reprinted in at least one black periodical, and one of them appeared as well in expanded form as a pamphlet published by the Council on African Affairs.[27] Meanwhile, Eslanda spoke about African views of the new United Nations at the plenary session of a conference sponsored by Buck's East and West Association, which over 600 librarians attended.[28]

In "A Negro Looks at Africa," one of the articles published in *Asia and the Americas,* Eslanda previewed some of the main themes of her book, especially the pride that black Americans could and should take in the achievements of Africans—just as other Americans took pride in the culture and accomplishments of their respective "old countries." Drawing on the work of anti-racist anthropologists such as Franz Boas, she described early African smelting of iron, the long-established systems of law among the Ashanti and the Hausa, and the domestication of cattle. She noted the inspiration of African art for modern art, and she suggested that the traditional communal ownership of land in Africa could likewise be an inspiration for contemporary society. Indeed, her essay prefigured in some ways the current "multicultural education movement."[29]

In "Proud to Be a Negro," Eslanda recounted a conversation on the plane leaving Africa with an arrogant European colonialist who pitied her son Pauli for being black. Eslanda declared firmly that "[Pauli's] color, his background, his rich history are part of his wealth. We consider it an asset, not a handicap." In addition to this assertion of black pride, she argued that racist attitudes had isolated European colonialists—and like-minded Americans—from the world of tomorrow, and that such attitudes would make their lives difficult. Africans and African Americans, meanwhile, in their long experience of fighting oppression, "have survived and grown strong." This strength was only increased in the ideological and strategic conflicts of World War II, Eslanda added, as Africans felt that the "Four Freedoms" and the promises for self-government of the Atlantic Charter should apply to them, and where an African governor of a French colony, Felix Eboué, took his stand with the Free French. One might note, however, that Eslanda, like the Council on African Affairs as a whole, expressed an unfounded optimism about French promises to restructure their empire in Africa to include more self-government.[30]

While Eslanda was buoyed by letters she received in response to her articles in *Asia,*[31] the response to the publication of *African Journey* itself was overwhelming:

The first printing was sold out on the day of publication, and it resulted in much greater demand for her services as a lecturer.[32] The African-American press was most enthusiastic. Ben Burns in the *Chicago Defender* called *African Journey* "perhaps the first really popular book ever written on the African Negro. It will make [American] Negroes hold their heads and shoulders high, proud to be Negro and African."[33] Prince A. A. Nwafor Orizu, a Nigerian living in the U.S., and a regular columnist on Africa for the *Pittsburgh Courier*, agreed that "the Negro in America must take pride in his African origin as a beginning of self-confidence which is the starting point of outward freedom." He wrote, with the kind of hyperbole that one would think only book publishers and ad-writers could make up, that Eslanda's book "opens a new page in the history of the black man in America," potentially as important as Marcus Garvey's movement for pan–African pride after World War I. Another columnist in the *Courier* also whole-heartedly endorsed the book, and described Eslanda's role on behalf of the Council on African Affairs and the decolonization movement at the founding conference of the United Nations in San Francisco in April 1945.[34] Constance Curtis in the *Amsterdam News* detailed Eslanda's dismaying descriptions of conditions of blacks in South Africa, but noted as well that the book brings the important "discovery" that Africans were "deeply interested in the colored peoples outside of their land," a point that Eslanda had discussed at length. Curtis added that Eslanda's view of Africa as an African American would be particularly interesting for her black readers: "It is good to see Africa through such eyes because it ceases to be the land of the big game hunter and the Pukka Sahib and becomes a land in which people live who are like many all of us know."[35]

White reviewers gave *African Journey* coverage that was just as prominent and just as favorable; both the *New York Times* and the *New York Herald-Tribune* reviewed it in their weekday and Sunday book columns. Ernestine Evans called *African Journey* "an excellent tourist book as well as a treatise on the color line," and a "starting point of real study" on Africa. She duly noted the political significance of Eslanda's discussion of the difficulty she encountered in obtaining visas, as "people who are counting grievances are not allowed to go where they please." Eslanda, like the other thirteen million African Americans, was beginning to count herself as one with the "ten million West Indians of color, the one hundred and fifty million blacks of Africa, and tentatively all the peoples of Asia," in the realignment of the world's peoples that would take shape in the post-war world.[36] While noting the poverty and discrimination Eslanda described, Evans, too, understood the importance of her descriptions of African achievements. She cited a few, such as temperature control mechanisms in traditional African housing, that the U.S. might learn from — "Federal Housing, please note," Evans wrote. Evans, writing in the *Herald-Tribune*, provided perhaps the most detailed and incisive review, but it was representative of the response. Helen Cain highlighted Eslanda's warning that "those who make the peace must not overlook a seething, brooding Africa." Francis Hackett noted with respect, albeit with regret, Eslanda's turn to the Soviet Union as a model for development of non-industrialized societies and for the creation of a non-racist modern society. Stuart Cloete, a liberal white South African — who said that to him "a zebra is a white beast with a black stripe; to Eslanda Robeson it is a black beast with a white stripe" — welcomed Eslanda's frankly "biased" approach in favor of black Africans, which might "make the white South

African wonder," as no other book has done, "what those whom he calls his servants think of him."[37]

Several reviewers contrasted *African Journey* favorably with John LaTouche's *Congo*, which appeared at the same time. LaTouche's book was based on a trip paid for by the Belgian government, and gave a favorable view of Belgian colonialism. Ironically, LaTouche was the author of the song *Ballad for Americans*, which Paul had helped make famous, and LaTouche himself reviewed Eslanda's book favorably.[38]

Eslanda went on staff with the Council for African Affairs in September 1945, a month after *African Journey* came out, and she participated in its work at the U.N. on behalf of decolonization over the next few years.[39] She was also active, along with Paul, in Henry Wallace's presidential campaign in 1948, and she became a leader of the Progressive Party in Connecticut and a candidate for Connecticut Secretary of State in 1948 and for Congress in 1952.[40]

But she also kept up her association with Pearl Buck, and the two women met regularly to prepare *American Argument*, which appeared in January 1949. This so-called "talk book," presented as an edited conversation with Buck's commentary, was part of a series that Buck published in which she presented critical views that she thought Americans needed to hear — Buck had earlier published her interviews with a Chinese agrarian reformer, a Russian woman who had grown up on a collective farm, and a German socialist and anti–Nazi refugee.[41]

American Argument was a wide-ranging dialogue covering Eslanda's background and the views of the two women on American society, Russia, race relations, gender relations and women's role, education and child-rearing, and many other issues. As Eslanda had done for the African people in *African Journey*, Buck kept the focus on Eslanda as a total person rather than just her "political" ideas as such. Indeed, some of the more interesting sections included Eslanda's discussion of her personal encounters with color prejudice by the light-skinned elite in the African-American community, and her observations on the different attitude toward the "finality" of marriage of Paul and herself, which only partly veiled their marital tensions.[42]

As many reviewers noted, the two women, Eslanda and Buck, agreed more than they disagreed, both excoriating American Cold War policies toward the Soviet Union, attacking U.S. militarism, denouncing the failure of the U.S. to work for decolonization, and bemoaning American women's preoccupation with families and housework rather than public affairs. Where the two disagreed was on tactics for change, with Eslanda defending Soviet policies, and even proposing that "liquidation" — yes, she used that term associated with the Stalinist regime — of the enemies of civil rights in the U.S. would be appropriate.[43] Buck, who portrayed herself as an "individualist," demurred from such measures, but nevertheless defended Eslanda from accusations of disloyalty, and agreed that the American ideology of individual rights had facilitated the denial of the collective rights of large numbers of Americans. While Buck made clear her own opposition to Communism, and tried to forestall criticism by declaring that she knew that Eslanda was no Communist,[44] the very fact that she brought out this book with Eslanda, just when attacks on Eslanda's and Paul's "loyalty" were about to reach their height, demonstrated her own rejection of Cold War ideology, and provided an important platform for Eslanda's ideas. Indeed, Buck structured the book to present a critique of American society from the perspective of an educated, professional, activist African-American woman, in order to puncture the complacency of white Americans who considered their society to be a democracy of all of its citizens.

Considering the political climate — U.S.-Soviet tensions were very high as the Berlin blockade and airlift were underway; the NAACP had recently fired Du Bois; Max Yergan, the former director of the Council on African Affairs accused Paul of leading a "Communist faction" of the group; and the heavily red-baited Wallace campaign had received very few votes— the critics' reaction to *American Argument* was quite positive.[45] There were, to be sure, a few wild denunciations. The ultra-reactionary *Plain Talk* called it an "anti–American interview" and accused both Buck and Eslanda of disloyalty to American principles, while the *Washington Star* implied that Buck had fallen for Eslanda's Soviet propaganda.[46]

But favorable reviews far outweighed such criticisms. The *Boston Herald* told readers that Eslanda's critique of the U.S. was worth considering, especially regarding the treatment of blacks, while the *San Francisco Chronicle* emphasized Eslanda's view that with more democracy at home the U.S. could become a force for progress in the world. The *St. Louis Post-Dispatch* pointed to the importance of both women's critique of the growing cult of domesticity in the U.S.[47] Mary Ross in the *New York Herald-Tribune* described the book as "serious but never pompous or preachy, that it cannot help but be stimulating to others who love America but are also troubled by certain qualities of our national life." Ross, like some other reviewers, made it clear that both authors love this country, and that they have unusual vantage points on this country, as both insiders and outsiders, Buck having grown up in China, and Eslanda having lived abroad for twelve years and looking at the U.S. as both an anthropologist and as one with dark skin.

The *New York Times* challenged Eslanda's views on the Soviet Union but declared the need to hear her viewpoint, while the *Saturday Review of Literature* urgently recommended the book to "the isn't-it-grand-to-be-an-American school."[48] Mary Margaret McBride, host of a popular radio show on which Buck often appeared as a guest, balked at inviting Buck and Eslanda to appear together because of the "Communist angle," but eventually relented.[49]

The African-American press also recommended the book to readers. The *Pittsburgh Courier* called it "must" reading, "a provocative but friendly argument, and one worthy of the serious reflections of all Americans— especially American women." The *Amsterdam News* said that both the political discussion and the human portraits of the authors revealed in the book were noteworthy. The *Chicago Defender* was less enthusiastic, but still respectful, calling Eslanda "a vigorous and interesting conversationalist."[50]

Despite the publicity and the reviews, however, the book did not sell well, as Buck later apologized to Eslanda.[51] But the publication and reviews of the book demonstrate the dialogue that Eslanda had with the mainstream of the literary community as late as 1949, as well as Buck's continuing dialogue with the left. That this association with Buck was helpful to Eslanda is made clear by the fact that Eslanda's lecture agency, in soliciting bookings in the 1950s, quoted extensively from Buck's effusive description of Eslanda in *American Argument*, as follows:

> [Eslanda] sees in herself every Negro in the United States, every poor white in a poll-tax Southern state, every black man, woman, and child in Africa, every untouchable in India, every colonial in Indonesia and Indochina, every woman anywhere who longs for equality.[52]

The two women continued to exchange friendly letters about politics and family for several more years. Buck congratulated Eslanda when she lashed out at the hate-mongers who tried to interfere with Pauli's marriage to a white woman, and commiserated with her when Eslanda was called before Joe McCarthy's Senate committee. In one particularly ironic twist, one of the times that McCarthyism hit Buck personally was when an invitation was rescinded under pressure from the House Un-American Activities Committee to speak at an all-black Washington, D.C., high school. The school was none other than Francis Cardozo High School, named after Eslanda's illustrious grandfather.[53]

Eslanda's experience at the United Nations in the 1940s led to a long stint during the 1950s as the UN correspondent for *New World Review*, a pro–Soviet magazine linked with the National Council for American-Soviet Friendship, an organization with which Eslanda, and Paul, were also associated.[54] On the whole, Eslanda did not defend Stalinism in these articles, although she certainly did not criticize it. Eslanda's writings plugged decolonization, opposition to the Cold War, the admission of the People's Republic of China to the UN, and the rise of the neutralist bloc as symbolized by the Afro-Asian conference in Bandung, Indonesia, in 1955, all of which coincided with Soviet policy but which a wider range of progressives could also support.[55] After a brief period in 1950 when she attacked the Nehru government in India for its persecution of the left, she soon became a particular booster of Nehru's independent foreign policy and of his UN representative, Krishna Menon, whom she had known in London.[56] Among Eslanda's most noteworthy articles were those in which she highlighted particular women leaders abroad and at the UN, carrying on the work of the small but energetic progressive women's networks in the years that some historians have called the "doldrums" of the women's movement.[57]

Paul and Eslanda Robeson (far right) relax with Soviet Premier Nikita Khrushchev (second left) near Yalta, 1958. Courtesy of Paul Robeson, Jr.

Even during the most difficult times in the U.S., with the weakness of the progressive movements in general in the 1950s and the attacks on the Robesons personally, Eslanda maintained a sense of optimism from her UN post, as she saw, slowly but perceptibly, the increased influence of Asians and Africans in world politics.[58] While these articles contained important analyses of this changing world scene as crystallized at the UN, they were not widely circulated and did not reach as many people as any of her three books had done.

Paul and Eslanda Robeson, 1965. Courtesy of Paul Robeson, Jr.

But Eslanda Goode Robeson did make her mark as a political writer and speaker, with a reputation tied to her husband's but a voice all her own. She made this mark in her analysis of Harlem and the black community in *Paul Robeson, Negro*; of African culture, European colonialism, and nationalist resistance in *African Journey*; and of the American and world scenes in *American Argument*; as well as in her active work for decolonization in the Council on African Affairs and in her journalistic endeavors towards the same end in *New World Review* and other publications.

Historian Arthur Schlesinger, Jr., in his polemic against multiculturalism, has claimed that current efforts to establish an identification of African Americans with Africa are artificial, that they do not flow from the logic of African-American history.[59] Eslanda Goode Robeson — light-skinned, middle-class, cosmopolitan — might be among the African Americans most likely to corroborate Schlesinger's thesis. But Eslanda, in fact, developed a strong cultural and political identification with Africa and Africans, even as she asserted her rights as an African American, and this identification made sense to important sectors of the black community at the time. This identification developed in the anti-colonial and anti-imperialist movement that gained momentum from the mid–1930s on, but was disrupted in the black community by the Cold War and McCarthyism.[60] The experience of Eslanda Goode Robeson, thus, shows both the shallowness of Schlesinger's critique and the importance of focusing renewed attention on the ways that African Americans in the mid–20th century interpreted their domestic experiences in a global, and especially an African and anti-colonial, context.

Notes

Note: For the sake of brevity, Eslanda Goode Robeson will be referred to in these notes as "EGR," while Paul Robeson will be referred to as "PR."

"Robeson Papers–Howard" refers to the Robeson Family Papers at the Moorland-Spingarn Archives, Howard University.

"Robeson Papers–Schomburg" refers to the Paul Robeson Papers in the Schomburg Collection, N.Y. Public Library.

"EGR Vertical File" refers to the Vertical File on EGR, microfilm 004:342 in the Schomburg Collection, N.Y. Public Library.

"Brown Papers" refers to the Lawrence Brown Papers in the Schomburg Collection, N.Y. Public Library.

"John Day Papers" refers to the John Day Co. Papers, Firestone Library, Princeton University.

1. Brenda Gayle Plummer, *Rising Wind: Black Americans and U.S. Foreign Affairs, 1935–1960* (Chapel Hill: University of North Carolina Press, 1996); Penny Von Eschen, *Race Against Empire: Black Americans and Anticolonialism, 1937–1957* (Ithaca: Cornell University Press, 1997), 4 and passim.

2. Martin Duberman, *Paul Robeson: A Biography* (N.Y.: Alfred A. Knopf, 1989). For a hagiographic portrait of EGR which ignores the marital conflict altogether, see Barbara Ransby, "Eslanda Goode Robeson, Pan-Africanist," *Sage: A Scholarly Journal on Black Women*, 3 (Fall 1986), 22–26.

3. For discussion of Cardozo's role in South Carolina politics, see Eric Foner, *Reconstruction: America's Unfinished Revolution, 1863–1877* (N.Y.: Harper & Row, 1988), 27, 102, 327 and passim; Joel Williamson, *After Slavery: The Negro in South Carolina During Reconstruction, 1861–1877* (Chapel Hill: University of North Carolina Press, 1965), 356–91 passim; and W.E.B. Du Bois, *Black Reconstruction in America, 1860–1880* (N.Y.: Antheneum, 1972 [1935]), 392, 395, 397–98, and passim.

4. EGR, *Paul Robeson, Negro* (N.Y.: Harper & Brothers, 1930).

5. Duberman, *Paul Robeson,* 1939–40, 613.

6. "A Negro Artist," *Times Literary Supplement* (22 May 1930), 432.

7. Harry Hansen, "The First Reader," *N.Y. World* (25 June 1930), 11.

8. Langston Hughes, "Ambassador to the World," *N.Y. Herald-Tribune Books* (29 June 1930), 1–2.

9. W.E.B. Du Bois, "The Brewing Reader," *The Crisis,* 37 (Sept. 1930), 313.

10. EGR, *Paul Robeson, Negro,* chapters 1 and 4, quotations here at 44, 46–47.

11. On EGR's mixed background, and the minor scandal which her light-skinned mother

caused by marrying "a dark man," see Duberman, *Paul Robeson,* 35–36. For an example of EGR "passing" for white, see EGR, *Paul Robeson, Negro,* 110–11.

12. EGR, *Paul Robeson, Negro,* 110–11.

13. Rose Feld, "Paul Robeson Viewed by His Wife," *N.Y. Times Book Review* (13 July 1930), 5; Hansen, "The First Reader." My evaluation of the reviews by Feld and Langston Hughes differ from Duberman's: cf. Duberman, *Paul Robeson,* 613.

14. William Soskin, "Books on Our Table," *N.Y. Evening Post* (25 June 1930), 9.

15. Stark Young, "Paul Robeson, Negro," *New Republic,* 63 (6 Aug. 1930), 345–46.

16. EGR, *Paul Robeson, Negro,* 154–55, 170–71. That EGR in these years was not free from elitist attitudes toward other blacks may be seen in correspondence with Paul's pianist, Lawrence Brown, in which she referred casually to the "niggers" in the telegraph office who might be reading her messages; see EGR to Lawrence Brown, 7 Mar. [1932?], Brown Papers, microfilm reel 1.

17. EGR, *African Journey* (N.Y.: John Day Co., 1945).

18. For discussions of gender relations and women's roles, see, e.g., EGR, *African Journey,* 41–42 (on a black South African nurse), 45–46 (on an African wedding), 91–93 (on the separation of men and women socially in Uganda), 104 (on women's role in traditional medicine), 108–09 (on the Ugandan herdswomen).

19. *Literacy Guild Review — Wings* (Aug. 1945), as quoted in EGR in Lawrence Brown, 15 July 1945, Brown Papers, microfilm reel 3. See also Richard J. Walsh (the book's publisher) to EGR, 28 April 1944, EGR correspondence, Robeson Papers–Howard. For the quoted passage of Pauli's, see EGR, *African Journey,* 51.

20. See EGR, *African Journey,* 32–33, 34, 82, 128, 149.

21. Duberman, *Paul Robeson,* 292.

22. *Ibid.*

23. *Book Review Digest, 1946 (with cumulative index 1942–46)* (N.Y.: H. W. Wilson Co., 1947), 927 (for entries on Africa), 1269 (South Africa), 999–1000 (China), 1134–35 (India). I include books on South Africa with the Africa total, but have excluded those focused solely on North Africa.

24. W.E.B. Du Bois, "The War for Race Equality," *Phylon,* 3 quarter (1942), 321. See

also Pearl S. Buck, *American Unity and Asia* (N.Y.: John Day Co., 1942), and Buck, *What America Means to Me* (N.Y.: John Day Co., 1943), and Peter Conn, *Pearl S. Buck: A Cultural Biography* (N.Y.: Cambridge University Press, 1996), chap. 7.

25. For brief reports on this rally of 8 April 1942, sponsored by the Council on African Affairs (which Eslanda and Paul had helped form), see "Pearl Buck Urges Mobilization of Negro and Colonial Peoples," *Opportunity* (April 1942), 119, and *In Fact* (20 April 1942), 3. For efforts by Paul to get Buck involved in the support movement for the imprisoned Puerto Rican nationalist leader Pedro Albizu Campos, see Buck to PR, 3 Aug. 1942, and PR to Buck, 28 Aug. 1942, in PR correspondence, Robeson Papers–Howard.

26. Buck to EGR, 12 Oct. 1943, and Walsh to EGR, 19 Nov. 1943 and 28 Apr. 1944, and EGR to Walsh, 7 May 1944, all in EGR correspondence, Robeson Papers–Howard. For discussion of a campaign EGR wanted to initiate outlawing segregation, see Buck to EGR, 10 June 1944, EGR correspondence, Robeson Papers–Howard, and see also Mary Braggiotti, "Tourist in Africa" (a profile of EGR), *Negro Digest*, 3 (Oct. 1945), 43–44. That EGR had originally intended to complete this book much sooner, and that she expected that her first publisher would print it, is clear from an article about the trip based on a letter from EGR to Harper & Brothers: Carolyn Marx, "Book Marks: Essie Robeson Writes from Africa," *N.Y. World-Telegram* (11 Sept. 1936), 31.

27. EGR, "A Negro Look at Africa," *Asia and the Americas*, 44 (Nov. 1944), 501–03; EGR, "Proud to Be a Negro," *Asia and the Americas*, 45 (Feb. 1945), 108. On Walsh editing the first article based on EGR speeches, see Walsh to EGR, 12 June 1944 and 17 July 1944, EGR correspondence, Robeson Papers–Howard. "Proud to Be a Negro," though not identified as such, was an advance publication of pages 150–52 of *African Journey*. For re-publication, see *Negro Digest*, 3 (Jan. 1945), 3–6, and *Negro Digest*, 3 (April 1945), 43–44 (under the heading "Is Black a Handicap?"), and see EGR, *What Do the People of Africa Want?* (N.Y.: Council on African Affairs/African Pamphlet Series, May 1945). Much of this material was reprinted much later as "Is African Civilization Backward?" *Freedom*, 3 (June 1953) 2.

It is possible that part of the delay in publication of *African Journey* was due to wartime paper restrictions that publishers faced; see Walsh to EGR, 28 Apr. 1944, EGR correspondence, Robeson Papers–Howard.

28. *People Through Books*, 1 (May 1945), 15, and 1 (June 1945), 6.

29. EGR, "A Negro Looks at Africa," and EGR, "Proud to Be a Negro." For other examples of the popularization of and controversy around Boas's anti-racist work, and for this early development of multicultural education during World War II, see Ruth Benedict and Gene Weltfish, *Races of Mankind* (N.Y.: Public Affairs Committee, 1943, 1946), and Robert Shaffer, "Multicultural Education in New York City During World War II," *New York History*, 77 (July 1996), 301–32.

30. For another contemporary treatment of the significance of Eboué's role, see Walter White, *A Rising Wind* (Garden City, N.Y.: Doubleday, Doran, 1945). On the overly generous evaluation of the Free French program for Africa, see EGR, *What Do the People of Africa Want?*, 21–22, and cf., in the magazine of the Council on African Affairs, "French Plan New Role for Africa in Tomorrow's World," *New Africa*, 3 (Feb. 1944), 1–2, and "Editorial," *New Africa*, 3 (Mar. 1944), 3.

31. See Walsh to EGR, 2 April 1945, responding to a letter from EGR not in the files, EGR correspondence, Robeson Papers–Howard.

32. EGR to Brown, 15 Aug. 1945, Lawrence Brown papers. For one lecture series announced at this time, see "Mrs. Franklin Roosevelt and Mrs. Paul Robeson to Serve as Lecturers for New Community School," *N.Y. Age* (11 Aug. 1945), 5. For a brief reference to EGR's speech about Africa to her sorority's national convention in Dec. 1945, see EGR to "Sorors in Delta Sigma Theta," 4 Aug. 1949, Robeson Papers–Schomburg (microfilm reel 1, frames 469–75).

33. Ben Burns, "Off the Book Shelf," *Chicago Defender* (25 Aug. 1945), 13.

34. Prince A. A. Nwafor Orizu, "Africa Speaks: Mrs. Robeson's Book Is a Challenge to the Negro in America," *Pittsburgh Courier* (25 Aug. 1945), 6; P. L. Prattis, "The Horizon: Mrs. Robeson Finds Herself Very Much at Home When She Visits 'Her People,'" *Pittsburgh Courier* (15 Sept. 1945), 7.

35. Constance Curtis, "About Books," *N.Y. Amsterdam News* (25 Aug. 1945), 13-A. See

also the earlier review of Eslanda's CAA pamphlet, in Curtis, "About Books," *N.Y. Amsterdam News* (14 July 1945), 13-A. Excerpts from the book were also featured under the heading "An American Negro Views Her 'Old Country,'" in the *Negro Digest*, 3 (Oct. 1945), 85–93, along with the reprint, on pages 43–44, of a feature article from the *N.Y. Post* about Eslanda's success with the book.

36. The phrasing of this review provides a striking confirmation of the thesis developed by Von Eschen, *Race Against Empire*.

37. Ernestine Evans, "An American Negro in Africa," *N.Y. Herald-Tribune Weekly Book Review* (12 Aug. 1945), 2; Lewis Gannett, "Books and Things," *N.Y. Herald-Tribune* (13 Aug. 1945); Francis Hackett, "Books of the Times," *N.Y. Times* (9 Aug. 1945), 19; Stuart Cloete, "Contrasting Appraisals of a Still-Dark Continent," *N.Y. Times Book Review* (12 Aug. 1945), 5; Helen Cain, "A Close-up of Africa's People by an American Negro Woman," *St. Louis Post-Dispatch* [Oct. 10, 1945?], clipping, EGR Vertical File; Margaret Williamson, "'Africans Are People,'" *Christian Science Monitor* (22 Aug. 1945), 14; George Streator, "Books of the Week," *Commonweal*, 42 (21 Sept. 1945), 555–56; John LaTouche, "In Africa Before the War," *Saturday Review of Literature*, 28 (25 Aug. 1945), 11–12.

For brief but positive references to race relations and social development of "so-called 'backward people'" in the Soviet Union, see EGR, *African Journey*, 47, 106–07, 153.

38. See the reviews cited in the previous note by Cloete, Gannett, and LaTouche.

39. See "Mrs. Robeson Joins Staff; Reception Honors New Book," *New Africa*, 4 (Aug.-Sept. 1945), 4, and Ruth Gage-Colby's tribute to EGR after her death on their work together before the Trusteeship Council of the UN, in *Freedomways*, 6 (Fall 1966), 340–42. EGR traveled briefly in Africa again in 1946; a brochure announcing an 11 Nov. 1946 lecture in N.Y.C. based on this trip may be found in EGR Vertical File.

On the CAA's campaign at the UN in the postwar years, see Von Eschen, *Race Against Empire*, 83–96, and on African-American appeals at the UN more generally see Carol Anderson, "From Hope to Disillusion: African Americans, the United Nations, and the Struggle for Human Rights, 1944–1947," *Diplomatic History*, 20 (Fall 1996), 531–63.

40. See, e.g., EGR publicity material, and EGR to "Sorors in Delta Sigma Theta," 4 Aug. 1949, Robeson Papers–Schomburg (microfilm reel 1, frame 74 and reel 1, frames 469–75, respectively).

41. Buck, *American Argument, with Eslanda Goode Robeson* (N.Y.: John Day Co., 1949); Buck, *Tell the People: Mass Education in China* (N.Y.: John Day Co., 1945); Buck, *Talk About Russia, with Masha Scott* (N.Y.: John Day Co., 1945); Buck, *How It Happens: Talk About the German People, 1914–1933, with Erna von Pustau* (N.Y.: John Day Co., 1947).

42. Buck, *American Argument*, 19, 22–23.

43. See esp. Buck, *American Argument*, 125–27.

44. For a revealing exchange on the issue, in which Eslanda charged in effect that Buck's "defense" of her as a non–Communist was a capitulation to Cold War thinking, see *American Argument*, 122–23.

45. Buck excised references to Eslanda's participation in the Progressive Party from the book, explaining to Eslanda that with publication in January 1949, such discussion would be dated; see Buck to EGR, 27 Sept. 1948, EGR correspondence, Robeson Papers–Howard. Buck probably felt as well that eliminating partisan references would help the book's reception.

46. Suzanne LaFollette, "Anti-American Interview," *Plain Talk* (Feb. 1949), 45–49, clipping, EGR Vertical File; Fletcher Isbell, "A New Dictatorship 'By the People' Is Given Hearing," *Washington Star* (30 Jan. 1949), clipping, Robeson Papers–Howard.

47. Helen Beals, "Pearl Buck Race 'Argument' Produces Varying Emotions," *Boston Herald* (26? Jan. 1949), and Jay Smith, "A Talk Book on Questions Facing World," *St. Louis Post-Dispatch* (6 Feb. 1949?), clippings, EGR Vertical File; P. M. Mezey, "Our Country," *S. F. Chronicle* (20 Feb. 1949), 19.

48. Mary Ross, "Native Grounds," *N.Y. Herald-Tribune Weekly Book Review* (6 Feb. 1949), 17; R. L. Duffus, "On the Defects of Society Today," *N.Y. Times Book Review* (23 Jan. 1949), 21; Mrs. Worth Tuttle Hedden, "Four Critical Eyes on U.S.A.," *Saturday Review of Literature* (5 Feb. 1949), 13. See also for similarly positive reviews, Olive Deane Hormel, "Challenge to Americans," *Christian Science Monitor* (17 Mar. 1949), 22, and M.P [anon. reviewer]., "Strong Views, Aptly Put," *Worcester Sunday Telegram* (23 Jan. 1949), clipping, Robeson Papers–Howard.

49. Richard Walsh, Jr., to Richard J. Walsh, 23 Dec. 1948, and EGR to Buck, memo, 11 Jan. 1949, both in Box 261, John Day Papers.

50. Thelma Thurston Gorham, "'American Argument' Features Women's Opposing Viewpoints," *Pittsburgh Courier* (26 March 1949); "News of Books & Authors," *N.Y. Amsterdam News* (29 Jan. 1949); Gertrude Martin, "'American Argument' Is General Accord," *Chicago Defender* (29 Jan. 1949), all clippings in Robeson Papers–Howard.

In addition, chapter one of the book was reprinted in *Negro Digest*, 7 (May 1949), 81–94. The *Baltimore Afro-American* reprinted sections as well; see Carl Murphy to John Day Co., 13 July 1949, Box 261, John Day Papers. The newly-organized Negro Reading Club also recommended the book to its members; see Leslie Jones to Buck, 28 May 1949, Box 267, John Day Papers.

51. Buck to EGR, 18 July 1951, EGR correspondence, Robeson Papers–Howard.

52. Press release [1954], Robeson Papers–Schomburg, microfilm reel 1, frame 71. The quoted passage may be found in Buck, *American Argument*, 196.

53. See various letters between Buck and Eslanda, 1950–53, in EGR correspondence, Robeson Papers–Howard.

54. For EGR's first article in the magazine see "World Woman Number One," *New World Review* [hereafter *NWR*], 19 (July 1951), 20–25; for her appointment to the staff as "editorial consultant on Negro and Colonial Questions," see editor's note, *NWR*, 20 (Aug. 1952), 3; for her own involvement with the National Council of American-Soviet Friendship, on which she served as co-chair of its Committee on Women, see "Why I Am a Friend of the USSR," *NWR*, 21 (Aug. 1953), 27–28.

55. For a representative sampling of articles, see: "The Cry for Freedom Rings Through Africa," *NWR*, 20 (Sept. 1952), 14–17; "Which Way for Africa?" *NWR*, 20 (Dec. 1952), 24–29; "Trust in Trusteeship," *NWR*, 23 (May 1955), 28–30; "UN + Bandung = Peace," *NWR*, 23 (July 1955), 26–29; "The Changing Face of the United Nations," *NWR*, 25 (May 1957), 9–12; "China and the U.N.," *NWR*, 25 (June 1957), 15–19; "The Accra Conference," *NWR*, 27 (Feb. 1959), 13–14.

56. For EGR's attack on Nehru after her return from a trip to the Soviet Union and China in 1949, see "USSR Visit Opened Eyes: Mrs. Robeson Regrets Having Defended Nehru," *Baltimore Afro-American* (28 Jan. 1950), clipping, Robeson Papers–Schomburg, microfilm reel 2, frame 962. For PR's opposition to Nehru at this time, see Duberman, *Paul Robeson*, 378–79, 698–99; apparently EGR's Jan. 1950 statement represented a change from her position of a few months earlier. For EGR's later appreciation of Nehru's foreign policies, see her articles, "Before and After Bandung," *NWR*, 23 (July 1955), 26–29; "Krishna Menon: A New Type of Diplomat," *NWR*, 24 (June 1956), 10–14.

57. See EGR's articles: "World Woman Number One" (on Soong Ching-ling [Mme. Sun Yet-sen]); "140,000,000 Women Can't Be Wrong" (on the exclusion of the Women's International Democratic Federation from consultative status at the UN), *NWR*, 22 (June 1954), 18–23; "Women in the United Nations" (on women delegates) *NWR*, 22 (July 1954), 7–10; "If the UN Seated China" (on women in the PRC), *NWR*, 22 (Aug. 1954), 21–23; "Women in the UN," *NWR*, 26 (Mar. 1958), 33–35.

On the difficulties of the U.S. affiliate of the Women's International Democratic Federation, see Amy Swerdlow, "The Congress of American Women: Left-Feminist Peace Politics in the Cold War," in *U.S. History as Women's History: New Feminist Essays*, edited by Linda Kerber, et al. (Chapel Hill: University of North Carolina Press, 1995), 296–312. On U.S. feminism in this period in general, see Leila Rupp and Verta Taylor, *Survival in the Doldrums: The American Women's Rights Movement, 1945 to the 1960s* (N.Y.: Oxford University Press, 1987), but on women's peace activists see also Harriet Hyman Alonso, *Peace as a Women's Issue: A History of the U.S. Movement for World Peace and Women's Rights* (Syracuse: Syracuse University Press), chap. 6, and Susan Lynn, *Progressive Women in Conservative Times: Racial Justice, Peace, and Feminism, 1945 to the 1960s* (New Brunswick: Rutgers University Press, 1992).

58. See, e.g., EGR, "The Rising Tide," *NWR*, 20 (Nov. 1952), 10; EGR, "Here's My Story" (guest column), *Freedom* (July 1953), quoted in *Paul Robeson Speaks*, edited by Philip S. Foner (N.Y.: Citadel Press, 1978), 569–70; EGR, "Peace, Friendship, and Progress," *NWR*, 22 (Nov. 1954), 29–32 (a speech presented at a *NWR* dinner honoring the Robesons); EGR, "Some Thoughts on Negro History Week," *NWR*, 23 (Mar. 1955), 20–21.

59. Arthur M. Schlesinger, Jr., *The Disuniting of America: Reflections on a Multicultural Society* (N.Y.: W. W. Norton, 1992), 82–83, 135.

60. I am following the framework here of Von Eschen, *Race Against Empire*.

Paul Robeson and Jackie Robinson: Athletes and Activists at Armageddon

JOSEPH DORINSON
Long Island University

Pablo Neruda, Nobel Laureate in Poetry, before his symbolic appearance in the film *Il Postino*, sang the praises of Paul Robeson —[1]

> Once he did not exist
> But his voice was there, waiting
>
> Light parted from darkness,
> day from night,
> earth from primal waters
>
> And the voice of Paul Robeson
> Was divided from silence.

Robeson's voice was unforgettable. *New York Times* critic Brooks Atkinson likened it to "a cavernous roar." Another writer described that unique bass/baritone as "sheer, carpeted magnificence." Even a notoriously nasty reviewer from the *Herald Tribune* felt compelled to describe Robeson's voice as "celestial."[2] That unique voice, silenced by the grand inquisitors in the 1950s and by death in 1976, uttered its

first cry on April 9, 1898, the day of his birth to Rev. William Drew Robeson, a runaway slave, and Maria Louisa Bustill, an educated woman. Growing up sanely in an absurd society rife with "Jim Crow" segregation, he enjoyed a spectacular career as a scholar-athlete. At Rutgers University he won varsity letters in football, basketball, baseball and track. He excelled in the classroom, too. Phi Beta Kappan, debate champion, valedictorian: Robeson towered above his classmates.

After graduating from Columbia Law School, he abandoned legal practice for the theater. He roared in the 1920s as Eugene O'Neill's *Emperor Jones* and as Oscar Micheaux's hero in *Body and Soul*. In 1928 Robeson electrified London audiences as Joe in Jerome Kern's *Show Boat*. Two years later, his Othello won rave reviews. After almost two decades abroad, Robeson returned to his native land. On November 5, 1939, he came to CBS Radio where he sang

Earl Robinson's *Ballad for Americans*. He was granted an honorary doctorate at Hamilton College in 1940 and the Donaldson Award in 1944 for his splendid Othello.

His meteoric rise brought him global fame. He seemed to embody the American dream in that giant frame. Larger than life, he was a natural for the role of good-will ambassador. On one of his many trips he visited the Soviet Union in 1934. It produced a mutual love affair with serious consequences. Like Othello, he loved not too wisely but too well. For the first time in his life, Robeson felt totally welcome, unfettered, adored — indeed lionized.

As long as the common enemy was Nazi Germany or Imperial Japan, Robeson enjoyed large fame and modest fortune. The American press rarely criticized either his personal beliefs or his public statements. In fact, Paul Robeson reached a high point in 1943 when he starred in a Broadway production of *Othello* and led a delegation of Negro leaders to a meeting of major league baseball owners and their czar, Kenesaw Mountain Landis, to petition for the entry of blacks into the citadel of our national pastime. Cordially received and effusively greeted by Commissioner Landis, Robeson had every reason to believe that he had earned stature in the eyes of white America and had paved the way for Jackie Robinson's entry four years hence. It seemed like a story crafted by and for a black Horatio Alger.

But another Alger — Hiss — then appeared. Whittaker Chambers accused Hiss of communism, and a new congressman, Richard Nixon, produced the "Pumpkin Papers," supposedly proving that he was. The Cold War heated up in 1947. The threat of Communist-led insurgency in Greece and Turkey, the rising popularity of Communist leaders (Togliatti in Italy, Thorez in France), the coup in Czechoslovakia in 1948, the triumph of Mao's armies in China in 1949, and the detonation of an A-bomb in Russia breaking our nuclear monopoly: all contributed to worsening relations between the two superpowers. And Paul Robeson was caught in the cross fire.

He told a Paris Peace Conference that, "It is unthinkable that American Negroes could go to war on behalf of those who have oppressed us for generations against the Soviet Union, which in one generation has raised our people to full human dignity."[3] Arnold Rampersad suggests that, wrenched out of context, Robeson's remarks were taken literally instead of ironically. This interpretation painted Robeson into a corner: colored red. Robeson returned from Europe angry and belligerent. He resented attacks on his patriotism. The famous singer defied "any errand boys … and Uncle Toms of the Negro people, to challenge my Americanism."[4]

Biographer Martin Duberman points out that Robeson retained support in 1949. The Council on African Affairs warned against a campaign to smear a man who stood up for civil rights. Even critics like Alfred G. Clausen raised a serious question: "Why did this man gifted as a singer, an actor, an athlete and a scholar prefer the restrictive regime of Russia to the democracy of his native land?" Clearly, the critic concluded that the answer resided in America's refusal to admit all members to full participation as citizens. Duberman's analysis is cogent. Robeson, he contends, feared a preemptive strike. Moreover, Paul Robeson, Jr., has found evidence of a big bang option that would have rained nuclear bombs on Russian cities in a nefarious program called "Project Boiler."[5] The elder Robeson firmly believed that the twin evils of racism and imperialism, endemic in America, constituted the gravest threat to humanity.[6] Hence his oft-repeated words delivered with passionate intensity: "And we shall not put up with any hysterical raving that urges us to make war on anyone. We shall not make war on the Soviet Union."

To rebut and isolate Robeson, HUAC hearings opened in mid–July. Alvin Stokes, a man of questionable repute, testified that Communists planned to set up a Soviet republic in Dixie. He characterized Robeson as the Kremlin's voice of America. Another paid informer, Manning Johnson, testified that Robeson was a Communist who harbored grand delusions. HUAC's attempt at a public display of Negro loyalty seemed to be gaining ground. A de facto double standard applied. While white Americans were required to name names, the preferred litmus-paper test for blacks was denunciation of Paul Robeson.[7] For a knock-out blow, Committee Chair John Wood of Georgia summoned a heavy hitter — Jackie Robinson — to rebut Robeson. The Brooklyn Dodger trailblazer felt constrained to comply.

As Robinson remembered this confrontation, he faced a dilemma. After extended discussion with wife Rachel, mentor Branch Rickey, and Urban League executive Lester Granger, the brilliant second-sacker framed a reply for his appearance on July 18, 1949, to "give the lie to statements by Paul Robeson." The summons invited skepticism and Jackie knew the score. He understood Robeson's rage and the white establishment's desire to get him. He realized that the target of HUAC was "an embattled and bitter man" who had suffered indignities from his Princeton childhood to his Rutgers college experience. Shunned in Nazi Germany while on tour in 1934, he was embraced in Soviet Russia. Nor was Robinson blind to the manipulation of his star-studded appearance. "I'm not fooled because I've had a chance open to very few Americans."[8] Robinson admitted that, although he lacked expertise in politics, he knew his people and their experience intimately. He, too, vowed to continue the struggle against racial discrimination in society as well as sports. He realized that to many blacks, as Arnold Rampersad writes, "Robeson was both a glamorous entertainer and a black man of unusual courage; among many whites, too, he was a highly respected, even revered figure."[9] Jackie did not want to tangle with the great singer-activist, but he could not accept Robeson's premise regarding the behavior of Negroes vis-à-vis the Soviet Union. Except for the stridently rhetorical and patently artificial last line that reaffirmed Jackie's determination not to squander his large investment in America "because of a siren song in bass," the rebuttal was fairly gentle. Indeed, Robeson qualified his critique of Robeson: "He has a right to his personal views and if he wants to sound silly when he expresses them in public, that is his business and not mine."[10]

Jackie felt that no one leader could speak for all African Americans, certainly no one who was pro–Soviet. Perceptively, he understood the dynamics of doubleness imposed on blacks: the external fight and the battle within. Unable to back down, blacks had to fight on both fronts. Full representation in American society depended on service — including military service — to the state. Quoting Jesse Jackson later in life, Robinson quipped: "It ain't our government, but it's our country."[11] Biographer Rampersad succinctly summarizes Robinson's delivery: "In homespun language, leavened only now and then by humor, Jack offered himself as both a humble man and one proud of his deeds; keenly opposed to racism in America but full of hope."[12]

Press coverage in the main reflected a strong anti–Robeson bias. The *New York Times,* for example, put Robinson's testimony on page one and added an editorial in support. But the paper did not dignify Robeson with a report on his press conference to answer the Dodger star.[13] In this remarkable two-hour exchange at the

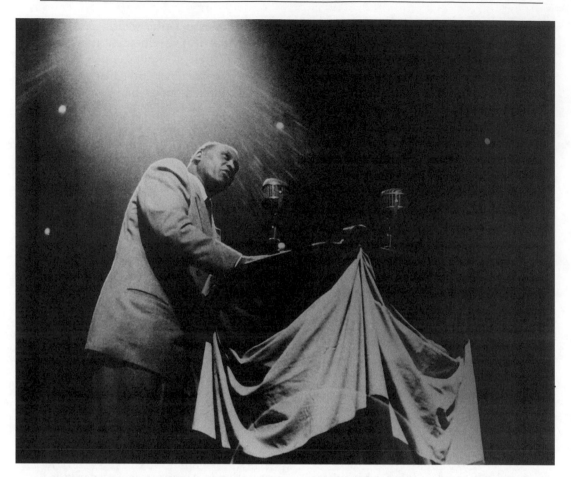

Robeson speaking at Madison Square Garden, shortly before he and Robinson were interrogated by the House Un-American Activities Committee. Courtesy of Paul Robeson, Jr.

Hotel Theresa, Robeson refused to be baited into a frontal attack on Robinson. "As a matter of fact, Jackie said he was for peace, and I am, too, so let's start fighting for it." Robeson offered to testify and urged Negroes to testify about their conditions in America. Robeson went on to blast the committee chair from Georgia for his defense of the Ku Klux Klan. He sneered at Congressman John Wood for his absence during Robinson's appearance, asserting that it was dictated by a refusal to address the witness as Mr. Robinson. Why didn't the committee summon Joe DiMaggio — Robeson wondered aloud — to testify on the loyalty of Italians? He went on to chide Robinson — albeit mildly — for playing ball

with the enemy. He clarified his Paris statement, stressing the peace option in the face of war fever. He conceded that eighty-five engagements had been canceled because of political reaction. He vowed to go on fighting. Robeson concluded by denying that he had written to Robinson in an effort to prevent his testimony or saying that blacks would not fight in a war against Russia.[14]

"Heavy hitters" like former first lady Eleanor Roosevelt also favored Robeson, as did 239 Brooklynites surveyed by *The Amsterdam News*. In contrast to the white establishment, the black press offered a more measured analysis. The Baltimore *Afro-American* featured a cartoon that depicted Jackie Robinson as a frightened little boy brandishing a huge gun tracking Robeson's giant footprints. The caption read: "The leading player in the National Baseball League is only a tyro as a big game hunter." Educator J. A. Rogers defended Robeson as a "loyal American."[15]

To his credit, Robeson refused to attack Jackie Robinson, "I have no quarrel with Jackie. I have a great deal of respect for him, he is entitled to his view. I feel that the House Committee has insulted Jackie, it has insulted me, it has insulted the entire Negro race."[16] Paul Robeson, Jr., agrees with this assessment. At the LIU [Long Island University] Robinson Conference, April 4, 1997, he put a different spin on the Robinson-Robeson controversy. His illustrious father had said, in effect, "Hell, no, we should not go" and not "Hell, no, we won't go." Both blasted racism. At one game the younger Robeson recalled that he wanted to get Jackie's autograph. Big Paul, however, demurred. He did not want to embarrass the Brooklyn Dodger star.[17]

The Peekskill Riots that followed show how polarized America had become. Unwavering in his support for the Soviet Union, Robeson suffered loss of income and, worse, a diminished audience. One year later his passport was revoked. Unable to travel, he lived under virtual house arrest in his own country. But he refused "to go gently into that good night." He raged against his persecutors. Critic Eric Bentley captures Robeson's feisty exchange with congressmen. By "any civilized criterion," he observes that the great singer was singled out for depersonalization by the American "power elite." This mirror image of Soviet treatment of dissidents began with the second Peekskill riot, in which Robeson was targeted for assassination. The honor guard, acting to protect him, flushed out two nests of snipers nestled in the foliage.[18] Unable to eliminate the man of courage, Robeson's enemies curbed his travel, curtailed his income, canceled his concerts, and consigned him to oblivion.

Bentley concedes that Robeson showed a flawed sense of history when he linked Stalin with Marx, an error that he shared with Communists globally. But the astute critic presciently points out that Robeson's defiant words anticipate the black freedom and black nationalist movements of a later decade. The testimony that he gave under duress on June 12, 1956, put him on a collision course that ultimately lead to a contempt citation. He proved more defiant than the inquisitors had reason to anticipate. Proudly, indeed contemptuously, he peppered the inquisitors with pointed questions of his own. It appears that the repeated denial of his petition for a passport freed Robeson from restraint and gave vent to a righteous indignation. He demonstrated utter contempt for the members—and rightly so. Witness, if you will, these words of defiance:

> Chair: "What do you mean by the Communist Party?"
>
> Robeson: "Would you like to come to the ballot box when I vote and take out the ballot and see?"
>
> Chair: "You are directed to answer the question?"
>
> After consultation with counsel, Robeson retorted: "I take the Fifth Amendment."

In response to continued badgering by counsel Arens, Robeson corrected the chronology regarding his alleged remarks about Americans' refusal to make war on the Soviets. In the absence of hot war, Robeson quipped: "So I was prophetic, was I not?"

Arens read Robeson's 1949 statements into the current record but persistently refused to allow the singer-activist to read his prepared statement. Robeson countered: "The Smith Act is a vicious document."

Rather than defend Stalin, perhaps an untenable stand anyway, Robeson attacked the American record that "wasted sixty to a hundred million black people dying in slave ships and on the plantations, and don't you ask me about anybody, please."[19]

Even if these figures are inflated, they cut to the heart of Robeson's fierce anger. And if Paul Sr. misjudged Stalin, he accurately captured black rage. He also anticipated the black militancy of Malcolm X. His finest hour, however, came when he blasted Chair Francis Walter for his authorship of bills to keep colored people out of America in favor of "Teutonic Anglo-Saxon stock." And in response to that old clichéd question posed by Representative Scherer, "Why do you not stay in Russia?" he replied, "Because ... my people died to build this country and I am going to stay here and have a part of it just like you."[20]

Paul Robeson was one of a handful of dissidents who spoke out against the grand inquisitors during "scoundrel time." Now that the Cold War is over, it is time to assess the confrontation or, more accurately, the set-up that pitted two African-American giants against each other. Right after the first Peekskill Riot, reporter Bill Mardo approached Jackie Robinson on August 28, 1949. He gave the Dodger star a newspaper account of this sordid event. Robinson angrily asserted that, "Paul Robeson should have the right to sing, speak or do anything he wants to. These mobs make it tough on everyone. It's Robeson's right to do or be or say as he believes. They say here in America you're allowed to be whatever you want. I think those rioters ought to be investigated." Perceptively, he observed that in this country "anything progressive is called Communism."[21] Bill Mardo demonstrates that the two alleged combatants were actually on the same side. He dubs them "a double play for the ages."

Near the very end of his life, Jackie Robinson admitted his error in an aptly named autobiography, *I Never Had It Made.* "However, in those days I had more faith in the ultimate justice of the American white man than I have today [1972]. I would reject such an invitation if offered now."[22] Although Robinson insisted that he never regretted the statement per se, in a searing confession he wrote: "I have grown wiser and closer to painful truths about America's destructiveness. And I do have increased respect for Paul Robeson who, over the span of that twenty years, sacrificed his career, and the wealth and comfort he once enjoyed because, I believe, he was sincerely trying to help his people."[23]

Unfortunately for the great singer, the divide and conquer strategy proved effective. Like a protagonist in a Greek tragedy, the heroic Paul Robeson was brought down, ostracized and exiled in his own land, the America that he had exalted in the famous *Ballad for Americans.*

While an older generation of radical white as well as black activists continues to honor the memory of Paul Robeson, young Americans are woefully ignorant of Robeson's contributions. Perhaps they need to hear the strains of "Ol' Man River" to induce what critic Edmund Wilson called "the shock of recognition."

Sing,
my friend,
never stop singing.
You broke the silence of the rivers
When they were dumb
because of the blood they carried.
Your voice speaks through them.

Sing:
Your voice unites
Many men who never knew each other.
Because you sing
they know that the sea exists
and that the sea sings.

They know that the sea is free,
wide and full of flowers
as your voice my brother

The sun is ours. The earth will be ours.
Tower of the sea, you will go on singing.

Notes

1. *Paul Robeson: The Great Forerunner* by editors of *Freedomways* (New York: Dodd & Mead, 1985), 244. Neruda's poem appeared in *Freedomways* magazine in 1971, and appears not to be included in any other edition of Neruda's works in Spanish or English. Neruda apparently wrote it for a celebration of Robeson in the United States. It is reprinted at the beginning and end of this essay courtesy of *Freedomways* and Esther Jackson. The biographical information that follows is largely culled from the same source, 319–322, which in turn was derived from Erwin A. Salk, *Du Bois-Robeson: Two Giants of the 20th Century: The Story of an Exhibit and a Bibliography* (Chicago: Columbia College Press, 1977). A more comprehensive chronology is found in Philip Foner, editor, *Paul Robeson Speaks: Writings, Speeches, Interviews 1918–1974* (New York: Brunner/Mazel, 1978), 27–46.

2. Martin Bauml Duberman, *Paul Robeson: A Biography* (New York: Alfred A. Knopf, 1988), 159.

3. As quoted by Ronald A. Smith, "The Paul Robeson–Jackie Robinson Saga and a Political Collision," in Jules Tygiel, editor, *The Jackie Robinson Reader* (New York: Penguin Dutton, 1997), 180. This excellent article, first published in the *Journal of Sports History*, 6 (Summer 1979), is the basis for my study; but I think it is too narrowly focused. Since its publication in 1979, additional information and a dramatic shift in Cold War dialectics provide an altered interpretation.

4. *Ibid.*, 357.

5. In a presentation at Rutgers University at Newark, February 21, 1998, the son of Paul Robeson cited documents released under the Freedom of Information Act.

6. Duberman, 354.

7. Victor Navasky, *Naming Names* (New York: Penguin Books, 1981), 187.

8. Jackie Robinson, *I Never Had It Made: An Autobiography,* as told to Alfred Duckett (New York: The Echo Press, 1995), 82–83; also see Jules Tygiel, *Baseball's Great Experiment ...* (New York: Oxford University Press, 1983), 334.

9. Arnold Rampersad, *Jackie Robinson: A Biography* (New York: Alfred A. Knopf, 1997), 212.

10. Duberman, 360.

11. Robinson, *I Never...*, 84.

12. Rampersad, 213.

13. Foner, 521, fn. 2.

14. *Ibid.*, 219–221.

15. Duberman, 361.

16. As quoted in Rampersad, 215.

17. Richard Sandomir, *The New York Times,* April 4, 1997; also from a tape recording of Robeson's paper.

18. Robeson, Jr., at a conference, "Climbing Jacob's Ladder," held at Rutgers University at Newark, February 21, 1998. Howard Fast made the same observation in a radio interview, which included this writer, on WGCH 1490 AM, Connecticut. This program, hosted by Jim Thompson, aired on February 22, 1998.

19. The testimony is largely culled from Eric Bentley, *Thirty Years of Treason: Excerpts from Hearings Before the House Committee on Un-American Activities, 1938–1968* (New York: The Viking Press, 1971), 768–786.

20. As quoted in David Caute, *The Great Fear: The Anti-Communist Purge Under Truman and Eisenhower* (New York: Simon & Schuster, 1978), 166.

21. Bill Mardo, based on an article he wrote for the *Daily Worker*, August 29, 1949, shared the interview with participants in the conference, "Jackie Robinson: Race, Sports and the American Dream," at Long Island University, April 3, 1997. This illuminating exchange is published by M. E. Sharpe (1999) in a book on Robinson edited by this author and Joram Warmund. Rampersad, *op. cit.,* 213, quotes Mardo on Robinson's reaction to the Peekskill debacle.

22. Robinson, *I Never...*, 84.

23. *Ibid.*, 86.

Paul Robeson, Peekskill, and the Red Menace

JOSEPH WALWIK
Manatee Community College

The weary, battered victims of an unforeseen riot gathered near a stage outside Peekskill, New York, on the night of August 27, 1949. The small group included the remnants of a concert audience that had traveled to Lakeland Acres picnic grounds for an evening concert by one of America's most remarkable performers, Paul Robeson. Instead, the concert-goers became witness to a night of ugly violence.

A protest march by local veterans in the early evening set the tone for the night and made the community's opposition to Robeson's presence explicit. Arriving concert-goers were jeered and insulted by a crowd who gathered near the site, then watched in horror as a cross was set afire on a nearby hillside. Robeson and the majority of the concert-goers never arrived, having been warned of trouble or turned away by the crowd. The few who had arrived early bore the brunt of the crowd's anger and eventually abandoned their efforts to control the picnic grounds. As they watched rioters make fires out of their camp chairs and music books, the concert-goers huddled before the stage and joined defiantly in singing "We Shall Not Be Moved."

Finally, two hours after the start of the riot, the police arrived; the injured received treatment and the rest safe escort out of the picnic grounds. Almost miraculously, there were no fatalities that night, although the threat of death was very real. Novelist Howard Fast, who was to have served as master of ceremonies for the evening, recalled, "at one point I knew I would die in that terrible fight in Peekskill."[1]

Shaken, but undeterred, the concert's planners quickly scheduled a concert for the following week and began organizing their own security to protect both performers and concert-goers. Peekskill townsmen likewise regrouped, adamant in their conviction that only a determined protest could safeguard community autonomy. The rising tension was aggravated by angry rhetoric, as charges of "Communist," "fascist," "Nazi," "Nigger-lovers," and "Jew bastards" were exchanged. The ensuing concert and subsequent riot represented far more than a spontaneous eruption: Both concert-goers and protesters entered the Peekskill area convinced of the need to defend fundamental American values. What was contested was not the music of Paul Robeson, but the very nature of American democracy.

"A Friendly Town"?

"Peekskill is a Friendly Town." At least that's what the sign at the town limits told visitors. Yet the veterans who protested Robeson's appearance might have added: friendly did not mean naive. The Peekskill veterans felt that their protest march was part of the ongoing international struggle between the United States and the Soviet Union. It was not Paul Robeson the singer whom they opposed, but Robeson the fellow traveler — the Communist — whom they could not abide. And it was his followers, un–American in their politics and only recently American in their heritage, who aroused the fears and suspicions of many of the Peekskill veterans. The veterans brought their memories of Hitler, Tojo, and Mussolini to the events in Peekskill, but they also recognized that this Cold War represented a new kind of conflict. Communism was the enemy, and Robeson, by virtue of his professions of love and fidelity to the Soviet Union, was merely an agent of the Kremlin. At best he was a dupe, at worst a traitor.

For the left-wing concert-goers, Robeson was not merely another singer, but a powerfully symbolic fighter for civil rights in America, against fascism in Spain, and against colonialism in Africa. By attacking the concerts the locals in Peekskill had accosted a near-sacred icon. Regardless of his stature among people on the left, Peekskill residents had no intention of making Robeson feel welcome.

When word of Robeson's proposed concert in Peekskill reached the public, the reaction from the area veterans' organizations was swift and unambiguous. Although he had appeared in the region in each of the previous three summers, in the summer of 1949 he attracted unwanted attention. Robeson's new notoriety stemmed largely from statements made at the April 1949 Congress of the World Partisans of Peace in Paris. Robeson, professing to speak on behalf of all American workers, said that, "our will to fight for peace is strong. We shall not make war on anyone. We shall not make war on the Soviet Union." There is some confusion regarding this statement because Robeson was quoted by the Associated Press as saying, "it is unthinkable that American Negroes would go to war on behalf of those who oppressed us for generations against a country [the Soviet Union] which in one generation has raised our people to the full dignity of mankind."[2] When these words were reported in the United States they helped to cement the outspoken Robeson's growing reputation as an "un–American." In Peekskill the *Evening Star* printed the wire service's report of Robeson's statement on page one under the headline "Robeson Says U.S. Negroes Won't Fight Russia."[3]

The Paris speech and his continued support of the Soviet Union made Robeson politically suspect in the tense atmosphere of the Cold War. Robeson's talents had not waned, but his politics were increasingly unpalatable to many Americans. Robeson sounded like a Communist, associated with Communists, and openly defended the Soviet Union. Even if he was not technically a Communist Party member, Robeson's public style placed him firmly in the Communist camp.[4]

Once the *Evening Star* confirmed that Robeson was indeed on his way to Peekskill, it printed a series of articles, editorials, and letters to the editor that left little room for doubt as to the paper's position on the upcoming concert. The August 23, 1949, *Evening Star* ran a front page headline reading "Robeson Concert Here Aids 'Subversive' Unit" and a controversial editorial entitled "The Discordant Note." "The time for tolerant silence that signifies approval is running out," wrote the editor. "No matter how masterful the decor, nor how sweet the music," Americans should not be duped into accepting communism in their own communities.[5] The paper also repeated the charges of the California Committee on Un-American Activities that the Civil Rights Congress, for whose benefit Robeson was appearing, was a "Communist dominated organization."[6] Although recognizing that Robeson had performed in the area before with little incident, the newspaper made clear that his welcome had faded by 1949 because over "the past several months Robeson has turned violently and loudly pro–Russian."[7]

The same edition also printed a letter to the editor from a local veterans' leader, Vincent J. Boyle:

> The present days seem to be crucial ones for the residents of this area with the present epidemic of polio. Now we are being plagued with another, namely the appearance of Paul Robeson and his Communistic followers.... It is an epidemic because they are coming here to induce others to join their ... ranks and it is unfortunate that some of the weaker minded are susceptible to their fallacious teachings unless something is done by the loyal Americans of this area.
>
> Quite a few years ago a similar organization, the Ku Klux Klan, appeared in Verplanck and received their just reward. Needless to say they have never returned. I am not intimating violence in this case but I believe that we should give this matter serious consideration and strive

to a remedy that will cope with the situation the same way as Verplanck and with the same result that they will never appear again in this area.

> The irony of this meeting is that they intend to appear at Lakeland Acres Picnic Area. If you are familiar with this location you will find that it is located across the street from the Hillside and Assumption Cemeteries. Yes, directly across the street from the resting place of those men who paid the supreme sacrifice in order to insure our Democratic form of government.
>
> Are we, as loyal Americans, going to forget these men and the principles they died for or are we going to follow their beliefs and rid ourselves of subversive organizations? ... If we tolerate organizations such as these we are apt to face a repetition of the past and in the near future.[8]

Boyle's letter expressed the concerns and strategies of this new kind of war. He likens communism to polio, an insidious disease that strikes at unsuspecting members of society. He raises the issue of his readers' loyalty as opposed to that of Robeson and his "Communistic followers." Drawing on local history, Boyle reminds his townsmen of how the Ku Klux Klan was expelled from nearby Verplanck and suggests similar action against Robeson. Finally, Boyle invokes the legacy of World War Two and reminds readers of the sacrifices made by the veterans now resting in the cemeteries across the street from Lakeland Acres.

This letter, along with the news stories and editorials of August 23, 1949, set the tone for the next two weeks in Peekskill. The "Discordant Note" editorial sanctioned opposition to Robeson with an official voice, while Boyle's letter served as a call to action. The issue at hand, according to the *Evening Star* and Vincent Boyle, was as much about local autonomy as it was about communism. Even if there was no way to legally prohibit the concert, other measures could be taken that would allow local citizens to express their opinions forcefully. For, while most Peekskill residents realized that it was not illegal to be a Communist, they certainly considered it un–American.

The *Evening Star* continued to print articles using words such as "Communist" and "subversive" in connection with Robeson, and local civic leaders quickly concurred. "There is no room in this community," said Lloyd Whitaker, President of the Peekskill Chamber of Commerce, "for any person or group of persons whose ideology advocates allegiance to any other form of government than that which we enjoy here in these United States of America." Allan Grant, Cortlandt Town Supervisor, let it be known that he was "openly opposed to such gatherings, where the sponsors are listed as subversive and against our American way of life." Grant also complained that American citizens were "powerless to act" until communism was outlawed. "Whether or not a subversive front operates far away or in our locality," Grant exhorted, "it behooves every believer in the Constitution of the United States to stand pat to see that the rights of the majority are not destroyed."[9]

On August 25, 1949, the Joint Veterans' Council (JVC), a body consisting of representatives of various veterans' organizations, convened a special meeting to discuss the Robeson concert. Even before the JVC could meet, the local posts of the American Legion and Veterans of Foreign Wars had already endorsed a protest parade as a means of taking a "definite stand against the appearance of Paul Robeson."[10] The JVC followed the lead of its members and called for a "peaceful and orderly" demonstration to be conducted "in the best traditions of our country. We can thus illustrate," the JVC statement continued, "the democratic form of expression and protest in contrast to the force and vio-

lence as practiced in Communistic and dictatorship countries." Although the JVC called for a peaceful demonstration, the parade was intended to be confrontational. The veterans planned to march along Hillside Avenue in front of the entrance to Lakeland Acres during the concert performance. A JVC statement in the *Evening Star* invited non-veterans to join them in the march, but asked that they "follow the orders of the ex–G.I.s who will be acquainted with the overall plan."[11] The protest march was carefully planned and organized, and clearly intended to physically confront the concert-goers.

Other community groups in Peekskill quickly lent their voices to the anti–Robeson chorus as the concert drew near. The Chamber of Commerce, Jaycees, Kiwanis Club, Knights of Columbus, and other civic organizations went on record as opposing Robeson's appearance.

Although they were few in number, there were dissenting voices. American Labor Party member Victor Sharrow, a resident of nearby Crompound, wrote an appeal to the State Attorney General claiming that the *Evening Star* was acting in an inflammatory manner and requesting police protection for the concert.[12] In a letter to the *Evening Star*, one area resident accused the newspaper and the parade organizers of losing "faith in the fundamental soundness of democracy [in order to] ... adopt one or more of the very methods of Communists which we detest in them." The greatest threat lay not in Paul Robeson or communism, but in what the results would be if "those who think of themselves as good Americans should become panicky and forget (if they ever fully understood and truly appreciated) the great value of Democratic principles."[13] These minority opinions were drowned in a sea of anti–Robeson and anti–Communist feelings.

In the days before the concert, the

Evening Star, the central player in the drama, defended itself against accusations, like those of Victor Sharrow, which blamed the paper for any trouble that might occur at the concert. In a rare front page editorial entitled "Music or Politics?" the newspaper made its reply:

> At no time, either in its columns or editorially, has the *Evening Star* ever advocated "violence" as a means of disrupting this, or any other kind of program. We did state, however, and do here reaffirm, our conviction that the time for tolerant silence that signifies approval has run out, and that it is high time to speak forth.

The newspaper justified this unusual use of the front page because of the recent "glib misrepresentations" by outside groups who were trying to "discredit the newspaper's opposition to the Robeson concert, which has been made strictly on patriotic grounds." The paper commended the veterans' plans for a peaceful demonstration and reasserted its position, concluding, "Violence? Absolutely not! Let such tactics remain elsewhere — in the trick bags of the undemocratic."[14]

On the day of the concert the paper fired one more editorial blast, entitled "Minority Intolerance":

> Sponsors of the Paul Robeson concert to be held this evening in Peekskill have protested to the County Executive and the District Attorney because the Peekskill *Evening Star* has told its readers in plain language just exactly the kind of man Robeson is and just who are his political sponsors.
>
> Those who protest this frank newspaper treatment are always the first to cry aloud for the right of free speech when they think their own civil rights imperiled. In fact the minorities that are the most vehement in demand of their own rights are the most intolerant in granting similar privileges to the majority.[15]

The *Evening Star* pursued its anti–Robeson campaign throughout the pages of the August 27 edition. The paper reminded its readers that the "Russia-loving Negro baritone" was going to sing that night for the benefit of a "Communist front organization."[16] The lines of conflict were clearly marked in the pages of the *Evening Star*; it was to be minority versus majority rights, outsiders versus locals, and "Communists" versus "Americans."

Joe Albertson, the editor of the *Evening Star*, had put his paper in the middle of the conflict, and on the day of the concert his message was clear: The rights of Robeson and his fans need not be taken too seriously because they obviously cared little about the rights of the majority in Peekskill. The degree to which the newspaper can be held accountable for the violence of August 27 is debatable. At the very least, though, its editorials and feature stories gave voice to and inflamed the anti-Communist, anti–Robeson sentiment in the community.

While the newspaper, veterans' organizations, and other town leaders all supported the protest parade, there is no evidence to suggest that any of them foresaw or planned the violence that followed. Ironically, Allan Grant asked the state police to send some troopers because he was worried that some "toughies" from New York City might come to the concert and cause trouble.[17] In reality, most of the concert crowd was drawn from people who vacationed in the Peekskill area.

Press Reactions

The Peekskill riot of August 27, 1949, did not long remain a local issue. News of the riot quickly spread across the country via the radio and wire services. The initial United Press coverage inaccurately told of how a "mob of young men tonight set fire to the stage at a picnic area near here [Peekskill] in trying to halt a scheduled concert by Negro Paul Robeson."[18] News of the riot at Lakeland Acres soon reached into American living rooms. In the days that followed, the Peekskill riot developed from a simple wire service story into a political lesson for the nation.

Throughout the Northeast the riot received both news coverage and extensive editorial commentary. From Washington to Albany, editorials on Peekskill exhibit a rhetorical consistency by embracing the Peekskill veterans' cause but denouncing the violence. In so doing, most editorialists take as assumed knowledge two important premises: 1) Robeson was, at the very least, a fellow traveler; and 2) Communist subversion represented a very real threat.

Even in the restrained *New York Times,* which strongly defended the rights of the concert-goers, the editor tweaked Robeson while upholding his right to sing in Peekskill: "Lamenting the twisted thinking that is ruining Paul Robeson's great career, we defend his right to carry his art to whatever peaceably assembled groups of people he wishes. That is the American way."[19] Other editors were less generous.

Most editorials did not protest the violence because of the injuries suffered, or even because of the violation of civil liberties, but because violence played into the hands of Communist propagandists. The editor of the *Philadelphia Tribune* spoke for many of his colleagues when he argued that anti-communism itself was not a legitimate excuse to riot because "those who are opposed to Communism can not destroy it with violence. Force and strong arm tactics are the handmaidens of communistic procedures. They love it. They thrive on it."[20] The editor of the Albany, New York, *Knickerbocker News* charged that the Peekskill veterans had actually weakened the cause of anti–Communism.

"We deplore any action that might tend to dignify, or perhaps even martyrize the Negro singer. And that," according to the editor, "is precisely what happened Saturday night in Peekskill." The editor further warned that the "danger is that the Red singer, who otherwise seems destined for involuntary obscurity, might gain stature through such incidents." Without mentioning the right of free expression, the editorial cautioned against even "peaceful demonstrations," as they tended to "lend undue importance" to controversial events such as the Robeson concert. And the onset of violence, "with its inevitable publicity, multiplies by many times the notice accorded." The *Knickerbocker News* did find a silver lining in the bad news that attended the Robeson concert. The publicity, although it probably provided fuel for the Communist propaganda mill, also served to expose Robeson "thoroughly" as a "self-appointed crusader for the Communists." Americans, argued the editor, need never be confused about Paul Robeson again, since he had proven himself to be "a disgrace to his race and country."[21]

Other publications also decided that the propaganda value of the riot to the Communists was the real story. The editor of New York's *Herald Tribune* condemned the violence in Peekskill because "Americanism cannot be defended by aimless violence or riotous demonstrations," as "Communists thrive in such an atmosphere of chaos." He claimed that the "veterans groups played into the hands of their opponents, either in righteous or misguided indignation." The editor underlined his point by asserting that the "Communists" not only provoked the conflict, but exulted in it as well. The riot created a "new set of martyrs," he argued, which was enough "in the Communist book, to make the concert a howling success." Despite the "provocative and offensive" statements Robeson would undoubtedly have made had the concert proceeded, the protesters should have been willing to "let the irony and the facts of the case stand as sufficient refutation of the charges of the concert's sponsors."[22] Even though he was willing to blame the protesters for falling into a trap set by the "Communists," the editor of the *Herald Tribune* charged that Robeson and his followers were subversives who, although technically the victims in the riot, had to be viewed with suspicion. Protesting subversion was not in itself wrong, argued the editor, but being lured into violence was inexcusable.

Newspaper editorials in Washington, D.C., focused their attention on the victims of the violence in Peekskill, but expressed little sympathy. While the Peekskill veterans were criticized for attempting to prevent the concert, thus "adopting the Communist technique and playing the Communist game," the concert-goers were held up for special ridicule. "The anguished outcries of Mr. Robeson should not be taken seriously," wrote the editor of the *Washington Evening Star,* because "they do not appeal to public opinion with clean hands." Unconcerned with questions of constitutional rights, the editor claimed that, so far as the "Communists" were concerned, "their shrill demands for the protection of the Bill of Rights ought to be appraised accordingly."[23] The editor of the *Washington Post* was somewhat less strident than his crosstown peer when he wrote, "it is hard to say which side is more to blame for this disgraceful and ominous episode." In the end, however, he concluded that Robeson, for "his disparagements of his native country and his fulsome glorification of Soviet Russia," deserved most of the blame. The *Post* editor reminded his readers that "since he [Robeson] has refused to deny that he is a Communist, he is open to suspicion."[24]

These editorials are remarkable for their willingness to take what amounts to a wartime attitude towards suspected sedition. Civil liberties rarely entered editorials, and then only to point out that those violently preventing the Robeson concert had adopted a "Communist tactic." Otherwise, the editors seemed to have few qualms about the suspension of free expression where Robeson was concerned. There is little concern that Robeson's rights were violated, only fear that the "Communists" would capitalize on the incidents.

While residents of other cities read about the riot in their daily newspapers, the people of Peekskill were still living in its wake. The *Peekskill Evening Star,* accused by many in the pro–Robeson camp of complicity in the violence, had its own interpretation of the riot. While the paper's coverage was filled with the same negative references, like "subversive," "Communist front," and "Russia-loving Negro," as other papers, its first accounts of the riot were more critical than supportive of the protesters and rioters.

The *Evening Star*'s August 29, 1949, editorial echoed its big city counterparts when lamenting the termination of the otherwise "orderly and peaceful" protest in violence. The editor of the *Evening Star* expressed regret over the personal injuries and property damage, but mostly worried that the "undemocratic show of leaderless disorder," which was "precipitated by a few unruly persons," occurred at a time when there was insufficient police protection to prevent violence and actually "played right into the hands of the concert supporters." Although the editor formally condemned the riot, he was obviously pleased at seeing the Communist issue brought out into the open. The Peekskill veterans, according to the editor, showed that they "are in no mood to appreciate the political gall of those who scream for rights and benefits as American citizens, only to use these sacred privileges to serve un–American ends."[25] Like those in Philadelphia, Albany, New

York City, and Washington, the editor in Peekskill was more than willing to ignore the subtleties of civil liberties in favor of sweeping anti–Communism.

In the aftermath of the riot the editor of the *Evening Star* condemned the violence, but without implicating individual protesters or rioters in any serious wrongdoing. The policy set the tone for both editorials on the events and the content of the news stories regarding the riot. In its first edition following the violence, the paper ran a front page story reporting "bitter" fighting when "nearly 300 young veterans and others battled a group of youthful Communist sympathizers." The young veterans, according to the story, could not be restrained and "drove Robeson sympathizers back down a dirt road leading to the concert grounds with their fists." When the deputy sheriffs on hand ordered them back to Hillside Avenue, "they circed [sic] around through the hills and wreaked destruction to the concert equipment and chairs." According to the newspaper account, the departing concert-goers were forced to run a gauntlet of log, rock, and barbed wire roadblocks as "the demonstrators secreted themselves along the dusty road as the first cars began speeding out of the grounds. As the vehicles bounced over the log, they rose in unison and battered the automobiles with a terrific barrage of stones."[26]

Based on this account, a strong case can be made that the veterans instigated the violence. The rioters were depicted as aggressive, semi-organized, uncontrollable, and, most importantly, clearly identifiable as veterans. By the time the next issue of the *Evening Star* hit the streets on August 30, the picture had become somewhat more clouded. In a front page headline, that edition reprinted the veterans' charges that "Armed Commie 'Goon' Squads" provoked the attack. This marked both a reporting and an interpretive shift for the paper. From this point forward, the *Evening Star* stopped portraying the veterans as aggressors and moved towards a position that claimed the veterans had not participated in the violence at all. One unidentified veteran told the newspaper that, "there wouldn't have been any trouble if the Communists had not imported 'goon' squads and armed them for trouble." The so-called "goon squads" consisted of men who were "dressed for violence. They wore old clothes and carried knives, blackjacks, brass knuckles, and clubs." Protest organizer Vincent Boyle told a reporter that it was "regrettable that the ugly face of mob violence was exposed after the veterans dispersed." Besides, said Boyle, Robeson's "patrolmen caused the riot when they came armed and with a belligerent attitude."[27]

The obvious contradictions in these stories were complicated by the fact that the veterans, had they actually dispersed and gone home, could not possibly have known who started the fight or whether anyone was armed. Nor did the fact that the police found no weapons among the concert-goers influence the newspapers' opinions. Whether this interpretive change was a conscious editorial decision or reflected new information gathered by the paper is not clear.[28]

The new account of the events did not implicate any individuals or groups from the Peekskill area who could be held responsible for the violence. Beginning on August 30, the *Evening Star* suggests that the Peekskill veterans were not the aggressors in the confrontation with the concert-goers; in fact, as the days passed, the veterans began to appear more like the victims in the riot. After all, it was one of their own, William Secor, who had received the most serious injury, and, according to Secor's account, that injury occurred only after the concert-goers started a fight. This abrupt reversal may also have been prompted by veterans who had a vested interest in protecting themselves from liability for the property damage caused by the riot. The veracity of the veterans' statements is even more suspect given that many who were used as sources by the *Evening Star* refused to give their names for fear of being held responsible for the damage at Lakeland Acres. While the veterans' organizations steadfastly maintained that their members were not at fault, some were clearly worried. Emphasizing the Communist threat allowed these men to shift attention away from themselves and lay the blame on Robeson and his followers. The August 30 editorial completed the shift by clearly stating that preventing riots could only be accomplished by removing the source of the violence — the subversive threat.

Ultimately, that was not the responsibility of the community, but of Washington. The national government compiled lists of subversives, but authorized few legal sanctions against them.[29] Although the *Evening Star*'s coverage of the riots is clearly biased against the concert-goers, this August 30 editorial raised an interesting argument. If citizens are told by trustworthy sources, in this case the Department of Justice, that a person or organization has loyalties that threaten the national welfare, how should the citizenry react when such organizations enter their communities? By this logic, it was government negligence that ultimately led to the riot. The *Evening Star* deplored the violence in Peekskill, as did most other papers, but the *Star* also offered a distinctly local perspective on the dilemma: If Paul Robeson represented the face of Communism in America, and Communism was the enemy, what were "good Americans" to do when confronted with subversive acts in their hometowns?

Notes

1. Howard Fast, *The Naked God* (New York: Praeger Publishers, 1957), 22.

2. Martin Bauml Duberman, *Paul Robeson: A Biography* (New York: Ballantine Books, 1989), 342. For his part, Robeson never disavowed the comments as reported by the Associated Press.

3. "Robeson Says U.S. Negroes Won't Fight Russia," *Peekskill Evening Star*, 21 April 1949, 1.

4. In his biography of Robeson, Martin Duberman concludes that Robeson never actually became a member of the Communist Party. At the time, the FBI had very different ideas. An internal FBI memo in 1949 reported that "Paul Robeson, singer and actor, was a member of the Communist Party and that his party name was John Thomas." R. W. Wall to H. B. Fletcher, 22 April 1949, FBI Freedom of Information Act Reading Room, Washington, DC, file #100-12304-122, section 3.

5. *Peekskill Evening Star*, 23 Aug. 1949, 4.

6. *Ibid.*, 1.

7. *Ibid.*, 3.

8. *Ibid.*, 4.

9. *Peekskill Evening Star*, 24 Aug. 1949, 2.

10. *Peekskill Evening Star*, 25 Aug. 1949, 1.

11. *Peekskill Evening Star*, 26 Aug. 1949, 1.

12. *Peekskill Evening Star*, 24 Aug. 1949, 1.

13. *Peekskill Evening Star*, 26 Aug. 1949, 4.

14. *Ibid.*, 1.

15. *Peekskill Evening Star*, 27 Aug. 1949, 4.

16. *Ibid.*, 1.

17. Allan Grant interview by Lt. R. W. Ficke, 29 August 1949, Dewey Papers, 5:222:36. Lt. Ficke confirms that Grant did indeed call him on 8-25-49 and ask for police protection.

18. *Washington Post*, 28 Aug. 1949, 1.

19. "Interrupted Concert," *New York Times*, 29 Aug. 1949, 16.

20. *Philadelphia Tribune*, 3 Sept. 1949, 4.

21. *Knickerbocker News*, 2 Sept. 1949, 3.

22. *New York Herald Tribune*, 2 Sept. 1949, 10.

23. *Washington Evening Star*, 30 Aug. 1949, 8.

24. *Washington Post*, 29 Aug. 1949, 6.

25. *Peekskill Evening Star*, 29 Aug. 1949, 4. The *Evening Star*'s first stories on the riot did not appear until Aug. 29, two days after the event, because the paper did not publish a Sunday edition.

26. *Ibid.*, 1–2.

27. *Ibid.*, 1.

28. It is, of course, conceivable that the editor of the *Evening Star* made a decision to change the tone of his paper's coverage so as to protect individuals from possible prosecution. However, it should be noted that the version of events which holds that it was non-veterans who instigated and carried out most of the violence corresponds to later investigations of the riots by the ACLU and the Westchester County Grand Jury.

29. *Peekskill Evening Star*, 30 Aug. 1949, 4.

Remembering Peekskill, USA, 1949

HOWARD FAST

The difference between myself and practically ever other author in this collection, except for Henry Foner and Lester Rodney, is—I would guess—some thirty-five years. I know that my subject is Peekskill, but I cannot resist one story about Paul Robeson which only I know, because it occurred at our dinner table many years ago.

It was a matter of a week before he was to go down to Washington with a subpoena from the House Un-American Activities Committee. He was morose. I had already made the journey to Washington with my own subpoena.

"Tell me what can I say?" Robeson asked.

I said: "It's very simple. You're not a Communist."

He said: "You do not understand. I can't do that. I sang in France to members of the resistance, and they were Communists; and I sang in Italy to the guerilla movement, and they were Communists; and I sang in the Soviet Union to the people who defeated the Nazis, and they were Communists. And I go to

Washington and that bastard asks me whether I'm a Communist and I say to him I'm not. How do I face anyone? How do I explain?"

So he went there and he said nothing at all. He said: "I refuse to answer your questions." He took his chances with jail, but they were not ready to jail Robeson. It is an interesting historical sidelight on a period.

When he was barred from every concert hall, when he was barred from every university except the black colleges—and if I am not mistaken, several black colleges barred him, too—he nevertheless sang at every black church that asked him to sing, every public meeting for civil rights, every public meeting when the cause was peace. He never refused. He would sing for twenty people; he would sing for a thousand.

So it was natural that sometime that summer—1949—the people who spent their summer months in upper Westchester County, New York, decided that they would have a great concert and that they would ask Paul to sing to them. These people were from workers' communities, summer cottages, very inexpensive little homes.

They formed a committee and they got some help from the Fur and Leather Workers' Union. They found a beautiful picnic ground in a sort of natural round hollow near Peekskill, and they telephoned me and asked me whether I would chair this concert. Paul Robeson would speak and sing there.

"Absolutely! I would be delighted to," I responded.

That's how I came to be at the concert. Women and children arrived an hour early in a big bus from northern Westchester, and what happened then, before the other concert-goers arrived, was an attack by a mob of hoodlums, joined by local police and Governor Thomas Dewey's state troopers, both groups willingly assisting and joining the hoodlums. This mob of about a thousand people closed the roads into this picnic ground about an hour before the concert was scheduled to begin. Paul never got there. The busload of women and children was there, about twenty people from the neighborhood had come early, and a handful of people from the Fur and Leather Workers' Union. I don't want to dwell on the concert because — as I said — Paul never got there. But it was a horrible, ghastly night where the intent and the purpose was to kill Robeson. And a new slogan was coined by the mob of hoodlums and police — an interesting new slogan. They threw it at us. They called us "white niggers." And that cry went on and on all through the night.

This was a terrible scene. There was a stone bridge that led into these concert grounds, and for some hours we were able to hold the bridge, about twenty of us. They were throwing a barrage of rocks at us. The fight went on all through the night. Finally, an FBI car rolled in. They had been there all the time watching this, and they finally decided to end it. So much for that first concert that never took place. It was a battle, not a concert.

The Fur Workers and others had a meeting the next day, and it was decided that this was a challenge to all decent people. And we scheduled a second concert. This time we got solid trade union backing. The second concert, curiously enough, was also in a picnic grounds, in a similar hollow. There are many such hollows in Westchester County, with a ridge of forested hills backing up the picnic grounds. We got there early. I say we, but not myself; a group of the trade unionists got there early. And they flushed out of the hills two men with high powered rifles who were posted up there to kill Robeson. We got rid of them. Then the trade unionists came in and they made a fantastic wall that was [about] two miles long of men standing shoulder to shoulder with arms linked. It was a show of discipline that was simply marvelous to see.

Robeson, who read everything that had been written about the first concert — the papers were full of it — eagerly and willingly agreed to speak and sing at the second concert, even though he knew that there were definite plans to kill him. When he arrived at the second concert, the concert organizers asked for a new group of volunteers. And they got about a dozen men eager to protect Robeson — two or three of them veterans of the Abraham Lincoln Brigade, which incidentally was another group that Robeson had sung to during the Spanish Civil War.

These men took a position in front of Robeson, in front of him against his objections, holding that his life was no more valuable than theirs. They took a position in front of him so that if there were any more riflemen posted up in the hills they would kill these men; they would not hit Robeson.

And Robeson stood up, facing thousands and thousands of people in that hollow, and he sang. He sang every song in his repertoire. It was a wonderful, wonderful afternoon. Marvelous afternoon! Nothing interrupted it until we began to leave the concert.

What had been prepared for us while we were in there, surrounded by a mile and a half of trade unionists with their arms linked, was a new trial by fire — under the guidance, and with the support, of the local and state police. And remember this when you talk of police tactics today, a trap was set to destroy us. The police willingly lent themselves to this effort. They piled rocks on every overpass, and there were many overpasses in upper Westchester. In those days the Hudson River towns were in a state of virtual decay. The police found plenty of drunks and hoodlums, and together they collected piles of stones on these overpasses. As we drove out of the concert grounds, the cars were pelted with rocks, many of them the size of watermelons. Pelted with rocks from the sides of roads, too. Every car going out of that picnic ground had to run through this gauntlet of shattered glass and smashed metal. It was like nothing I had ever seen. Some of the World War II vets who were there said they had never encountered anything as threatening, as horrifying, as those two concerts.

Paul, happily, got away unhurt. There was no official apology for this assault. Governor Dewey said not one word in protest, although we had dozens of photographs of his state troopers as part of the crowd in the assault, and photographs of local police joining the crowd in rock throwing. Well, anyway, this is the story of Peekskill. It's a story that should be investigated, researched, and written about. It's an important event in American history.

I will tell just one other story. I went to see *Othello* before I met Paul. I looked at this man. I watched this play. I said I must do something about this. So I wrote a book called *Freedom Road*. And I wrote it with only one purpose in mind. The moment the manuscript was finished I gave it to Paul. I said: "This is for you. I wrote it for you. And you must play the part." For twenty years we tried and no one in Hollywood would touch it with a ten-foot pole. And finally, because Muhammad Ali, a good, generous, sweet man, was willing to play the part of Gideon Jackson — and only because he was willing, NBC agreed to make the film. But, unfortunately, while Muhammad Ali had the stature, the brains — everything else — he had no voice. And so we never had a chance to hear that grand voice that was like no other in the world.

Paul Robeson, *Freedom* Newspaper, and the Korean War

LAWRENCE LAMPHERE
Cornell University

The outbreak of the Korean War in June 1950 was a turning point in the life of Paul Robeson. Robeson's career declined rapidly after his 1949 Paris speech, in which he suggested that African Americans would not participate in wars against socialist countries,[1] but it was only after the start of the Korean conflict the following year that Robeson was deprived of his passport.

After losing his right to travel, one of the most important tools that Robeson used to reach his public was *Freedom* newspaper, a black-oriented newspaper that he and his associates published in New York City from late 1950 through 1955. Several characteristics of *Freedom* set it apart from nearly all American newspapers. These included a regular column from Robeson, support for Robeson's passport struggle, in-depth coverage of the labor movement, and opposition to American military involvement in Korea. Robeson contributed to a number of publications during the early 1950s, but *Freedom* was the only one in which he had a regular column. *Freedom* is thus an indispensable source for understanding Robeson's political views. This paper examines *Freedom*'s coverage of the Korean War and related issues, and analyzes Robeson's views on Korea in the context of his broader international perspective.

My examination of *Freedom*'s Korean coverage addresses several questions related to the historical significance of Paul Robeson. To what extent was Robeson's opposition to our involvement in Korea reflective of African-American opinion? How did *Freedom*'s coverage of the war compare with that of other black newspapers? How did the desegregation of the military during the Korean War influence black opinion? How did the rise of McCarthyism during the Korean War influence black opinion? Perhaps most important — what were the connections between Robeson's views on Korea and his views on other political issues?

Paul Robeson, a world traveler who

studied numerous European, African, and Asian languages, was deeply interested in many different countries and peoples. By the early 1930s Robeson was a staunch supporter of the Soviet Union. Even before that he had a deep interest and identification with the African continent. In the late 1930s, while living in London, Robeson helped found the Council on African Affairs (CAA). The CAA was not a mass organization, but, in the words of one historian, it "helped keep the issue of colonial liberation on the U.S. agenda and provided links to anticolonial networks and African liberation groups."[2]

After World War II Robeson clearly wanted to focus more on political activism and less on the artistic side of his career. In 1947 he declared that he was abandoning his concert career in order to "talk up and down the nation against race hatred and prejudice." In part, this decision was due to Robeson's displeasure with post-war international developments. He was disturbed by the worsening of American-Soviet relations, the hesitancy of European colonial powers to grant independence to their possessions, and the rise of anti–Communist hysteria in the United States. All these developments, according to Robeson, were inextricably linked with race relations. He interpreted European colonialism as a manifestation of racism. Robeson remarked on several occasions that many of the most aggressive American anti–Communists were also supporters of segregation and European colonialism.[3]

Despite all of his interest in international affairs, Robeson does not appear to have paid much attention to Korea before 1950. This should not be surprising; before 1950 Korea was regarded even by most experts on international affairs as of secondary importance. Long "a pawn in Far Eastern power plays,"[4] Korea was divided after World War II by a mutual agreement between the United States and Soviet

Union. By 1949 Communist North Korea and capitalist South Korea were independent nations. Both the North and South Korean governments wanted to reunify the peninsula, and were willing to use military force towards that end; between 1946 and 1950 a civil war claimed thousands of lives.[5]

The North Korean invasion of South Korea on June 25, 1950, took the American people by surprise and reinforced the image of a monolithic Communist conspiracy. To most Americans, the invasion was an obvious case of Communist aggression.[6] The question of the origins of the Korean War had a divisive impact on the American left. Henry Wallace, whose 1948 presidential bid Robeson had supported, resigned from the Progressive Party shortly after the outbreak of the war, in response to the Progressives' opposition to American military involvement.[7] Wallace's resignation deprived the Progressive Party of its most popular leader and increased Robeson's importance as a symbol of the left. The outbreak of fighting in Korea had the effect of pushing Robeson into a closer alliance with Communists, who shared his view of the Korean situation, and driving him away from more moderate potential allies.[8]

Robeson's interest in Korea after 1950 should be understood in the context of his many international interests and political commitments. Robeson generally analyzed the Korean situation in relation to other international developments in countries such as South Africa, Kenya, China, and Viet Nam.

In his first major speech following the outbreak of the Korean War Robeson made his position clear. On June 28, 1950, three days after the North Korean invasion, Robeson addressed a capacity crowd at Madison Square Garden: "I have said it before, and say it again, that the place for the Negro people to fight for their freedom is here at home — in Georgia, Mississippi, Alabama, and Texas— in the Chicago ghetto, and right here in New York's Stuyvesant Town." Robeson linked the Korean situation with various African issues throughout the war, and he asked his Madison Square Garden audience to consider the possibility of black Americans being sent to fight not only in Asia but also in Africa. In Robeson's words, it would be a "travesty" if black American youth were "called on to one day put down these brave African peoples. What mockery that black Americans should one day be drafted to protect the British interest in Nigeria whose proud people cannot be held in bondage for another ten years. Fail to stop the intervention in Korea, and that day may come."[9]

Robeson also mentioned the beginning of mass protests against the new apartheid system in South Africa, and called for similar action by black Americans. At a rally in Harlem in September 1950 Robeson asked his audience a question that probably struck a powerful chord: "If the people of South Africa rise up against the Malan fascist government, wouldn't it be unthinkable for us Negroes to support those who would send us to shoot down our African brothers?"[10] Robeson's linkage of Korea and South Africa is especially significant. The North Korean invasion convinced American policy makers of the need for a massive nuclear build-up, thereby increasing the importance of uranium from southern Africa. Historian Thomas Borstelmann notes that South African support for the American role in Korea led "to a series of agreements in late 1950 that firmly established American support for the apartheid regime."[11]

In August 1950 Robeson became one of a long list of Americans who were deprived of their right to travel during the Cold War. He had planned to perform in Europe in August and September, but the State Department declared his passport void, claiming that Robeson's presence abroad would be "contrary to the best interests of the United States." At a subsequent meeting with Robeson, State Department officials clarified their position, telling him that he had no business talking about American racism in foreign countries. The loss of his passport prevented Robeson from earning large sums of money as he had in the 1940s. For by 1950 Robeson was not welcome in major American concert halls but was still in demand in Europe.[12]

In late 1950 Robeson and his associates formed *Freedom* newspaper, largely as a means for Robeson to inform African Americans about his struggle for the right to travel abroad. The newspaper's contributors included W.E.B. Du Bois and renowned African-American cartoonist Ollie Harrington. The young Lorraine Hansberry, who would later win fame as the author of *A Raisin in the Sun,* was an assistant editor at *Freedom. Freedom* editor Louis Burnham was one of Henry Wallace's campaign managers; prior to that he was Executive Director of the Southern Negro Youth Congress, a left-wing group that battled discrimination in the South from the mid–1930s through the late 1940s.

In a December 1950 interview Burnham outlined the mission of his new newspaper. *Freedom* was "part of the Negro press ... one more newspaper among the more than 200 now being published. But it's also a different kind of Negro newspaper." According to Burnham, six characteristics of *Freedom* set it apart from the rest of the black press: 1) A working class orientation, as opposed to the middle class values of traditional black newspapers; 2) Emphasis on African Americans' close ties with the labor movement; 3) Advocacy of third party politics; 4) Emphasis on the plight of African Americans and their struggle in the South; 5) Support of the movement for world peace; 6) In-depth coverage of Africa, Asia, and Latin America, particularly movements against colonialism.[13] In one of his *Freedom* columns Robeson echoes Burnham's criticism of the black press, stating that *Freedom* "must address itself to the eagerly awaiting masses, must become a fearless fighter for our full rights.... It must become a voice such as does not exist in the Negro press at this time."[14]

Paul Robeson and his associates may have been correct in their belief that an opening existed for a radical, black-oriented newspaper. However, *Freedom* would only survive five years, and in its last two years was not able to publish every month. *Freedom*'s demise was due mainly to the pressures of McCarthyism, which made most African Americans hesitant to be associated with Robeson in any way. Robeson, unlike some of his associates, would never see the inside of a jail cell, but he was followed everywhere he went by FBI agents. Robeson concerts were the best opportunity for Robeson to distribute his newspaper — the price of admission often included a subscription to *Freedom*, but the FBI ensured that concert attendance was often light. Concert-goers were photographed and their license plate numbers recorded. Robeson fans with government jobs could thus be pressured into not supporting his concerts. Various state and municipal governments often made it impossible for Robeson to secure a large concert facility, limiting him to churches and union halls with relatively small capacities.[15]

Most of the organizations with which Robeson was involved — most importantly the Council on African Affairs and the National Negro Labor Council — faced constant harassment from the federal government. The government's attacks forced the black Left organizations to devote much of their time and money to legal defense efforts. This left precious little for new projects— such as the promotion of *Freedom* newspaper.

Freedom was one of the few American newspapers to oppose American military involvement in Korea.[16] Every issue carried a call for peace in Korea, and Robeson spoke out against the war in many of his columns. *Freedom* generally avoided the question of the origins of the war, and concentrated instead on war-related issues of special interest to African Americans. *Freedom* attempted to appeal to black readers by contrasting the federal government's aggressiveness against communism with its relative inaction on civil rights. In the February 1951 issue Robeson related the war to the recent execution of the Martinsville Seven, a group of young African Americans convicted of rape in Virginia.[17] Robeson, like many African Americans, believed that they were innocent. A *Freedom* editorial reflected his anger at the verdict: "The loud-mouthed braggarts who sell the American way of life to so-called 'backward' peoples have fed the blood-stained maw of white supremacy with the precious lives of seven sons of the Negro people ... the blood-letting in Korea has driven our rulers mad. Their military campaign against the colored peoples of Asia has let loose the vilest passions of Anglo-American 'superiority' which threaten to drown the lives and liberties of Negro Americans in a sea of blood."[18] March 1951's issue featured an article from Benjamin J. Davis, Jr., the Communist Party's most prominent African-American leader. In Davis' words, "Wall Street and Truman have brought out such Negro misleaders as Walter White, Roy Wilkins, Edith Sampson, Adam Powell, and A. Philip Randolph and set them singing tunes of war to the Negro masses. When these so-called leaders accepted the pats on the head and the crumbs from the Jim-Crow table of the white ruling class in return for supporting the war program, they betrayed the whole struggle for Negro rights."[19]

To what extent was Robeson's opposition to the Korean War reflective of African-American opinion? In some respects it was; on other war-related issues, however, Robeson was either wrong or out of touch. Contrary to Robeson's 1949 prediction in Paris, young African-American men registered for military service during the Korean War in record numbers. Military historian Morris J. MacGregor notes that blacks in the Army rose from 10.2 percent in April 1950 to 13.2 percent by December 1952. The main cause was the willingness of blacks to enlist; the black percentage of first-time enlistees "jumped from 8.2 in March 1950 to 25.2 in August, averaging 18 percent of all first-term enlistments during the first nine months of the war."[20] The Korean War led to the creation of integrated armed forces for the first time in American history, and was also the start of black overrepresentation in the Army that continues to this day. It is also important to note that the war opened opportunities in defense industries for many black workers.[21]

Almost no mainstream African-American leaders and newspaper editors accepted Robeson's view of the Korean war. In general, they were quick to express support for American military involvement in Korea. A. Philip Randolph declared that the North Korean attack proved that "Russia is bent upon world conquest."[22] In late June the NAACP convention passed a strong anti–Communist resolution.[23] In Harlem Congressman Adam Clayton Powell, Jr., up for reelection in November, declared his renewed opposition to Communism.[24] In January 1951 Powell announced "that for the duration of the war he would, in the interest of unity, suspend his attempts to get antisegregation amendments to military appropriations."[25]

While Robeson was clearly wrong on some issues, most notably the willingness of African Americans to serve in the military, my reading of the black press and the

statements of civil rights leaders suggests that African Americans were significantly less enthusiastic about the war than white Americans. It is also clear that black skepticism towards the war increased over time. Robeson's statements on some war-related issues were, in fact, accurate reflections of what many African Americans were thinking.

Several reasons explain the relative lack of black enthusiasm towards the Korean War. One of the most important was the treatment of black soldiers by the military justice system. Between August and October 1950, thirty-two blacks and only two whites were convicted of "misbehavior in the presence of the enemy," the military's term for cowardice. The most publicized case was that of Leon Gilbert, a black lieutenant accused of cowardice for refusing to carry out an order that many people regarded as suicidal.[26] In January 1951 NAACP official Thurgood Marshall traveled to Korea and occupied Japan to examine the treatment of black troops, especially the court-martial issue. On his return to the United States, Marshall expressed sharp disappointment with the level of racism within the military.[27]

Many African Americans were offended by the comments of military officers who publicly criticized the battle performance of black troops. This was an especially sensitive topic that had arisen in World War II. Some evidence suggested that black troops performed less effectively than white troops, due to the lower educational level among blacks and morale problems caused by segregation.[28] In Korea, historian George Lipschitz notes that the all-black "Twenty-fourth Infantry Regiment won the first U.S. victory of the conflict near Yechon in July, but it came in for criticism once the fighting began to go badly for the American side."[29] Military historians differ on the performance of black troops in Korea, but, judging from editorials in the black press and the statements of black leaders, the result was an increase in black skepticism towards the war.[30]

Apart from racial issues, the entry of the Chinese into the war in November 1950 appears to have increased black skepticism towards American involvement.[31] In October, following the success of the Inchon landing, American troops crossed the 38th Parallel into North Korea. In November the Chinese counterattacked and pushed the Americans back into South Korea, ending American efforts to reunify the peninsula. The entry of the Chinese threatened to turn the conflict into a world war, and many of America's European allies were horrified by the turn of events.[32]

By late 1950 even the most moderate black leaders and newspaper editors began to express their support for the war in extremely guarded language. In November Howard University president Mordecai Johnson told the CIO convention that the so-called free world comprised "probably the most ruthless dominators and exploiters and humiliators of human life that ever spanned the pages of history."[33] The tone of one *Pittsburgh Courier* editorial from December 1950 was particularly strong: "[Asians] look to our record of arrogance and exploitation in the past and they have a feeling of hatred for us. This is true in Korea as in China...."[34] At about the same time, *Cleveland Call and Post* editor W.O. Walker echoed these sentiments. He argued that "every American soldier that has been killed in Korea has died in vain," and added that, "American soldiers should not be there in the first place."[35]

Robeson used his column to address many issues related to the war. He spoke out strongly in the Leon Gilbert case, citing it as an example of the folly of black support for the war effort. In one column Robeson remarked, "If Adam Clayton Powell and Walter White are so anxious to prove their patriotism, why don't they rush over to Korea and take the place of Lt. Gilbert and his other co-fighters who face white supremacy frame-ups in a Jim Crow army?"[36] In another column Robeson argued that, "no frameup of a Lieutenant Gilbert could ever happen in a Chinese people's army. No soldiers from one of the many minority peoples of China would be driven to mass courts-martial because their skin might be a little darker, or their language might be slightly different. No sections of either the Korean or Chinese armies are set apart to do all the menial labor while others do the fighting, or whenever the going gets really rough, are set up to be sacrificed while picked lighter skinned units are allowed to withdraw."[37]

Despite his outspokenness on war-related issues, military developments in Korea made it difficult for Robeson and *Freedom* newspaper to build a strong following. The problem was the lack of an emotionally charged war-related issue that *Freedom* could use to mobilize black opinion. Most of the dramatic events of the war, such as the entry of the Chinese, occurred before *Freedom* newspaper appeared.

The firing of Douglas MacArthur in early 1951 removed one issue that *Freedom* could have used to broaden its readership. Along with their doubts with respect to his attempt to reunify Korea, most black leaders resented both MacArthur's apparent indifference towards the desegregation of the armed forces, and his acceptance of racial segregation in occupied Japan.[38] In one *Freedom* column, written around the time of MacArthur's firing, Robeson asked his readers to "take a look at Japan since MacArthur's occupation. It's a Jim Crow country."[39] In response to MacArthur's dismissal, Baltimore *Afro-American* columnist James Hicks suggested that "there won't be any sad songs for General MacArthur from the tan yanks on the front lines in Korea."[40] MacArthur's replacement, General Matthew Ridgeway, believed in military integration. By 1952 it was clear that, as the Pittsburgh *Courier* noted, "complete integration [is] becoming more and more an actuality."[41] By this point, then, Robeson's criticism of a Jim Crow army did not carry the same weight.

Apart from his *Freedom* columns, Robeson criticized American policy in Korea in numerous speeches. In the early 1950s he was the keynote speaker at the annual convention of the National Negro Labor Council (NNLC), a left-wing group of labor activists that included many members of unions expelled from the CIO in the late 1940s.[42] The NNLC played an important role in organizing Robeson's concerts and selling subscriptions to *Freedom* newspaper. At the NNLC conventions Robeson always restated his 1949 Paris comments on black military participation, but was more careful to relate this question to developments in Africa. At the November 1951 NNLC convention Robeson emphasized developments in Egypt and the Gold Coast: "England is calling upon us to save them in Egypt.... We Negro people and the workers in America must understand that tomorrow the English will be calling upon this government to come and save them in the Gold Coast, to come and save them in Nigeria, to come and save them in a Federation of the West Indies crying for their independence. What will we do then? Will we go? I say, NO, not move a step."[43]

By 1952 the repatriation of prisoners of war had emerged as the major stumbling block in cease-fire negotiations. The United States charged that most of the POWs had no wish to return to North Korea. The North Korean government responded that the POWs were being intimidated and coerced by the South Korean and Nationalist Chinese guards at the camps. While it is probably true that some of the North Korean POWs were intimidated, it is clear that many of them, in fact, had no desire

to live under communism.[44] The POW issue raised questions of individual liberty that Robeson and *Freedom* newspaper could not answer easily. In one *Freedom* article, Robeson's wife Eslanda suggested that something like the intimidation that the North Koreans alleged "must have happened."[45]

Throughout 1952 Robeson continued to criticize the war in his columns and in speeches, asserting in one issue of *Freedom* that "U.S. troops have acted like beasts, as do all aggressive, invading, imperialistic armies."[46] At the 1952 NNLC convention Robeson again emphasized his opposition to black participation in any American war against African or Asian people: "I said more than three years ago that it would be unthinkable to me that Negro youth from the United States should go thousands of miles away to fight against their friends and on behalf of their enemies.... Well, I ask you again, should a Negro youth take a gun in hand and join with British soldiers in shooting down the brave people of Kenya?... I say again, the proper battlefield for our youth and for all fighters for a decent life, is here; in Alabama, Mississippi, Georgia ... in every city and at every whistle stop in this land where the walls of Jim Crow still stand and need somebody to tear them down."[47]

Robeson on several occasions discussed the relevance of the Korean War to the 1952 presidential elections. Robeson, along with the Communist Party, argued that Eisenhower's candidacy reflected Wall Street's desire for world conquest. The Korean War was seen as part of a conspiracy to roll back the Chinese revolution and conquer all of Asia.[48] In his first post-election column, Robeson asserted that Eisenhower was "moving as fast as possible towards an extension of the war," and that this "would mean an end to our struggle for civil rights." Somewhat more perceptively, Robeson noted that "there are real threats of attempting to support France on a major scale in Indo-China." Robeson also continued to voice the increasingly far-fetched hope that African Americans would form the base of an anti-war movement, despite the fact that they continued to enlist at a higher rate than whites. One early 1953 *Freedom* article on military discrimination argued that blacks would "fight for peace and oppose this suicidal policy"[49]; but there was, in fact, no sign that this was happening.

Despite charges by Robeson and the Communists that he was a warmonger, Eisenhower ended the Korean War six months after taking office. Interestingly, *Freedom* had no comment on the cease-fire, which suggests that Robeson and his associates sometimes preferred to ignore developments that contradicted their preconceived view of international affairs.

However, Robeson's comment about Indo-China shows that his interpretation of Eisenhower's election was not all wrong. At the 1953 NNLC convention Robeson discussed the Viet Nam issue again. After repeating his opposition to European colonialism in Africa, Robeson stated, "No one has yet explained to my satisfaction what business a black lad from a Mississippi or Georgia share-cropping farm has in Asia shooting down the yellow or brown son of an impoverished rice farmer ... we must not approve the squandering of billions of American taxpayers' money on the 'dirty war' in Indo-China — we must insist that the French rule in France and leave the Vietnamese to govern themselves."[50] A few months later, in a *Freedom* column entitled "Ho Chi Minh Is the Toussaint L'Ouverture of Indo-China," Robeson restated his Paris declaration in words that foreshadowed developments in the 1960s: "I ask again: Shall Negro sharecroppers from Mississippi be sent to shoot down brown-skinned peasants in Vietnam — to serve the interests of those who oppose Negro

liberation at home and colonial freedom abroad?"[51]

The historical legacy of Robeson's opposition to the Korean War defies easy categorization. Certainly Robeson can be criticized for underestimating African-American willingness to serve in the military, as well as for a naive attitude towards Communism. If examined in isolation, Robeson's views sometimes seem to be incorrect. As suggested earlier, however, when examined in an international context these same views sometimes appear more reasonable.

The connection that Robeson repeatedly identified between Korea and Viet Nam is an important key to understanding the historical significance of his opposition to the Korean War. Many historians have argued that American involvement in Korea paved the way for disaster in Viet Nam.[52] Robeson deserves credit for his ability to see this.

Robeson's views on China were also prophetic in some respects. With China, as with the Soviet Union, Robeson refused to condemn the human rights abuses committed in the name of building socialism. However, Robeson's consistent invocation of the nationalist content in the Chinese revolution shows that he had a deeper understanding of Chinese history than many anti–Communists. In the early 1950s few people would have predicted that China would still be Communist even after the Soviet Union collapsed. It is unlikely that Robeson would have been surprised by this development.

Another important point is that Robeson consistently linked his opposition to the Korean War with vigorous opposition to both European colonialism throughout the African continent and the new apartheid system in South Africa. Robeson was wrong on the willingness of African Americans to fight against Communism in Asia, but it remains an open question as to what would have happened if the federal government had ever sent large numbers of black troops to fight against African freedom movements. Robeson's opposition to the Korean War illustrates the importance of examining his views in the broadest possible international perspective.

Notes

1. Martin Duberman's biography emphasizes that Robeson's remarks in Paris were misquoted, but this may not be as significant as Duberman suggests; see Martin Bauml Duberman, *Paul Robeson: A Biography* (New York, Ballantine Books, 1989), pp. 342–9. The important point is that Robeson stated on many occasions *after* April 1949 that African Americans should not participate in wars against either socialist countries or non-white countries.

2. Penny Von Eschen, *Race Against Empire: Black Americans and Anticolonialism, 1937–1957* (Ithaca, New York: Cornell University Press, 1997), p. 17.

3. Duberman, *Paul Robeson,* pp. 296–311, 317.

4. Walter LaFeber, *America, Russia, and the Cold War, 1945–1996* (New York: McGraw-Hill, 1997), p. 99.

5. Jon Halliday and Bruce Cumings, *Korea: The Unknown War* (New York: Pantheon Books, 1988), pp. 24–62.

6. Alonzo L. Hamby, *Man of the People: A Life of Harry S Truman* (New York: Oxford University Press, 1995), pp. 538–9; Callum MacDonald, *Korea: The War Before Viet Nam* (New York: Free Press, 1986), pp. 29–30.

7. Richard J. Walton, *Henry Wallace, Harry Truman, and the Cold War* (New York: Viking Press, 1976), pp. 349–51.

8. David Shannon, *The Decline of American Communism: A History of the Communist Party of the United States Since 1945* (New York: Harcourt Brace, 1959), pp. 210–13.

9. Philip S. Foner, ed., *Paul Robeson Speaks* (New York: Brunner/Mazel Publishers, 1978), pp. 252–53.

10. *Daily Worker,* September 9, 1950.

11. Thomas Borstelmann, *Apartheid's Reluctant Uncle: The United States and Southern Africa in the Early Cold War* (New York: Oxford University Press, 1993), p. 137.

12. Duberman, *Paul Robeson,* pp. 393–96.

13. *Daily Worker,* December 31, 1950.

14. *Freedom,* February 1952.

15. Duberman, *Paul Robeson,* pp. 381–403.

16. On the lack of widespread opposition to the war, see M.E. Mantell, "Opposition to the Korean War: A Study in American Dissent" (Ph.D. diss., New York University, 1973).

17. For details of the case, see Eric Rise, *The Martinsville Seven: Race, Rape, and Capital Punishment* (Charlottesville, Virginia: University of Virginia Press, 1995).

18. *Freedom,* February 1951.

19. *Freedom,* March 1951.

20. Morris J. MacGregor, Jr., *Integration of the Armed Forces, 1940–1965* (Washington, DC: Center of Military History, United States Army, 1981), p. 430. The Cleveland *Call and Post,* July 15, 1950, noted that while blacks made up only one eighth of Cleveland's population, they accounted for one third of new enlistments.

21. William H. Harris, *The Harder We Run: Black Workers Since the Civil War* (New York: Oxford University Press, 1982), pp. 128, 130.

22. Pittsburgh *Courier,* July 8, 1950.

23. Baltimore *Afro-American,* July 1, 1950; for criticism of the resolution see the California *Eagle,* June 30, 1950.

24. *Amsterdam News,* September 16, 1950.

25. Charles Hamilton, *Adam Clayton Powell, Jr.: The Political Biography of an American Dilemma* (New York: Atheneum, 1991), p. 194.

26. For representative African-American coverage of the Gilbert case, see the Baltimore *Afro-American,* October 21, November 4, 1950, and the *Amsterdam News,* October 21, December 2, 1950.

27. Michael D. Davis and Hunter R. Clark, *Thurgood Marshall: Warrior at the Bar, Rebel on the Bench* (Secaucus, New Jersey: Carol Publishing Group, 1992), pp. 125–32; Carl Rowan, *Dream Makers, Dream Breakers: The World of Justice Thurgood Marshall* (Boston: Little, Brown and Company, 1993), pp. 159–69.

28. Bernard Nalty, *Strength for the Fight: A History of Black Americans in the Military* (New York: Free Press, 1986), pp. 162–81.

29. George Lipschitz, *A Life in the Struggle: Ivory Perry and the Culture of Opposition* (Philadelphia: Temple University Press, 1988), p. 50.

30. For angry African-American reactions,

see the *Crisis*, October 1950, and the *Amsterdam News*, November 25, 1950.

31. Gerald Gill, "Afro-American Opposition to the United States' Wars of the Twentieth Century: Dissent, Discontent, and Disinterest" (Ph.D. diss., Howard University, 1985), pp. 85–87.

32. LaFeber, *America, Russia, and the Cold War*, pp. 117–19; William Stueck, *The Korean War: An International History* (Princeton, New Jersey: Princeton University Press, 1995), pp. 117–18, 130–32.

33. Philip S. Foner, *Organized Labor and the Black Worker, 1619–1981* (New York: International Publishers, 1981), p. 284.

34. Pittsburgh *Courier*, December 23, 1950.

35. Walker quoted in *Freedom*, February 1951.

36. *Freedom*, February 1951.

37. *Freedom*, May 1951.

38. Nalty, *Strength for the Fight*, pp. 258–59.

39. *Freedom*, May 1951.

40. Baltimore *Afro-American*, April 21, 1951.

41. MacGregor, *Defense Studies: Integration of the Armed Forces*, pp. 445–47; Nalty, *Strength for the Fight*, pp. 259–60; Pittsburgh *Courier*, August 4, 1951.

42. On the NNLC, see Foner, *Organized Labor and the Black Worker*, pp. 293–311.

43. Foner, *Paul Robeson Speaks*, p. 291.

44. Rosemary Foot, *The Wrong War: American Policy and the Dimensions of the Korean Conflict, 1950-1953* (Ithaca, New York: Cornell University Press, 1985), pp. 174–76.

45. *Freedom*, February 1952.

46. *Freedom*, January 1952.

47. Foner, *Paul Robeson Speaks*, pp. 332-33.

48. Shannon, *The Decline of American Communism*, p. 208.

49. *Freedom*, February 1953.

50. Foner, *Paul Robeson Speaks*, p. 367.

51. *Freedom*, March 1954.

52. Halliday and Cumings, *Korea: The Unknown War*, p. 204; LaFeber, *America, Russia, and the Cold War*, pp. 107–08; Stueck, *The Korean War*, p. 367.

Music, Film, Theater

A Dream Betrayed:
Paul Robeson and the
British Film Industry

JERRY HOLT
Shawnee State University

"I must keep fighting until I'm dying," Paul Robeson used to sing, changing the more defeatist lyric "Tired of livin' and feared of dyin'" from the *Show Boat* song "Ol' Man River." And, of course, every single day of his life was a fight: it's all recorded in, among other sources, the big biography by Martin Duberman (p. 214).*

Reading that massive tome, I found out more about Robeson's public and personal battles than I probably ever wanted to know. I learned of the many times he nearly lost his life; of the bloody Peekskill episode; of his persecution at the hands of the FBI; of J. Edgar Hoover's personal vendetta against him. I learned — think of this — that Paul Robeson was the first American to ever be banned from national television — in 1951, in response to his im-

pending appearance on Eleanor Roosevelt's talk show. I contemplated the tragic life of a man who could receive standing ovations and be turned away at a hotel in the same city on the same night. I gained some understanding, in short, of what it must have meant to be a successful, brilliant, working artist who also happened to be a man of color at the true dawn of civil rights activism in this country.

And yes, I learned that Robeson fought every step of the way. He used his voice and he used the stage and he spoke out politically — and he attempted to use the medium of film. Like so many others who have shared that epiphany of the possibilities of our single most important twentieth century art form, Robeson believed that film could sometimes be what it was

All references in this essay are to Martin Bauml Duberman's biography, Paul Robeson: A Biography (New York: New Press, 1989). They are indicated by page numbers in parentheses. Robeson's films are The Emperor Jones (1933), Sanders of the River (1935), Show Boat (1936), Song of Freedom (1936), King Solomon's Mines (1937), Big Fella (1937), Jericho (1937), The Proud Valley (1940), and Tales of Manhattan (1942).

meant to be: truth at twenty-four frames per second. He himself said it best: "I thought I could do something for the Negro race in films—show the truth about them and about other people too" (p. 213).

But, of course, Robeson lived in a time, not unlike our own, in which truth was a precious commodity. Indeed, I think if I had to point to one single incident recorded in the Duberman book which cuts to the bitter core of the absurdity that this individual faced, it would be the moment in September of 1946 when Robeson led a seven-person delegation to the White House to ask President Harry Truman to support anti-lynching legislation. Again— think of that: anti-lynching legislation. This world-renowned giant of the stage and concert hall on a sad pilgrimage to the aptly named White House to ask for legislation against the lynching of his people. And think of Truman's response: He cut Robeson short and said that he was concerned about lynching, but the time was "not propitious" for passage of a federal bill. When Robeson, who had come there, as he put it, to "be polite, but not excessively polite" (p. 307), told Truman that if the federal government refused to defend its black citizens against murder, blacks would have to defend themselves, Truman declared the interview at an end and walked out.

How would one make a film which captures the hopeless absurdity of such an exchange? It would be a monstrous task. And yet, every single filmmaker who ever approached Robeson, on this side of the Atlantic or the other, held out that very promise to induce him to offer his talent to the camera. And, in the end, virtually every one lied. Robeson summed it up this way: "I used to do my part and go away feeling satisfied—thought everything was okay. Well, it wasn't. The industry is not prepared to permit me to portray the life and express the living interests, hopes and aspirations of the struggling people from whom I come…. They will never let me play a part in a film in which a Negro is on top" (p. 213).

Those words "on top" embodied, certainly, a much more modest hope: Robeson would have been pleased with a finished film which depicted people of color as human beings with some degree of complexity. Such a hope was what took him to England in 1936, where he began a six-film cycle that would offer him to the public in a variety of incarnations. Some would approach the majestic, like 1940's *The Proud Valley*, his own favorite film. Some would be downright silly—and some would give us glimpses of the man as we today would perhaps like to have seen him. But in all the films one thing remains clear. In a different world, Robeson could have been that most elusive of mythic figures: a movie star. The chemistry that makes stars is a kind of magic. The director Howard Hawks once summed it up by saying: "The camera just likes certain people." And at six-two and 240 pounds, the camera liked Paul Robeson. Loved him, in fact. The inner strength and pure conviction of the man shone through even in the most ridiculous of vehicles.

After his forays into American film and even a surrealist effort named *Borderline*, which also featured Robeson's wife Essie, Robeson accepted an offer from the Korda Brothers, producer Alexander and director Zoltan, to appear in a film based on the Edgar Wallace novel *Sanders of the River*. In the summer of 1934 the Kordas certainly seemed to have what Robeson was looking for: Forerunners of David Lean's brand of cinema, they liked epics with personal stories at the center. In fact, they would be the team that made *Cry, the Beloved Country* in 1952, a critique of South African apartheid which certainly would have appealed to Robeson's sensibilities. In 1934 they had taken on a project that appealed to Robeson even more: They wanted to create the most incisive film look to date at African tribal culture. To that end they had already spent five months in Central Africa and had shot 160,000 feet of film, which included virtually every aspect of native life. Robeson screened the footage, which showed indigenous music, dancing, and rituals, with great interest, deeming it "magnificent." Full of optimism, he turned down an offer from the Chicago Opera to do two performances as Amonasro in *Aida*, an engagement that would have brought him a thousand depression-day dollars per performance and nation-wide publicity. The role Robeson was to play was not, of course, Sanders, an officer of the British Crown. Robeson would be Bosambo, a tribal chief—and the true protagonist of the film. "For the first time since I began acting," he told reporters, "I feel that I've found my place in the world, that there's something out of my own culture which I can express and perhaps help to preserve—for I'm not kidding myself that I've really gotten a place in Western culture, although I have been trained in it all my life" (p. 179).

Would that the film Robeson had in mind had ensued. Even as filming progressed at Shepperton, where the Kordas had recreated the Congolese village that would be the center of the film, things looked good. "Every scene and detail of the story is faithfully accurate," Robeson said early on. "I am sure [that this film] will do a lot towards the better understanding of Negro culture and customs." As for the Kordas, Robeson's wife Essie, who was on location, felt them worthy of nothing but praise: "They know their business thoroughly and are human beings" (p. 179).

Indeed. During the last five days of shooting, what had looked so promising turned very different. The Kordas now dropped in what Robeson called "an imperialist angle," flaunting a colonialist

sympathy utterly out of synch with the rest of the story. The point of the film is that a white presence in Africa is all that preserves it from barbarism and chaos. The film is racist enough to justify an outraged Robeson's 1938 statement that, "It is the only one of my films that can be shown in Italy and Germany, for it shows the Negro as Fascist States desire him — savage and childish" (pp. 179–180).

Sad to say, the film as it stands now offers us such outsized caricatures that it probably plays for audiences as campy fun. We know what we are in for from the credits: The British are called "Keepers of the King's Peace," and we are supposed to sympathize with them (after all, they are surrounded by savage Nigerian hordes that are "governed by a handful of white men"). The effort comes off like some grotesque combination of an especially bad Tarzan movie and an especially prissy *Masterpiece Theater*. The location footage is intercut in a way which makes the Africans look almost bestial. That meticulous collection of authentic African music — it gets lost. Robeson's tribal chief is repeatedly called upon to sing a "war-song" that one critic described as sounding irritatingly like the marching song from *The Vagabond King*. Beyond the anachronistic music we have the dialogue, at times transcendently bad. Sanders to a native: "You go now, and if you pester me again my arm will go mad." A premonition of Dr. Strangelove, perhaps?

The credits also boast the casting of "authentic tribal members," and this, in a way, is true. Most of the 250 extras in the film were blacks recruited from English port towns, and they had largely been born in Africa. They even came from the tribes being depicted. But when they dance to what sounds like light opera, they lose all credibility, and, thanks to the Kordas, they are therefore placed in the unhappy position of betraying their own culture. Note the noxious advertising blurb used for the film's initial release: "A million mad savages fighting for one beautiful woman! ... until three white comrades alone pitched into the fray and quelled the bloody revolt" (p. 180). Robeson felt actual guilt over the film — although not more, I hope, than whoever it was who wrote that blurb. Nonetheless, Robeson said: "I committed a faux pas which, when I reviewed it in retrospect, convinced me that I had failed to weigh the problems of 150 million native Africans. I hate the picture" (p. 182).

Robeson tried again in Britain — in 1936, the same year he would film *Show Boat* in this country. But *Show Boat* was, for him, rehashed stage work — and the British *Song of Freedom*, by contrast, looked very promising. In fact, it is nowhere near as bad as *Sanders of the River*. Robeson plays a London dock worker — a singing dock worker, of course — who is revealed to be the legendary King of the African province of Casanga. We know this from the beginning of the film, but John Zinga, the character Robeson plays, does not find it out until after he has emoted on the docks enough to be discovered and launched as a concert singer. He abandons that career to return to his people, taking with him his wife. Mrs. Zinga, scene-stealingly portrayed by Elizabeth Welch, is a no-nonsense sort who works as an equal partner with John pretty much throughout the film. While *Song of Freedom* has its share and more of silly moments, it does live up to Robeson's claim that he had been given "a real part to play for the first time." His John Zinga is intelligent and shrewd, and nobody's lackey. *Song of Freedom*, by the way, came from Hammer Films — the same group which, in the 1950s, would offer all those Christopher Lee horror movies to the drive-in trade in this country.

The year 1937 would bring three British efforts from Robeson. The first, *King Solomon's Mines*, is a reasonably faithful adaptation of the H. Rider Haggard novel. Robeson plays Umbopa, initially a servant but — once again — in fact an African chief, who in the course of the story helps the white men find the legendary mines and regains his own throne in the process. The real problem with this film, even more so than in others, is the discordant use of modern music — show tunes, really — which Robeson must sing. The film did boast 27,000 extras, not one of whom seems to like the music any better than Robeson. It is in this film that I first noticed a posture on Robeson's part that would stay with him throughout ensuing cinematic performances. He's up there and he's turning in the day's work — but in his eyes you can read another comment. "This isn't my real job," he seems to be saying, in a sort of private communion with the audience — much the same look Elvis bore through most of his film work. You come to appreciate that look after screening several Robeson films: It becomes a window on a suffering performer who is aware of the shabby material with which he is dealing.

The second 1937 film, *Big Fella*, was a mistake from the outset. It was another Hammer project, to be directed by J. Elder Wills, who had done *Song of Freedom*, and to costar Elizabeth Welch, who had acquitted herself so well in that earlier film. The project also offered a character role as a cafe proprietress for Essie Robeson, which she took to with relish. But Essie seems to be the only one who had any fun; this story of yet another singing dockside worker who finds a runaway and then, at the parents' behest, helps rear the boy, is pure corn syrup. Robeson's role even veers dangerously close to the kind of stereotyping he had sworn to avoid: His character reverts far too easily to the carefree life of the docks at film's end. Oddly, the original title was changed: It was *Banjo*, the name of Robeson's character. Why that name conjured plantation humor as a title and not as a character name is mysterious — but Robeson deserves great credit for doing what he could with the part in any case; between incongruous songs and layers of script sweetness he does manage to make at least some flesh and blood out of celluloid. His Banjo is a decent anyman who happens to be black, and Robeson gives him a nice, lived-in feeling.

Jericho, the last 1937 film, was shot partly in Egypt. The Robesons spent a month in Cairo and were taken with it. Essie Robeson wrote: "We can find a double in Harlem for everyone we've seen here. It's great fun to see an enormously rich country like this, where the colored folks are the bosses!" (p. 209). This would be in stark contrast to the film itself, for in the making of *Jericho* nobody seems to have been in charge. The basic problem is a plot with too many things happening. Robeson plays Jericho Jackson, a medical student drafted into the army, who rescues some other soldiers but who gets court-martialed anyway, deserts while everybody else is singing Christmas carols, and makes his way to North Africa. There he becomes a sort of Lawrence of the Nile, until he meets and marries the daughter of a desert chieftain, living out his days as a hero because he has brought medicine to these people. Honest, I didn't make that up. Along the way he sings, of course — usually at inopportune moments. The whole thing doesn't work — or, to quote critic Bosley Crowther: "...out of respect to Paul Robeson and his magnificent baritone voice, the less said about *Jericho* the better" (p. 210).

What remains is *The Proud Valley*, from 1940. This was Robeson's favorite film, and it is easy to see why. A sort of musical version of *How Green Was My Valley*, the film depicts the struggles of Welsh coal miners in 1938. Robeson plays David Goliath, an unfortunate name for a pretty good character. David is a wanderer who takes up residence in the community of miners, initially embraced, as usual, because he can sing. But in this film he just sings better, since these miners become a soaring choir at the drop of a pickax. Given that conceit, however, the rest of *The Proud Valley* plays rather realistically, especially the elements having to do with labor organization, a leftist theme that appealed to Robeson's politics. And race is handled in a way that, in the year after *Gone with the Wind*, must have seemed downright refreshing. "Don't like him because he's black," the foreman asks his men of Robeson. "Aren't we all black down in the pits?"

The Proud Valley was produced by Michael Balcon, a legend of British cinema who had a hand in projects ranging from Robert Flaherty's classic *Man of Aran* to Oscar-winner *Tom Jones*. If for nothing else, though, Balcon would be known for his early discovery of a shy, overweight title card designer named Alfred Hitchcock, who did very well for Balcon and for himself. Clearly Balcon knew talent, and he was eager to work with Robeson. The young director of *The Proud Valley*, Pen Tennyson, who Robeson liked very much, would end up a tragic footnote in film history: He was killed early in World War II after having completed only three films. For that matter, the Robesons themselves barely escaped wartime danger. As they wrapped the picture, London mobilized its anti-aircraft guns and blackouts went into effect. Robeson went to the set before dawn and returned to his flat each night by underground tunnel. It was a harrowing time, but Robeson felt the film was worth it. He believed in this one.

At the end of *The Proud Valley* Robeson's character dies in the mines after saving the lives of his fellow workers. In this outcome it is possible to find a reasonable symbol for Robeson's own political battles and his last years of isolation. It is also perhaps possible to find a metaphor about

Top: Still from *The Proud Valley.* Courtesy of Paul Robeson, Jr. *Bottom:* Soviet film director Sergei Eisenstein greets Paul Robeson on his initial visit to the Soviet Union in 1914. Courtesy of Paul Robeson, Jr.

Robeson and film. He had the highest hopes, most of them never realized, that his concerns would be realized in British film in ways they were not being realized in the United States. But the bottom line for the movie industry then and now is the box office. The films of this period mostly made money, and those profits enriched the state of a predominantly white industry, just as they would have in this country. And Robeson was left feeling not only cheated but sacrificed to the compromises of Caucasian commerce — abused on both sides of the Atlantic. It remains a sad coda that Robeson, while visiting his beloved Russia, did meet the great Sergei Eisenstein, who saw in this American a great potential film talent. They planned to collaborate, but somewhere between upheaval in Russia and upheaval in America, this was lost to time, another hopeless hope.

In sum, the British film industry did badly by Robeson. Deeply committed to the possibilities of the medium and always ready to rise to the demands of a worthwhile role, Robeson was seduced by promised significance and abandoned by cutting room conventionality. But he believed, in the words of the late Jimmy Stewart, that film could be what we all want it to be: precious little pieces of time. And so he tried, again and again. He didn't win the struggle: He was clearly no stranger to that. I began this paper with Robeson's rewrite of a slave lament, but I might look to the poetry of the equally oppressed Irish to close it: Because Robeson had such hopes, with film as with life, he did take up his ladder where all those ladders start — in the foul rag and bone shop of the heart.

Paul Robeson and Classical Music

WILLIAM PENCAK
The Pennsylvania State University

Paul Robeson's career as a musician mirrored his refusal to disavow his political radicalism and support of international revolution. Unlike the other great African-American singer of his day who possessed a flawless classical technique, Marian Anderson (1897–1993), Robeson refused to sing opera or German, French, and Italian art songs—the core of the classical repertoire: "I do not understand the psychology or philosophy of the Frenchman, German, or Italian. Their history has nothing in common with the history of my slave ancestors. So I will not sing their music or the songs of their ancestors."[1] Compared to great opera singers Lawrence Tibbett, Enrico Caruso, and Feodor Chaliapin — all of whom sang popular and folk songs— Robeson nevertheless refused to accept a role in *Aida* and become "one of the hundred mediocre singers" who ventured into the classical realm.[2]

Part of the reason Robeson shunned the world of opera was that he described his voice as "embarrassingly delicate," and incapable of projecting in large houses.[3] The *London Times* confirmed this assessment in 1936, noting that he did "not easily sustain a song even of the caliber of Gretchaninoff's 'A Player.'"[4] But Robeson would no more perform elite music than he would espouse elite ideas, and opted instead for performing the songs of the oppressed to audiences all over the world in both their own and the original languages. Introducing a collection of "Songs of the Red Army and Navy," he wrote:

> In many lands the arts, and especially music, have been cut off from the general life of the nation. They have become the source of enjoyment for a comparative few — a so-called elite — who feel that culture should be somewhat unapproachable except to their own understanding — and at times completely nonunderstanding — selves.

Noting that, thanks to the New Deal, America had begun "cultural sharing" of "the great creations of mind and spirit" through government-sponsored art and music, he regretted that during the 1940s this promising trend was cut off by "those forces that even today refuse to make the slightest sacrifice for the advancement of the good life — that do not really want an enlightened and sensitive citizenry."[5]

Early in his career Robeson felt a "responsibility to his people, who rightfully resented the traditional stereotyped portrayals of Negroes on stage and screen." He therefore resolved that "if the Hollywood and Broadway producers did not choose to offer me worthy roles to play, then I would choose not to accept any other kind of offer."[6] Similarly, he devoted the first five years of his concert career exclusively to singing African-American songs, and then expanded his programs to include the songs of other oppressed groups.[7] The songs of the Russian and "Jewish people, with whom I have been especially close,"[8] were particularly dear to him. Notable among these performances are his bilingual renditions of "The Song of the Volga Boatmen," in which the boatmen's chant merges imperceptibly into both the Russian and English verses, and the defiant "Song of the Warsaw Ghetto" in both English and Yiddish: "It was a people midst the crashing fires of hell, That sang this song and fought courageous 'till they fell." To the traditional Hebrew prayer of the oppressed, "Good Day to Thee O Lord God," he adds the Germans to the Romans, Persians, and Babylonians as tyrants from whom the Jews cry to be relieved.

Similarly, Robeson would regularly perform the popular Jerome Kern/Oscar Hammerstein show tune "Ol' Man River," which many have mistaken for a spiritual. But he continued to sing it apart from the musical *Show Boat* — whose plot deals with prejudice against a "white" performer who is discovered to be part black — only because it eloquently expressed the plight of African Americans. Robeson also changed the words to ennoble those who suffered and struggled, but thereby provoking a quarrel with lyricist Hammerstein who told Robeson to write his own songs rather than change his. Robeson altered the final line from "I'm tired of living and scared of dying" to "I must keep fighting until I'm dying." Two other changes substituted "There's an old man called the Mississippi" for "Niggers [later darkies] all working on the Mississippi" to open the song, and "you show a little spunk [for you get a little drunk] and you land in jail."[9] Robeson transforms the frightened Joe who accepts his plight and drinks to relieve his anguish into a militant waiting to explode.

On the other hand, Robeson rejected most classical music for reasons of principle. As he wrote in the *London Daily Herald* on January 5, 1935: "With the Renaissance reason and intellect were placed above intuition and feeling. The result has been a race which conquered Nature and now rules the world. But the art of that race has paid the price. As science has advanced, the art standards of the West have steadily declined. Intellectual art grows tenuous, sterile."[10] One of the few operatic pieces Robeson performed, perhaps only once, was Orfeo's invocation — a song of despair mourning his Eurydice — from the opera of that name by Jacopo Peri, one of the first operas written at the turn of the seventeenth century before tonality had triumphed.[11] Robeson preferred anonymous songs, "the creation of a mass of people ... derived from social communication" among "the oppressed": "I have sung my songs all over the world.... I found that where the forces have been the same, whether people weave, build, pick cotton, or dig in the mines, they understand each other in the common language of work, suffering, and protest."[12]

Nevertheless, Robeson did, on occasion, sing classical music, and with great beauty. Furthermore, he brought to whatever he sang — spirituals, protest songs, or folk ballads — the most subtle expression and perfectly refined classical singing technique. That is, he never resorted to the whispers, shouts, grunts, and sobs that

Paul Robeson sings, accompanied by his long-time associate Larry Brown, at the Moscow Conservatory, 1936. Courtesy of Paul Robeson, Jr.

even classical artists use to milk their audiences for cheap sentimental thrills. For instance, in "Joe Hill" he emphasizes the word "strike" to great effect by not breaking the line but merely raising the volume. In "Were You There When They Crucified My Lord?" he colors his voice to create a sense of nearly unendurable sorrow without the slightest distortion or loss of tone when singing very softly. Furthermore, Robeson always resisted the temptation to end songs on loud high notes: "I have never tried to sing A-flat while the audience held on the edge of its collective seat to see if I could make it."[13] The British critic W. H. Breare expressed it best:

> Paul Robeson ... has an extraordinary voice, but he knows how to use it so that the tones and phrases pour forth without effort — naturally, [in] the full sense of the term. His tone is always lyrical, it flows like a deep river which has not a

ripple on its surface.... One hears almost incessantly in others a beautiful tone spoilt by a sudden harsh element introduced therein by some fault of vocal production. It is Robeson's knowledge of the office of the breath which enables him to achieve the emotional shades or effect which is as real as life...[14]

Robeson claimed that, "I care nothing — less than nothing — about what the lords of the land, the Big White Folks, think of me and my ideas."[15] Yet by performing the people's music using a superb classical technique he was in effect reaching out to them, too, demonstrating that folk songs and spirituals could be as beautiful as Schubert or Mozart. Nothing gave Robeson more pleasure than to discover a classical composer such as Stravinsky "borrowing from Negro melodies," which he found much more fruitful than "Negro musicians ... labouring with Beethoven and Brahms."[16] He praised modern classical composers Mussorgsky, Bartók, Janáček, Vaughan Williams, Duke Ellington [note the inclusion!], George Gershwin, and others for incorporating the "old Pentatonic modal folk music ... just as Bach based much of his music on the ancient modal folk chorales."[17] In the same manner, Robeson noted that African culture "deeply influenced the great artists of our time—a Picasso, a Modigliani, a Brancusi, an Epstein."[18] He also took great pleasure in noting that among those people he saw in the Soviet Union, thanks to the government's cultural education program, "art was closely wedded to life." "Eager and enthusiastic audiences" heard "Bach, Mozart, Beethoven, Chopin, Debussy, Moussorgsky, Tchaikovsky, Prokofieff, Shostakovitch, [and] Gershwin" as "their daily bread and wine."[19]

While Robeson's insistence that the pentatonic (five-note, piano back key) scale lay at the root of all folk music is dubious,[20] what cannot be questioned is his belief that the highest pinnacle classical music could achieve only approached "the mainstream of world music" by incorporating folk melodies.[21] Just as he claimed that "the character of a nation is determined not by the upper classes, but by the common people, and that the common people of all nations are truly brothers in the great family of mankind,"[22] the quality of classical music improved as it approached the purity of folksong.

Hence, when Robeson did perform classical music, he presented it as folksong. He sang it either in the common language of his audience or alternated verses in the original language with a translation his auditors would understand. He thereby sought to demonstrate the consonance of people's music and struggles throughout the world. Furthermore, all the classical music he sang was about struggling against oppression or a plea for universal harmony

and brotherhood. He offered Smetana's "Zvornost" or "Freedom" in both Czech and English. A religious man, Robeson sang Bach's "Christ Lay in the Bonds of Death," which begins sorrowfully but then proclaims the resurrection. Robeson commenced his piano-voice version of Beethoven's "Ode to Joy" from the Ninth Symphony, retitled as the "Song of Peace," with the words "Brothers, sing your country's anthem, Shout your land's undying fame," which at first glance has a tinge of the jingoism he abhorred. But the glory of this nation, which could be any or all nations, is the achievement of peace and fraternity: "None shall push aside another, none shall let another fall; March beside me, O! my brother, All for one and one for all."[23] Robeson hints at what a marvelous Sarastro he would have made in Mozart's *The Magic Flute* with his recording of "O Isis and Osiris." With these words the benevolent ruler of a realm devoted to universal brotherhood blesses a young couple about to embark on their struggle against the forces of evil. He also performed Beethoven's "Creator's Hymn"—the song "Die Ehre Gottes aus der Natur"—in which all nature proclaims the glory of the creator.[24]

Robeson sang Mendelssohn's "Lord God of Abraham" from the oratorio *Elijah* on various occasions as yet another prayer for deliverance from oppression.[25] In the film *The Proud Valley* he did so as a miner performing as soloist with a choral society. Unlike the films of contemporary singers Josef Schmidt, John McCormack, and Beniamino Gigli—who respectively mixed their operatic repertoires with German, Irish, and Italian folk and popular songs—Robeson did not star in films that were basically excuses to film a recital. An actor before he was a singer, Robeson and his art became, in film as in life, an integral part of the struggle being portrayed.

A composer dear to Robeson's heart was Modest Mussorgsky (1839–1881). Even here, however, he only seems to have performed carefully chosen selections: the songs "Saul," "The Song of the Orphan," "After the Battle," and "The Song of the Flea," and Boris's "Clock" and "Death" scenes from *Boris Godunov*. Based on a poem of Byron, "Saul" urges the Israelites to conquer or die; the poor orphan is near death as he begs in vain for food from a "dear, kind, good gentleman"; Death roams the battlefield among the corpses as the only victor; courtiers are forbidden by a capricious monarch to scratch themselves lest they injure his pet flea, a satire on the absurdities of upper-class etiquette and obsequiousness. "The Death of Boris" is the touching good-bye of a tragic ruler to his people in troubled times. In the opera's "Clock Scene"— which Robeson performed at his 1958 return to Carnegie Hall — the troubled monarch who sought to save his people but was undone by conspiracies all around him becomes a symbol of Robeson's own persecution.[26]

The classical composer Robeson discussed most favorably was the Czech Antonín Dvořák (1841–1904), who lived in the United States and incorporated Negro folk melodies into some of his compositions. Robeson recorded, in English, "Songs My Mother Taught Me," and "Going Home," the spiritual-inspired folk tune that is the germ of the second movement of the "New World Symphony" No. 9. The classical song he discussed most in depth was Dvořák's "By the Waters of Babylon," which he recorded in Czech. In this "searing outcry of an enslaved people against their oppressors ... from ancient Judea these words of the 137th Psalm had crossed the vast reaches of time and distance to stir the hearts of the Negro slaves in our own Southland." African-American abolitionist Frederick Douglass compared the American South to Babylon in describing the evils of slavery and predicting ultimate deliverance. "Half a century later the gifted

Dvořák came to our country, studied the melodies and lyrics of Negro song, and drew upon its richness for his own creations— and so, in this way, the words of this very song must have traveled back across the ocean with him; and I am told the song was especially popular among the Czech people during their years of suffering under the terror of nazi occupation."[27]

Perhaps the culmination of Robeson's effort to use music to unify the peoples of the world was his performance of "The Song of the Rivers." Unable to leave the United States in the fifties because his radicalism appeared sufficiently close to Communism — he was friends with leading Communists and praised Communist countries, although he never belonged to the party — Robeson was obliged to make the recording for this film with music by Dmitri Shostakovich and words by Bertolt Brecht from his brother's Harlem residence. Honoring the people who worked on the Mississippi, Ganges, Yangtze, Volga, Amazon, and Nile rivers, Robeson sang the words in several languages.[28]

Robeson was not alone in his musical ideas. He was a friend of British composer Ralph Vaughan Williams (1872–1959),[29] whose four lectures at Cornell University in 1954, published under the title *The Making of Music*, also argued the need for modern classical music to incorporate folk tunes to regenerate itself. Vaughan Williams maintained that what was most appealing in the great composers derived from their ability to develop folk material beautifully: "It never occurs to ... people that Mozart, Beethoven, and Schubert came from the humbler classes and were doubtless imbued from childhood with the popular music of their country ... we can claim Mozart and Beethoven as nationalists as much as Dvořák and Grieg."[30] Among Americans, Vaughan Williams praised Aaron Copland —"the tradition of the white spiritual unconsciously affects his music"[31]— Gershwin, and "the beautiful melodies of Stephen Foster." These composers towered over "those American composers who wrote symphonic poems, for which they were not emotionally ready, [and] are forgotten, while the work of those who attempted less but achieved more has become the foundation on which a great art can rise."[32]

In a related vein, critic Henry Pleasants has argued that "serious music is a dead art.... What we know as modern music is the noise made by deluded speculators picking through the slagpile." Pleasants, too, finds African-American music, especially jazz and blues, a solution to the woes of moribund classicism: "It is ... possible to see the history of American popular music in the twentieth century as a successful effort by practicing musicians to fight free of the obstacles to spontaneous musical invention represented by formal composition.... The jazz accomplishment is simply defined. It has taken music away from the composers and given it back to the musicians and their public."[33]

Unlike Pleasants, Robeson had mixed feelings about blues and jazz. He never performed jazz, although he did record "The St. Louis Blues" in 1934, and in 1941 teamed up with Count Basie and lyricist Richard Wright to produce a blues tribute to boxer Joe Louis. Classical critic Irving Kolodin praised Robeson's contribution as "majestic" and the whole song as "a high credit to everyone involved."[34] Robeson noted that in effect he had heard the blues in the songs "of my father's people from the plantations of North Carolina," as sung in the form of hymns by African-American congregations.[35] But he found spirituals and folk songs preferable to blues because the latter "express[ed] the emotional state of the individual," frequently a lament for a lost love, instead of the collective strivings of a people, as in folk, work, or protest songs. After completing a successful program of Polish, Russian, and Romanian songs in the Soviet Union, Robeson refused the crowd's demand for "The St. Louis Blues."[36]

Similarly, Robeson praised jazz musicians such as Dizzy Gillespie and Charlie Parker: "I ... have been both stimulated by their imaginative creations and a little astounded by their incredible technique and musicianship."[37] Others he considered "memorable" were Count Basie, Chick Webb, Ella Fitzgerald, and the "incomparable" Duke Ellington and Modern Jazz Quartet — whom he compared to Shakespeare and the Elizabethans. Thelonious Monk "floored" him.[38] He grouped jazz with the songs of Stephen Foster as a "brilliant instance" of "the immense influence which Negro folk music has had on the development of the musical culture of the peoples of the USA." But while he admired virtuosity of jazz musicians, Robeson could be critical of what he considered their spiritual failure. He claimed that "commercial jazz has prostituted and ruthlessly perverted many splendid models of Negro folk music and has corrupted and debased many talented Negro musicians in order to satisfy the desires of a capitalist society."[39]

Perhaps this judgment provides a clue as to why Robeson the musician, apart from his political radicalism, is less honored today than he ought to be. Folk music was important in the 1930s and 1960s when communal protest movements searched for anthems which could be remembered and sung by masses of people. But as American society has become more conservative, individualistic, and integrated, if not less exploitative and covertly racist, jazz and blues and those who perform them have become the foundation of the nation's musical culture, a small minority of classical aficionados excepted. Like Joe Hill, Paul Robeson still lives through his art, although his CDs are hardly best sellers.

But as he would be the first to point out, music signifies the circumstances and aspirations of a community. That the age-old music he championed is not America's music at the new millennium is not a criticism of him, but of us. Perhaps we need to recover Paul Robeson's dream that a society can be more than a mishmash of fundamentalist fanaticism, security-obsessed selfishness, pecuniary corruption, and a war against the poor rather than a war against poverty to appreciate his art in its full glory.

Abbreviations

RG — *A Paul Robeson Research Guide, A Selective Annotated Bibliography,* Lenwood G. Davis, compiler (Westport, Conn.: Greenwood Press, 1982).

MD — Martin Duberman, *Paul Robeson: A Biography* (New York: Alfred A. Knopf, 1988).

PRS — *Paul Robeson Speaks, 1918–1974,* Philip S. Foner, editor (Larchmont, N.Y.: Brunner/Mazel, 1978).

HIS — Paul Robeson, *Here I Stand* (New York: Othello Associates, 1958).

PRCM — The Paul Robeson Collection Microfilm (Bethesda, Md.: University Publications of America, 1972), copies of material at the Schomburg Branch of the New York Public Library, with a guide by David H. Werning.

Notes

1. Paul Robeson, interview in *New York World-Telegram,* August 30, 1933, in PRS, 85.

2. For Tibbett, *New York Daily News,* October 21, 1935; Caruso, *New York Daily News,* April 25, 1925; Chaliapin, *New York Evening Post,* May 5, 1925, in RG, 361, 329.

3. M. Danishewsky, *Picture Goer Weekly,* London, October 26, 1935, 28, in RG, 361.

4. *London Times,* January 20, 1936, in RG, 361.

5. Paul Robeson, "Introduction to Songs of the Red Army and Navy" (1941), PRCM, reel 2, #365–367.

6. HIS, 59.

7. HIS, 57.

8. HIS, 12.

9. MD, 369, 604; *New York Age,* June 18, 1949, in RG, 482.

10. Paul Robeson, interview in *London Daily Herald,* January 5, 1935, in PRS, 92.

11. Concert program, Jefferson City, Missouri, January 23, 1947, PRCM, reel 2, #645. Since there is no complete collection of Robeson concert programs, it is impossible to rule out that he sang other classical works. However, that with few exceptions (such as this) the same composers and songs keep reappearing suggests strongly he limited himself to these pieces, many of which he recorded — see discography in RG 771–779.

12. Paul Robeson, interview with Julia Dorn, summer 1939, PRS, 130–131.

13. Notes to Monitor record album MPS 580.

14. W. H. Breare, "Paul Robeson's Technique," *The British Musician and Musical News,* vol. 9, no. 7, July 1933, 158–159, in RG, 358.

15. HIS, 12.

16. Paul Robeson, interview in *London Daily Herald,* January 5, 1935, PRS, 92.

17. Spellings are Robeson's in his "Some Aspects of Afro-American Music," December 1956, in PRS, 439.

18. Paul Robeson, "The Negro Artist Looks Ahead," November 5, 1951, in PRS, 300.

19. Paul Robeson, "Introduction to Songs of the Red Army and Navy" (1941), PCRM, reel 2, #365–367.

20. MD, 438.

21. Paul Robeson, "Some Aspects of Afro-American Music," PRS, 439.

22. HIS, 56.

23. Words printed on occasion of First English performance on March 11, 1956, at Manchester, program in PRCM, reel 2, #733.

24. Concert programs, New Orleans, October 23, 1942, and New York, October 9, 1952, PRCM, reel 2 #s 600, 708.

25. Concert programs, New Orleans, October 23, 1942, and Jefferson City, Missouri, January 23, 1947, PRCM, reel 2, #s600, 645.

26. See discography in RG, 771–779; concert programs for New Orleans, October 23, 1942, Roxbury, Massachusetts, November 4, 1952, New York, February 6, 1955 (at which he also sang the Schubert "Lullaby"), PRCM, reel, #s 600, 675, 718.

27. Paul Robeson, "Bonds of Brotherhood," *Jewish Life,* November 1954, PRS, 392–393.

28. HIS, 406, 435, 449.

29. PRS, 406, 435, 449.

30. Ralph Vaughan Williams, *The Making of Music* (Ithaca, New York: Cornell University Press, 1954), 50–51.

31. *Ibid.,* 25.

32. *Ibid.,* 59.

33. Henry Pleasants, *The Agony of Modern Music* (New York: Simon and Schuster, 1955), 3, 175–176; see also his *Serious Music and All That Jazz* (New York: Simon and Schuster, 1969).

34. Discography, RG, 775; *New York Sun,* November 28, 1941, in RG, 466.

35. Paul Robeson, "The Related Sounds of Music," September 1957, in PRS, 443.

36. Harrison E. Salisbury, *Americans in Russia* (New York: Harper and Brothers, 1985), 194–195, in RG, 257.

37. Paul Robeson, in *People's Voice,* November 29, 1947, 14, in RG, 44.

38. Paul Robeson, "Thoughts on Music," in *Paul Robeson: Tribute and Selected Writings,* ed. Roberta Dent, et al., (New York: Paul Robeson Archives, 1976), 72–73, in RG, 115.

39. Paul Robeson, "Songs of My People," July 1949, originally published in Russian, in PRS, 213, 217.

"A Symbol, Representing My People": Marian Anderson's Way, *Not* Opposed to Paul Robeson's

WILLIAM PENCAK
The Pennsylvania State University

On Easter Sunday, April 14, 1939, Marian Anderson sang at the Lincoln Memorial in Washington, D.C. Some 75,000 people, about half of them black, attended; the concert was broadcast by radio throughout the nation, and filmed. Through this performance, the Memorial and its environs were transformed from a site that commemorated past achievements into a vast outdoor theater where people, especially black Americans, have ever since called attention to discrepancies between America's claim to stand for liberty, justice, and equality and the nation's actual practices.

This transformation of the Memorial from shrine to civic forum was effected by "The Lady from Philadelphia"—as a 1957 Edward R. Murrow television documentary about her concert tour through Asia was called. For unlike Paul Robeson, who changed the words of "Ol' Man River" to say "I must keep fighting until I'm dying,"

Anderson refused to answer insults, criticize racists, or participate in partisan politics. Instead, in keeping with the life of the Savior in whom she devoutly believed, she hoped to shame and then transform bigots through the dignity of her person and the quality of her art. In an interview she granted in her nineties to the Greater Washington Educational Telecommunications Association (WETA) for a documentary of her life that appeared in 1991, "Miss Anderson," as everyone referred to her, explained that she "wasn't a fighter" like Robeson, although she emphasized that such people were "very, very necessary." She rather numbered herself among those "who hope that if they are doing something worthwhile it will speak for them."

Marian Anderson did not seek out her role as a major figure in the history of civil rights. Born in Philadelphia in 1897, she sang almost exclusively in black churches and other segregated venues until 1924, at which time members of her congregation — the Union Baptist Church — raised enough money to send her abroad. The supportive environment of churches and friends in what was perhaps the nation's most secure and conservative black community led to her life-long faith and efforts to avoid controversy. As her accompanist, the Finnish pianist Kosti Vehanen, wrote: "this was one of her most beautiful characteristics — she is so far removed from anything that might be considered sensational or in opposition to any one or any organization…. She likes to win any victory purely with the implement of her great art."[1]

But victories she did win, and students of the civil rights movement may endlessly debate the value of her strategy as compared to more militant ones. As she wrote in her autobiography, furthering the cause of civil rights was one purpose of her great musical gift, which dawned on her when she decided to perform the Lincoln Memorial Concert: "I don't like a lot of show…. I studied my conscience. In principle the idea was sound, but it could not be comfortable to me as an individual. As I thought further, I could see that my significance as an individual was small in this affair. I had become, whether I liked it or not, a symbol, representing my people."[2]

But Anderson had, in fact, been such a symbol from her first appearances in Europe, where she integrated the realm of classical music, much as Josephine Baker did the theatrical avant-garde at the same time. Anderson was a sensation, sometimes singing over a hundred concerts a year between 1924 and 1935, from Britain to Scandinavia and the Soviet Union. She won praise from conductor Arturo Toscanini who claimed that a voice like hers was heard only once in a century, a remark publicized all over the world. Only in 1935, when impresario Sol Hurok signed her up

for a concert tour of the United States, did she begin to win recognition in her own country. Here, too, her popularity was instantaneous, with *New York Times* music critic Howard Taubman praising her as one of the world's greatest singers in reviewing her Town Hall debut.

Although "no fighter," Anderson played an important role in the civil rights struggle even before the Washington Concert. First, in Europe, she had integrated her programs: Black spirituals appeared alongside opera arias and European art songs. Her recordings, too, reflected this variety. As European critics and music-lovers proclaimed her equality with the greatest singers in the world, her choice of songs proclaimed the spirituals of her people were just as beautiful as the masterpieces of classical composers. John McCormack, the great Irish tenor, had earlier done the same for his people's music.

Second, upon her arrival in the United States, Anderson and her manager, Sol Hurok, arranged for her to sing in the South, where segregation in theaters had previously meant blacks sat in the balcony, whites in the orchestra. But the words "separate but equal" could also provide a loophole to subvert separation in the name of equality. All of her contracts insisted that seating in both orchestra and balcony be divided between the races. Eventually, she banned separate seating from her concerts entirely, even though she realized that thereby many people who wanted to see her could not. As Hurok noted: "She makes no complaint, creates no issues, offers no angry protest at the indignities that have been visited upon her because of her color…. And by being herself she has won citadels that have never been breached by doughtier warriors."[3]

Thanks to Marian Anderson, American blacks did more than see a black woman applauded by whites for the highest cultural achievements. Especially in the

South, many of them, for the first time, actually made their way into the concert hall, in seats just as good as their white neighbors, where they were exposed to her effective juxtaposition of spirituals with the classics. Conversely, many American whites heard a black artist sing what they considered to be "their" music better than they had ever heard before.

Anderson claimed that her appearances in the South were "victories." In her autobiography, she explained her strategy. People were prejudiced because of "fear," which she termed "a disease that eats away at logic and makes man inhuman." It was a lack of personal knowledge between blacks and whites that fueled segregation. Anderson noted that once, when an emergency situation compelled the races to travel together, "Negroes and whites talked to one another; they shared their newspapers and even their food. The world did not crumble." She was careful to note many kindnesses she received from whites throughout her life. "A whole group should not be condemned because an individual or section of the group does a thing that is not right," she argued, applying to whites the same logic they ought to apply to blacks. Anderson considered it her mission to create a favorable impression "that will make it easier for those who follow."[4]

Anderson would do even more for civil rights after Sol Hurok's initial arrangements for her Washington debut fell through. The best venue in the city was Constitution Hall, owned by the Daughters of the American Revolution. Interestingly, from the time the hall opened in October 1929 (the month the stock market crashed and the Great Depression began) until 1935, black artists, including tenor Roland Hayes—Anderson's personal hero, and with whom she had sung as a young woman in Philadelphia—had appeared in the hall. But as the New Deal reforms of the thirties turned much of America politically to the left, they provoked a reaction among some conservative institutions such as the DAR.

The manner in which the DAR denied Anderson use of the hall was, if anything, more insulting than the denial itself. At first, the management claimed the hall was booked on the day requested. When Hurok offered several alternative dates, they were booked too. Suspecting a lie, he enlisted another impresario who asked if the same dates were available for a white artist: they were. Only then did the hall's manager reveal a clause which read "white artists only" in the terms on which the auditorium could be leased, meanwhile expressing his personal opinion to Hurok's assistant Martin Feinstein: "No Negro will ever appear in this hall while I am the manager." The DAR's refusal to be forthcoming with the real reason for the refusal suggests changing times in America. Racists were becoming reluctant to be identified as such and preferred to find other means of keeping society separate and unequal.

Nevertheless, although a Gallup poll revealed 67 percent of the public supported Anderson's right to sing, the DAR had a legal point. They claimed to be following customs fairly universal throughout the land, and they were. For instance, to avoid staying in a segregated hotel in the nation's capital, Anderson was the invited guest of former Pennsylvania Governor Gifford Pinchot and his wife Cornelia Bryce, who was even more radical than Eleanor Roosevelt. Even when she sang in New York, Anderson was required to stay at a hotel in Harlem, the downtown hotels being segregated de facto. And it was ironic indeed that several members of the New York Metropolitan Opera—which only permitted Anderson to sing as its first black artist in 1955—joined in the protest. Among those who urged that she sing there was the Norwegian soprano Kirsten Flagstad—another apolitical woman who would be criticized, in her case for staying in her homeland during World War II to remain with her husband, a collaborator with the racist Nazi regime. Yet another signer was baritone Lawrence Tibbett, who sang *The Emperor Jones* at the Met because its doors were closed to Paul Robeson (who had triumphed in the role on film and stage).

But even then, the controversy was not over. "The Marian Anderson Concert Committee" next sought to rent the auditorium of the city's Central High School, which at the time was all-white. At first the District Board of Education denied the request, using as an excuse the premise that school grounds could not be used for profit-making concerts. When Congressman James McGranery, who represented the Philadelphia constituency where Anderson lived, asked them to produce their records of auditorium usage for the past five years, the Board changed its tune: In this "emergency" the auditorium could be used for the concert. But the Board's real objection came to the fore when Howard University, which was sponsoring the concert, and the black press insisted that the performance at Central High School would serve as a precedent for integrating educational facilities in the District. When the Board insisted that the contract for the premises acknowledge that no precedent was being set in this "emergency" situation, Anderson, Hurok, and the University turned down the offer.

As with the DAR, the Washington Board of Education had at first used a transparently fallacious argument, hoping the trouble would go away or that an America where segregation was still the rule rather than the exception would take its side. The DAR at first appealed to sanctity of contract — Constitution Hall had been rented — the School Board to the notion that public property ought not to be used for private ends. And in a technical sense, they won. Although Eleanor Roo-

sevelt resigned from the DAR — other liberal members started an abortive organization with the same initials, Descendants of the American Revolution — and both the DAR and the Board were widely criticized, the fact remained that there was no legal remedy available had Anderson, let us suppose, insisted on a lawsuit. In fact, at the time, segregation could be enforced in a number of arbitrary ways and ignored in others: Washington's National Theater permitted blacks to perform but not to sit in the theater, the exact opposite of Constitution Hall less than a mile away. Railroads allowed blacks to accompany whites in "segregated" cars as long as they were clearly servants or nurses. And as Anderson noted when crowds rushed backstage to congratulate her after concerts, segregation was never practiced there.

In retrospect, no one considers the fact that Anderson was excluded from the two halls a defeat. In fact, her world-famous concert, attended by Supreme Court justices, congressmen, and cabinet members, was a victory for civil rights — just as the Scopes Trial, another technical defeat, was a victory for evolution. The Roosevelts did not attend — Eleanor was on tour, and Franklin's New Deal coalition included a lot of Southern Democrats — but made amends by inviting Anderson to the White House to meet the King and Queen of England. Harold Ickes, the Secretary of the Interior whose department arranged the concert, introduced Anderson in a speech.

Although it may be uncharitable to criticize so well-intentioned a man who did so much good by staging the concert, it is hard to overlook the fact that Ickes turned Anderson's performance into the gift of two great dead white men. His speech paid tribute not only to Lincoln the Emancipator, but to Thomas Jefferson — the author of the Declaration of Independence, rather than the slaveowner, one must presume, although in the year *Gone with the Wind* appeared on the screen, few sensed probably any contradiction. Ickes stated: "For genius has touched with the tip of her wing this woman, who, if it had not been for the great mind of Jefferson, if it had not been for the great heart of Lincoln, would not be able to stand among us today a free individual in a free land." Anderson herself appears here as the passive recipient of a gift of genius that owes thanks to a great nation and its great men. Ickes did not mention the efforts of black Philadelphians to finance her vocal education and the concert, or the good will Anderson had fostered through her tours as an historical agent in her own right.[5]

Anderson did not speak at the concert; she sang. She let her singing speak for her, as she did when she was presented with the Bok Award for the Philadelphian who had done the most for the city: "I am no speaker, but I do remember that I ended in song."[6] But her program suggests not only a celebration, but a critique of the nation that only had to give her the opportunity to sing out-of-doors because it had denied her the freedom to sing indoors, a freedom that was never a problem in the supposedly less-free countries of Europe. Perhaps I am overinterpreting what, after all, would have been a typical Marian Anderson concert. But friends who sing in gospel choirs tell me there is always a reason certain songs are chosen for a service or performance. And the Lincoln Memorial songs convey significant messages.

After she sang "America" or "My Country 'Tis of Thee," Anderson sang the program's only opera aria: "O mio Fernando" from Donizetti's *La Favorita*. It is the lament of the "favorite" Leonora, mistress of the King of Spain. She cannot marry the man she truly loves because he has learned of her previous status. It is not hard to see in Leonora's air the history of black women forced into concubinage with white masters, or black people denied legitimacy and acceptance by white Americans despite their sincere desire for equality that only turned to separatism and radicalism when spurned. At the conclusion of the song, Leonora desperately cries that she will only find happiness and pardon in Heaven.

The theme of Donizetti's aria is thus similar to that of the spirituals which concluded the concert: "Gospel Train," "Trampin'," and "My Soul Is Anchored in the Lord." Before them came Schubert's "Ave Maria," a piece Anderson loved so deeply that in the 1991 documentary she could only say that it had "its own message for me which transcended other things." Here a "maiden"—which Anderson probably was until she married several years later—prays for both herself and for others she names, for the good and happiness of the world.

Then followed the spirituals: The "Gospel Train" is leaving for a better world, and it makes sense to be a passenger. "Trampin'" is about trudging through this world on the way to a Heaven "where the streets are paved with gold." America, of course, held out this promise to immigrants and citizens, as well as to Southern blacks who came North (such as Anderson's mother, a schoolteacher in Virginia who became a floor cleaner at Wanamaker's Department Store in Philadelphia). By including this song, Anderson subtly suggested that the American dream is but a secular second-best to what should be the Christian's true purpose. As she later wrote, "the Negro made images out of the Bible that were as vaulting as his aspirations. He had a desire to escape from the confining restrictions and burdens of the life he led. The making and singing of a song constituted an act of liberation, even it if was one that lasted only briefly in the imagination."[7]

To reinforce this religious message

and the fact that America had not lived up to Ickes' praise, I suggest we compare the triumphant high note with which Anderson ended the concert — "My Soul Is Anchored in the Lord" — with the unusual way she sang "America." Here, she sings the tune in high registers except for the last line, where "Let Freedom Ring" drops down to her effective lower register. Why does not "freedom ring" with the same clarion tones as the first three lines of the song? Her vocal coloring suggests to me that she is affirming — or demanding — a freedom that does not yet command the same respect as the "fathers [who] died" and the "pilgrims." Also, for a black woman — especially one who will shortly sing about spiritual pilgrimage — fathers and pilgrims take on different meanings than those the song usually suggests. There is a tinge of defiance as well as sadness, at least as I hear Anderson's interpretation of "America."

Much like her slave ancestors, Anderson did not always tell people what was on her mind. For instance, she refused to answer questions about the Lincoln Memorial Concert in public. "I don't know anything except what you have all seen in the newspapers. I have no opinion to offer."[8] Even over a half-century later, when asked to comment on the event, Anderson maintained the same tact and implacable dignity. She would only say that she "thought it was an unfortunate time for the people who were involved," but, "it's over; it's like beating a dead horse." Privately, however, upon hearing of Eleanor Roosevelt's resignation from the DAR, she told her accompanist: "What a wonderful woman she is! She not only knows what is right, but she also does the right thing."[9]

I only detected one sign of anger in my studies of Miss Anderson. In the 1991 film she explains that the proudest day of her life was when she told her mother's supervisor at Wanamaker's that "Mother will not be in tomorrow. You can get someone else to clean your floor." Immediately, she qualified the remark: "Of course, I didn't say that, but I meant it." In her autobiography, Anderson was less reticent: "We would have been blind if we had not noticed how weary she was at times. It was borne in on me that she must be freed from her bondage."[10]

Anderson spoke sometimes of the need for humility; that is, the need to realize an exceptional person like herself could only exist if she were supported and appreciated by a host of "ordinary" people. "Whatever we have may depend upon what other people have done to make it possible — food, clothing, and even the way we live and work." Probably remembering her mother, she added that "a cleaning woman makes a contribution to the well-being of the most successful executive by keeping his office free of dirt and clutter.... Even the highest needs some contribution from those he may regard as the lowest."[11]

Like the Savior in whom she so fervently believed, as portrayed in "The Crucifixion," a spiritual which she sang with unbearable poignancy, Anderson "didn't say a mumblin' word." She sang out with vigor and beauty: That was her "speech." She was explicitly aware that she became "a symbol, representing my people," which she never could have done if she had taken a more intellectual or political approach to her career, thereby alienating a significant segment of the public by engaging in controversy. And she knew Paul Robeson was "very, very necessary" as well.

Notes

1. Kosti Vehanen, *Marian Anderson: A Portrait* (New York: McGraw-Hill, 1941), 241–42.

2. Marian Anderson, *My Lord, What a Morning* (New York: Viking, 1956), 189.

3. Sol Hurok, *Impresario* (New York: Random House, 1946), 123.

4. Anderson, *My Lord*, 36–37, 174–76, 189.

5. Vehanen, *Marian Anderson*, 243–44.

6. Anderson, *My Lord*, 196.

7. *Ibid.*, 187.

8. *Ibid.*, 136.

9. *Ibid.*, 238.

10. *Ibid.*, 67.

11. *Ibid.*, 173–76.

"You Know Who I Am!"
Paul Robeson's *Ballad for Americans* and the Paradox of the Double V in American Popular Front Culture

KEVIN JACK HAGOPIAN
The Pennsylvania State University

The "Double V" campaign — victory over fascism abroad, and victory over racism at home. The World War II era demanded a variation on W.E.B. Du Bois' famous "double consciousness" of black America — simultaneously to pull together with other groups in an unprecedented statement of national unity against the fascist threat from overseas, and to make a strong stand for its own group interest, for economic justice, and against fascism at home. The period of the war was studded with epochal demonstrations of incipient black power within the ideal of the Double V, including A. Philip Randolph's March on Washington movement, the Tuskegee Airmen, and the Port Chicago Mutiny.[1] The war years marked an emerging consciousness of black power among many resentful whites as well, who often responded with demonstrations of their own, including the horrendous Detroit riots of 1943 and other racial collisions in El Paso and Port Arthur, Texas, in Springfield, Massachusetts, in Hubbard, Ohio, and in Harlem. In a hundred less dramatic ways, including job actions, individual hate crimes, and even legislation, many whites, North and South, defiantly restated the Jim Crow social and cultural standards the war was bringing under such sharp scrutiny. The large role played in the war effort by African Americans put the Double V on the national policy agenda and brought "the Negro question" to the front pages of the white press.[2] As the nation worked fitfully to resolve the paradox of the Double V, the stakes for black Americans were great and were marked by the most widely-sustained drive for economic justice and civil rights for the race since Reconstruction. Roi Ottley and Walter

White, in the two most widely-read moderate treatises on race written during the war, captured the new dynamism and uncertainty of race relations in their titles. Ottley's 1943 book on social conditions was entitled *New World a' Comin'*, and White's reflective account of his meetings with black troops in various theaters of war and encampments, published in 1945, was called *A Rising Wind*.[3]

The paradox of the Double V was precisely focused in the remarkable collaboration between two white composers, Earl Robinson and John LaTouche, and the performer Paul Robeson. Robinson and LaTouche's cantata *Ballad for Americans* represented an assertion of the social pluralism of the American Left's Popular Front in a form both accessible and serious. *Ballad for Americans* is a musical dialogue, a conversation between two allegorical forces over the nature of Americanism. In *Ballad for Americans*, an initially-skeptical chorus encounters a commanding individual American presence (Robeson, in the 1939 premiere of the piece on radio, in the best-selling recording which followed, and in many public performances during the war years) who is knowledgeable about the contributions of the average man and woman to American history and to contemporary American society. The story of *Ballad for Americans*' huge success as Popular Front iconography, and its dismayingly immediate compromise by forces of ideological reaction, foreground the difficulty that Popular Front culture had in dealing with racial equality in America. The interpretation of *Ballad for Americans* by Paul Robeson offered an analytical yet compassionate understanding of the pitfalls of pluralist ambitions to a huge national audience, and in so doing, provided an example of racial responsibility in Popular Front culture.

The Popular Front period of the Communist Party of the United States lasted from 1935 to 1939, the year of *Ballad for Americans*' premiere. During that time the Party became committed to a cultural program which would make more vivid its commitment to unity of action and ideological consensus with other Left and progressive groups in a specifically American setting. One of the Popular Front's most energetic initiatives was to encourage a program of civil rights and integration for African Americans.[4] Party Leader Earl Browder's statement in 1936 that "Communism is 20th Century Americanism" was evidence that the Party was also seeking a heretofore implausible marriage of nationalism with Left thought during these years. By the time the Popular Front consensus began to crumble in 1940–1941, due to American liberal anxiety over the Nazi-Soviet Pact, Browder's simplistic formulation was vital to the American cultural realm. Further, the Party itself supported black cultural production, fostering experiments in black theater, history, and music.[5]

The late 1930s and the era of World War II saw the development of a middle-brow audience for a more loosely-construed Popular Front ideology. As the influence of the Communist Party on artistic work declined, and semi-official and unofficial cultural agencies (as well as private individuals) took up the creative reins, the result was a confluence of ideas and means we might well call a culture of American affirmation.[6] The presence of this new audience often shifted the tone of Popular Front culture away from the explicitly political and toward an inclusive, upbeat cultural nationalism. The type of cultural material produced during these years was diverse. Included was the period's folk song revival, the many WPA arts projects, Martha Graham's ballet *Appalachian Spring*, the work of writers like biographer Carl Sandburg, poet Stephen Vincent Benét, and novelist John Steinbeck, and even the Broadway musical *Oklahoma!* All these works stressed the common ancestry of American democracy and folk culture, an ancestry that could knit together diverse American groups, including classes, ethnicities, and regions, in the common project of the fight against fascism, and in the process build a new America where these differences would be subordinated to a new national vision of fairness and equality.

The cultural practices in media such as drama, photography, the novel, dance, and music that emerged from these assumptions had four characteristics: social realism and a documentary impulse; cultural nationalism; sentimental populism; and, most important for our purposes, an ideology of unity and common purpose across all the old borderlines of class, race, and ethnicity. These attributes marked a turning away from early 1930s strident social criticism for Left artists in favor of a celebration of what one contemporary anthology jubilantly called "American stuff." For the war effort, this shift had profound influences; it meant that a large cadre of Left artists who in the early 1930s had angrily criticized American capitalism ended the decade as boosters of idealized American traditions and "types." The ideal of Popular Front unity, and the cultural forms which presented that unity, supported American participation in World War II not only as a response to totalitarianism, but as expressive of American national traits. As Malcolm Cowley wrote in 1943 without exaggeration, "This time the radicals are more patriotic than the conservatives."[7]

The Popular Front ideology of brotherhood tested anew the resolve of the influential black middle class, caught between assimilationism and modeling after white institutions on the one hand, and an ongoing fascination with race separatism on the other hand, motivated by continu-

ous rebuffs of assimilationist desires. The black press during the time *Ballad for Americans* made its first impact in late 1939 and throughout 1940 unconsciously reveals this bipolarity. In the Chicago *Defender* during this period, for instance, news of sorority cotillions, charity teas, and Jackie Robinson's gridiron prowess at UCLA shares the same issues with stories describing the purchase by the state of Mississippi of a new portable electric chair, the stalling of Federal anti-lynch laws in Congress yet again, and another desperate appeal to save the Scottsboro Boys from execution.[8]

Black artists were also aware of the conflict between assimilationist ambitions and separatist solace. Duke Ellington's civil rights review *Jump for Joy* (1941), his symphonic essay on African-American history *Black, Brown, and Beige* (1943), and Langston Hughes' long poem *Freedom's Plow* (1943) stand out as leading examples of black Popular Front art. All three were among the most elaborate works their authors' had yet produced, and each told an impressionistic and prideful history of the race in America. All three works found supporters among white tastemakers and critics, and all had mass audiences. Excerpts from Ellington's *Black, Brown, and Beige* were recorded, with an explanatory prologue by critic Barry Ulanov, and circulated free to American troops as part of the "V-disc" program. *Jump for Joy* produced several hit songs and initiated a collaboration between Ellington and Orson Welles on the latter's ill-starred documentary film project *It's All True.* Hughes' poem was performed on a nationwide radio broadcast by actor Paul Muni, and was read by Hughes at mass rallies for the war effort. All three works sought to reconcile a bitter past with a hopeful future for the race through modernist forms and reference to folk elements, but all three works avoided the romantic pluralism that was a keystone of much of the culture of American affirmation. Clearly, when it came to racial harmony, while hopeful, these black artists were reluctant to unhesitatingly endorse the ambitions of Popular Front culture as fact.[9]

If the ideal of brotherhood at the center of Popular Front culture was to have validity, the test would come not merely in the way its artwork employed rhetoric about otherness, but how that Popular Front culture accommodated otherness in its own practices. The grandeur of *Ballad for Americans* for modern (2001) listeners lies not in the lost dream of Popular Front unity, but in the way Paul Robeson used *Ballad for Americans* against itself, as a critical inquiry into brotherhood denied.

Robeson's version of *Ballad for Americans* remains definitive. However, several other artists have recorded it, including, most notably, Bing Crosby, as well as Sammy Davis, Jr., Odetta, and Brock Peters. Metropolitan Opera star Lawrence Tibbett's radio performance followed Robeson's premiere within a few days, and many others, including opera singers Jules Bledsoe and James Melton, performed the song before the end of the war. It was this second career, sparked by Robeson's electrifying performance, which made it seem that *Ballad for Americans* had fulfilled the dream of Popular Front culture, its combination of wide circulation and the creation of an imagined community of singers and listeners from many backgrounds presenting a miniature of the Popular Front utopia.

The cantata *Ballad for Americans* had its source in the fertile soil of Popular Front culture at its zenith. Earl Robinson was a Left composer and Communist Party member who had been active in the early 1930s Composer's Collective with Aaron Copland, Mark Blitzstein, Elie Siegmeister, Alex North, and others, nearly all of whom became fascinated by the possibili-

ties of melding folk styles with the forms of classical music. He had written for several WPA shows, including a revue with poet John LaTouche called *Sing for Your Supper*, the finale of which was called "The Ballad of Uncle Sam." Robinson had also written "Joe Hill" and several songs based on American folk and history themes. He would, before the end of the war, write "The House I Live In" (which, like "Joe Hill," Robeson also sang frequently) and another extremely popular exercise in musical Americana, the cantata *The Lonesome Train*. He was later the author of the popular civil rights song "Black and White," and devoted his life to progressive causes in almost every media before his death in 1991.

LaTouche's résumé was similar. He had an even stronger grounding in the folk song revival than Robinson, and had collaborated on the International Ladies Garment Workers' Union show of 1937, *Pins and Needles*. For Robinson, LaTouche, and several other Popular Front composers, the cantata form allowed them to blend high style and seriousness of musical purpose with folk materials in order to present the ideology of the Popular Front in an aesthetic form that middlebrow audiences would find appealing.[10]

Robinson knew Norman Corwin, the young radio impresario, and suggested that Corwin use "The Ballad of Uncle Sam" in his new radio series on Americanism, *The Pursuit of Happiness*, a collage or magazine-style show which had already featured Raymond Massey reading from Robert Sherwood's play *Abe Lincoln in Illinois*, and Ray Middleton singing a song with a theme much like *Ballad for Americans'* cross-section of the nation entitled "How Can You Tell an American." Robinson auditioned the piece for Corwin, who in turn had Robinson perform it again for CBS executives. Bill Lewis, an enthusiastic CBS vice-president, allegedly said, "Wouldn't

Robeson knock the hell out of this!" In fact, Robeson had already been contacted to do an episode of *Pursuit of Happiness*, but his price of a thousand dollars was too steep for Corwin. Corwin relented, and in late October of 1939 Robinson and Robeson met to begin rehearsals.

Robinson recalled the rehearsal experience as extraordinarily cooperative, the only disagreements with Robeson coming on the subject of pitch; Robeson insisted on recording in lower keys to take advantage of the combination of his trademark bass intonation and the additional power that a microphone gave him in these lower vocal ranges. But a week of piano and voice rehearsals at Robeson's apartment in Harlem's Sugar Hill confirmed Robinson's profound respect for Robeson. As in other creative settings, Robeson was genuinely responsive to strong coaching.

Corwin renamed the piece *Ballad for Americans*, and it premiered on November 5, 1939, at 4:30 PM. Mark Warnow, music director from radio's *Your Hit Parade*, conducted Ralph Wilkinson's lush orchestrations, and Lyn Murray conducted the large, New York–based, amateur choral ensemble Robinson called the American People's Chorus, which he had formed in 1937 to sing protest and folk songs. The song was an instant hit. A studio audience of six hundred in the Broadway theater that CBS was using as a studio responded with a sustained ovation for several minutes. Calls and letters by the hundreds flooded the studio for days, causing the network to repeat the performance on New Year's Day, 1940. In columns and reviews the next week the critical response was equally ecstatic: 20,000 copies of the sheet music were purchased in the first year. The song was recorded for Victor as a special four-sided release, and was a huge success in this form, selling 40,000 copies by the end of 1940 at $2.00 per album.

Ballad for Americans was the hit of Robeson's recital repertoire during the war years. He added the song to his concert repertoire for his highly successful mid-year tour in 1940, and performed it in a special production with the Hall Johnson choir at the Hollywood Bowl that same summer before the largest crowd ever to attend an event there. Surviving concert programs show that Robeson sang *Ballad for Americans* regularly, either at the very end of his recitals, or just before intermission. In especially lavish concert settings, a local orchestra or chorus was used to add drama to the performance of *Ballad for Americans*. It is also probable that he used it as an encore piece. Robeson performed the song less often after the war, but did so on several occasions when Robinson joined him, such as during Robeson's ten-day, 27 concert tour of Hawaii in 1948. The song was emotionally reprised at Robeson's 1955 birthday concert.

Merely by virtue of its inclusion in Robeson's repertoire, *Ballad for Americans* became a political song. During the war years, Robeson frequently performed the song not only at war bond rallies but also at public meetings of civil rights organizations, such as the 1942 meeting of the Southern Conference for Human Welfare in Nashville. Eleanor Roosevelt, who had been in attendance, wrote in her "My Day" column the next day that hearing Robeson sing *Ballad for Americans* had been "a thrilling experience... It always stirs me as a ballad, but last night there was something peculiarly significant about it."[11] *Ballad for Americans*' popularity led to the surveillance of Earl Robinson by the FBI as early as December 7, 1940. He would be blacklisted during the McCarthy era a decade later.

Despite these impressive notices, *Ballad for Americans*' possibilities as a radical anthem auguring real social change were limited, because its textual ambivalences allowed it to be instantly adopted as a musical paean to existing American equality. The markers of this middlebrow success were inescapable. Deems Taylor named *Ballad for Americans* as the best record of the month, in *Redbook* magazine. Lawrence Tibbett sang the song on radio a few weeks later on the *Ford Hour*, although Robeson was then a vocal supporter of a well-publicized strike at Ford. Eugene Ormandy announced plans to schedule *Ballad for Americans* on three concert programs in the following year's Philadelphia Orchestra season. Stanley Marcus, of the Neiman-Marcus department stores, presented 75 copies to the public schools of Dallas to encourage tolerance. *Time* magazine reported that the Victor recording was the most requested song at the RCA exhibit at the New York World's Fair during the summer of 1940. Within months after the song's release on record, high school choruses, church choirs, glee clubs, and community orchestras were performing it. An Army choir sang it for the Queen of England. Thirty-six Boy Scouts sang it in Gimbel's basement as a come-on for holiday shoppers. *Reader's Digest* called it simply "the finest piece of American propaganda."

As a result of the success of *Ballad for Americans*, LaTouche was considered by the Theater Guild as the librettist for *Oklahoma!* and Robinson won a Guggenheim Fellowship to work on yet another cantata, this one based on Carl Sandburg's *The People, Yes*. MGM bought the rights to the song, intending to use it in the Mickey Rooney–Judy Garland film *Strike Up the Band*. Such widespread acceptance of *Ballad for Americans* made it briefly known as "America's second national anthem."

Ballad for Americans' verses are ambiguous on the issue of future social change. The piece was designed by Earl Robinson in a series of four "movements," together documenting the progressive forward sweep of American history. In its retelling

of American history, *Ballad for Americans* recites specific moments every schoolchild could recognize as advancing American ideals of freedom (the Revolutionary War, Gettysburg), and names as American heroes a similarly normative catalog of greats, including the founding fathers and Lincoln. (LaTouche's text does include names most Americans would not have recognized, Revolutionary War patriots Chaim Solomon and Crispus Attucks.) The iconic instances and figures of American working class heroism in that same history (Haymarket, Homestead, Ludlow, Eugene Debs, Tom Mooney, the Lincoln Brigade) are not mentioned. References to the working class, in fact, are localized in the song's litany of specific occupations, such as "mechanic" and "truck driver"; organized labor is not referred to. The lyric even appears subtly to celebrate American expansionism and the economic conquest of the continent. The result of these textual attributes was to focus *Ballad for Americans* on progress achieved rather than progress denied, reflecting the self-congratulatory mode of an essentially conservative consensus rather than the radical agenda for change to which much of the Left was still committed. In this way, *Ballad for Americans* revealed the fatal flaw in the culture of the Popular Front: its accommodation of the same forces of reaction in a cultural sphere to which it was implacably opposed in the realm of ideology.

The single public controversy that the song engendered during its triumphal first year reflected this consensus. The Republicans included *Ballad for Americans* at their convention in the summer of 1940. The song was sung by white baritone Ray Middleton. Although Earl Robinson later claimed that Robeson had been invited to sing *Ballad for Americans* but had declined due to a scheduling conflict, many felt that Robeson was excluded because of his race and his emergent radicalism. The *New Yorker* reported that Earl Robinson's reaction to having the Republicans use the song was an enthusiastic one. "Fantastic!" he said, "we wrote the '*Ballad*' for everyone."[12] Indeed, the week before it had been used at the Communist Party Convention. The convention episode revealed how easily the song's premise could be extended to the point of burlesque. That point was reached when MGM eventually used the song in *Born to Sing*, a 1941 B movie version of *Strike Up the Band* with Virginia Weidler and Douglas MacPhail, in which starstruck teenagers stage a lavish patriotic revue. *Ballad for Americans* is the climax of the show, with what Robinson accurately described as "outlandish" choreography "involving pyramids and revolving stages."[13] A profile of John LaTouche in *Collier's* joked that he would have to give up his artsy, bohemian existence in Greenwich Village, as the success of *Ballad for Americans* was causing an identity crisis for the left-wing songwriter.[14]

Ballad for Americans became so much a part of mainstream America's self-congratulatory discourse on "tolerance" that leading black intellectual Alain Locke, writing in *Opportunity*, found it trite when compared to William Grant Still's cantata *And They Lynched Him on a Tree*, as well as the white composer Roy Harris' Popular Front symphony *Challenge 1940*, when the three works were performed together on June 25th, 1940, at Lewisohn Stadium in New York. The occasion was a concert featuring the New York Philharmonic, with Artur Rodzinski conducting and other musical organizations participating, before an appreciative audience of 13,000. (*Ballad for Americans* was again conducted by Mark Warnow, who had premiered the piece on radio, and again augmented by a large choir, probably the American People's Chorus.) The Lewisohn Stadium concert was mounted to showcase musical

themes of Americanism in the context of the war effort, and included American music from folk songs to advanced modernist compositions. The audience included Eleanor Roosevelt, who met with Robeson after the show and congratulated him.

While the audience was apparently appreciative, Locke was impatient with what he saw as *Ballad for Americans*' smug tone. In his judgment, "democracy today needs sober criticism, even courageous chastising." What Locke called Still's "inspired indirection" made *Ballad for Americans* seem obvious and insipid. It was work such as *And They Lynched Him on a Tree*, said Locke, uncompromisingly modernist and downcast, that would be remembered as "*the* ballad for democracy."[15]

Yet middlebrow white critics continued to champion Robinson's opus. The *New York Times* critic reviewing the Lewisohn Stadium concert felt "*Ballad for Americans* served as an effective explanatory forward for the concert, a framing story for the much more musically complex Still and Harris compositions," and recounted a rapturous audience reaction to the piece.[16] *Time* patronized Still's *And They Lynched Him on a Tree* for its dissonance and pessimistic tone, calling the evening an unqualified triumph for Robeson and *Ballad for Americans*.[17]

Locke was tired of *Ballad for Americans*' use as a placebo for real American inclusiveness that was at best still only a hope. "We're black, brown, and beige," ran a recitative in an early draft of Duke Ellington's composition of that name, "and we're red, white, and blue!" Ellington struck this phrase from the score before its premiere as an overstatement, and perhaps as too premature a declaration of common purpose. Yet, this affirmation was exactly the sort of excited rhetorical bridge between group and nation that dedicated Popular Front artists such as Earl Robinson made the core of their work. Ellington, at least, could not ignore promises long unkept in favor of promises newly made.[18]

Ballad for Americans used the nation's most recognizable black voice to speak for the vision of Popular Front pluralism, a pluralism which included race. That vision was trumpeted to mass audiences, both white and black, in unprecedented numbers. Was *Ballad for Americans*, then, perhaps the most obviously integrated cultural text produced for mass audiences during the Popular front period, a meaningful riposte to racism in its day? Or was it merely another romantic gesture toward racial harmony which, through an overly celebratory mood, failed to address the deep schisms among groups in American society?

When Norman Corwin discussed with me his choice of a name for what La-Touche and Robinson had called "The Ballad of Uncle Sam," he emphasized that he wanted it to be called *Ballad for Americans*. Indeed, in the tradition of Popular Front culture, there is a joyful, hectoring tone about the *Ballad for Americans*; it is a boisterous lecture on what its listeners *ought* to feel about brotherhood. In his history of the folksong revival movement in America, Robert Cantwell presents the song as Robinson and LaTouche undoubtedly intended it:

> The *Ballad*'s essential statement is an affirmation of political and social entitlement against the backdrop of a sense of powerlessness, invisibility, and marginality compensated ... by dignity, strength, and inclusion in numbers. It sketches in a series of verses a revolutionary theme as it is embodied in the patriarchs of the Revolutionary War and in Lincoln as the Great Emancipator. "Nobody who was anybody believed it," Robeson the narrator sings of these historical crises — setting the revolutionary dream against the class-based language of status and celebrity on the one hand,

and on the other, of urban anonymity, cultural invisibility, and immigrant powerlessness.[19]

Yet, the episode of the Republican Convention is circumstantial evidence of the extreme conflictedness of *Ballad for Americans*. Michael Denning, in his *The Cultural Front*, reports that *Ballad for Americans* had been so often used as a substitute for the brotherhood it sang of that it became a metonymy for New Left critics, such as Christopher Lasch, in their rejection of the Popular Front's "sentimental nationalism" as a lost opportunity for American socialism. Such criticism began with Robert Warshow's influential 1947 *Commentary* essay "The Legacy of the Thirties," in which he argued that *Ballad for Americans* was the pinnacle of a pseudo–American art movement that he saw as manipulative and cynical, a movement he termed "banal," "false," and "affected," and a defusing of radical energies in formal and historical self-righteousness.[20]

Ever since, Left social critics have reiterated Warshow's use of the song as an evocation of the Popular Front delusion of brotherhood, and criticized the cantata form which is so integral to *Ballad for Americans'* affect as an index of the period's Europeanized middlebrow musical affectations. Stanley Aronowitz and Maurice Isserman indicted the song by name in their denunciations of Popular Front culture. Historian Warren Susman called it a "pseudo-folk ballad," comparing it to the coy brand of "people's culture" practiced by Norman Rockwell, and said that it typified the excesses of Popular Front culture: "Out of it came an absurd vision of the American past, a peculiar notion of American society in the present, a ludicrous attitude toward American culture in general. At a most crucial juncture in American history American socialists helped us little in understanding ourselves or the world." Sidney Blumenthal argued that *Ballad for Americans*, far from endorsing a meaningful Left position, in fact supported populist conservativism, or what he called the "democratic *schwarmerei*" of Ronald Reagan, who often said his favorite song was Earl Robinson's other Popular Front opus, "The House I Live In."[21] Yet, none of these denunciations address Paul Robeson's transformative presence in his rendition of *Ballad for Americans*.

Robeson arrived in the United States from Europe in October 1939 to begin rehearsals for Roark Bradford's play about the black folk hero, *John Henry*. Robeson had spent much of the years 1932 to 1939 traveling. He had seen African colonialism, German fascism, Soviet communism, and the Spanish Civil War first-hand. These years transformed him politically from a progressive integrationist to a Communist. Robeson returned not as simply a concert singer with political sympathies, but as a committed political activist who intended to use the medium of song as he had at the Loyalist camps in Spain, to preach a passionate message of brotherhood and resistance. As he had in Europe, Robeson quickly and wholly dedicated himself to Left and anti-fascist causes, though much of the most radical of this work was out of the eye of the mass audience. His political activities during the war years, including speaking, concertizing, and writing, were as prodigious in number as they were varied in venue. He was as likely to be found singing for workers at a war plant as he was speaking before a conference on racial equality, broadcasting for Russian War Relief or stumping for FDR's 1944 re-election bid, saluting a union gathering or performing at West Point. He seemed to be everywhere, and everywhere he was cheered by disparate audiences. For the Left during these years, he was politically ubiquitous.

Robeson was also now keenly aware of the negative power of retrograde imagery of blacks, no matter how well-intentioned a product of compromise such imagery was. In 1942, after a disappointing experience on the film *Tales of Manhattan*, Robeson foreswore work in commercial films until he could be assured that portrayals of blacks in cinema would be free of racist stereotypes. His self-consciousness about his status as the exponent of his race to whites had increased dramatically during the 1930s.

For middlebrow America, however, the persona of Paul Robeson the Broadway and film star still dominated its perception of this complex public figure, largely because Robeson's maturing political views were ignored or simplified in published interviews and profiles in the mainstream national press around the time *Ballad for Americans* was first performed.[22] For most listeners to *Pursuits of Happiness*, Robeson's character during these years was symbolized by his appearance as the first black Othello in a major production of the play beginning in 1942, not by his increasing outspokenness on matters of race and class in America. Appreciation of Robeson's success on stage and screen could be regarded by whites as proof of their own even-handedness, and by the black bourgeoisie as another in a line of black "firsts," such as the accomplishments of Jesse Owens and Dr. Charles Drew. This slippage between the sympathetic but apolitical resonance of the "old Robeson" of *Show Boat* days and the resolutely political "new Robeson," a spokesperson for a host of Left causes, allowed Robeson to trade on the political naivete that is a large part of *Ballad for Americans*' premise, as written by Robinson and LaTouche. By the time of the anti–Robeson riot in Peekskill, New York, in August 1949, Robeson's public personality had absorbed the explicitly political and ideological electricity he had, in fact, been generating since his return to America in 1939. *Ballad* could never again be sung by him without a heavier freight of irony than Robinson and LaTouche's fundamentally optimistic song could bear.

It is thus instructive that Bing Crosby recorded *Ballad for Americans* in 1940, shortly after Robeson's version was first heard. For Crosby's own stage persona possessed the bashfulness that made the song's sentiments seem fresh, plausible, and anything but ironic. What had been a confrontational presentation of LaTouche's lyrics as a set of propositions declaimed to a skeptical audience in Robeson's version now became a characteristically Crosbyian set of intimate asides, eradicating the ethos of conflict and guilt in the song, an ethos that Robeson had made a structuring norm of his performance. *Ballad for Americans* becomes a different song in the voices of these two performers. As sung by Bing Crosby, *Ballad for Americans* celebrates an American ideological consensus, while Robeson's version honors a truly pluralist America; the distinction is subtle, but significant.

Crosby's version grapples uncomfortably with *Ballad for Americans*' message of eventual, almost inevitable ethnic, class, and especially race harmony. Crosby had a long history of minstrelly homages to the black voice of spirituals and the blues on disc, on radio, and in movies during the 1930s and 1940s, an act of strained cultural revision that was a longstanding practice in American popular music.[23] His recording of a song so obviously identified with Robeson suggests conflicting possibilities: either that Robinson's oft-stated vision of a color-blind nation, in which anyone could sing *Ballad for Americans*, was a reality, or simply that *Ballad for Americans* was not the essay in revolutionary social change Robinson, among others, always believed it was. A darker, third reading of Crosby's version looms—that Robeson's

very popular performance of the song was so strong in its implications of the inevitability of massive social change that Crosby's interpretation was required by the contemporary American society of the time to rectify the threat to the status quo. Indeed, if we consider Robeson's the definitive version of the song, many of the versions of *Ballad for Americans* during the era of the war years suggest a covering up of its revolutionary implications, a salving-over of the manner in which Robeson made the song work against its own optimism by revealing the gaps and fissures in the American image of pluralism.[24]

In any case, the phrase "You know who I am," when sung by Crosby, enjoins an audience to imagine the song as sung by "Bing Crosby," a specific character familiar through his many appearances on radio and in movies. By contrast, and strikingly for one who was, as a performer, perhaps even more *sui generis* than Crosby, Robeson's identity in *Ballad for Americans* was calculatedly that of a representative black man, and he carried more cultural experience through the refrain "You know who I am" than Crosby could muster. Crosby's fully assimilated, even commodified Irish ethnicity could simply not compete with the force, and the fact, of Robeson's blackness.

The "nobody" of Paul Robeson's *Ballad for Americans* is thus not a stylized Popular Front Everyman, an amalgam of traits of every imaginable group identification. Instead, it is always the same black "nobody" that Bert Williams sang about, sad-eyed and smiling wistfully. In that commanding stage presence and with that gigantic, often accusing voice, Robeson used *Ballad for Americans* subtly, to demand the repayment of debts long owed in exchange for an endorsement of the bright dream of Popular Front American citizenship. In Robeson's version of *Ballad for Americans* there is a constant, productive tension between a bitter past and a bright but conditional, even hypothetical, future.

That future remains in the hands of whites, who in 1940 own the power structure. To the white chorus of *Ballad for Americans* Robeson would always and forever be a black man, something which celebration of his countless "firsts" only confirmed. When he sings to the chorus his catalog of nations, races, ethnicities, and religions, he dares them to imagine the black man as anything but black. His aloneness and anonymity against the white mass is itself cultural baggage, and their inquiry, "Who are you, mister?" can't help but sound surprised and petulant. Robeson's upbeat answer of a list of many origins maddeningly refuses to acknowledge these categories as meaningful designations, including that of race. For Crosby, the chorus are his confederates throughout, while for Robeson they are, initially, antagonists, and only later, near the end of the song, are they his allies, finally converted to his position by the strength of his ideas, stated firmly and compassionately. Here, Robeson is able to use the power of his own performance persona to strong and different effect than that generated by the conceit of his representing an "average" black man. That a chorus taken from any group of ordinary Americans could possibly be ignorant of Bing Crosby is understood in the song humorously, as an American cultural impossibility. Similar ignorance of Robeson's almost equally well-known voice speaks of a willed disinterest in black America by the same white chorus. Throughout, Robeson's interpretation tends to flatten Robinson's topography of progress into a series of allusions to squandered chances for fairness and too-frequent martyrdoms. Robeson's interpretation turns a romance of pluralism into a lecture on difference.

To the end of his life, Earl Robinson saw his and John LaTouche's song as color-

blind, and its success as a vindication of the grand dream of the Popular Front. Yet the signifying spark that Robeson brought to *Ballad for Americans* in his characterization as a representative black man gave the piece an authenticity as a social tract it sacrificed in many of the subsequent performance settings its very popularity inspired. We cannot do more than speculate on the causes of the immense popularity of the Robeson version of *Ballad for Americans* among ordinary Americans, black and white, in its day. But it is clear that, however Robeson's status as a radical political figure was underappreciated by the mass audience, something in his interpretation of Robinson and LaTouche's cantata vibrated deeply within that audience. It is tempting to imagine that they heard, *and understood*, a great, solemn, and tender voice telling them of the hard work they had yet to do as individuals to win the dream of American pluralism.

As he reflected on the success of *Ballad for Americans* late in his life, Earl Robinson acknowledged this unique contribution of Robeson's to the life of his song, although he mistakenly saw the issue solely in terms of Robeson's persona as an internationalist and a progressive, not in terms of the American racial spokesmanship persona that Robeson used when he sang *Ballad for Americans*:

> So if my career received a vigorous jolt into public recognition by Paul Robeson's singing of *Ballad for Americans*, it can also be said that his career and the cause of equality also got a lift ... with each singing of the piece, with Big Paul there or a thousand miles away, *his* America hung in the concert hall like a great, fraternal democratic aura.[25]

Norman Corwin worked with Robeson again in 1945. His comments then could just as easily summarize Robeson's work in *Ballad for Americans*, and the manner in which Robeson had managed to avoid both a rigid ideological reading of the song and a romantic undercutting of its most troubling implications:

> It was an amazing performance, civilized, poised, penetrating, neither emotional nor intellectual, but communicated straight from the heart, or whatever chamber it is from which absolute conviction flows.[26]

The many other recorded versions of *Ballad for Americans* have faded from public memory, and the song has rightfully become reidentified with Robeson. It is Robeson's conviction, rather than Crosby's consensus, which we listen for in *Ballad for Americans*, and what saves the song from its now ignominious history of cooptation. Paul Robeson tested the Popular Front's claims of brotherhood. He found them ambitious but wanting. And having found them wanting, he said so, in his version of *Ballad for Americans*.

Earl Robinson was right about the depth of Robeson's impact. With each singing of the piece, Robeson's interpretation hangs in the concert hall like an aura. When Norman Corwin spoke to me of first staging *Ballad for Americans* sixty years ago, that aura persisted in his own voice. Said Corwin, "He radiated strength. Strength of character, strength of conviction. He is a shining figure in my memory."[27] In Paul Robeson's *Ballad for Americans*, that figure still shines today.

Notes

The author wishes to express his deep appreciation to Norman Corwin for sharing his recollections of the creation of *Ballad for Americans* and his work with Paul Robeson.

1. Robin D.G. Kelley, "The Riddle of the Zoot: Malcolm Little and Black Cultural Politics During World War II," in *Malcolm X: In*
Our Own Image, Joe Wood, ed. (New York: Doubleday, 1992), 155–182; Nat Brandt, *Harlem at War: The Black Experience in World War II* (New York: Syracuse University Press, 1996); Association for the Study of African American History and Life, *African Americans and World War II* (Washington, DC, 1994); Neil A. Wynn, *The Afro-American and the Second World War* (New York: Holmes and Meier, 1993); and Robert L. Allen, *The Port Chicago Mutiny* (New York: Warner Books, 1989).

2. Geoffrey Perrett, *Days of Sadness, Years of Triumph* (Madison: University of Wisconsin Press, 1973), 143–154, 310–324, 357–367; and Lawrence R. Samuel, *Pledging Allegiance: American Identity and the Bond Drive of World War II* (Washington, DC: Smithsonian Institution Press, 1997), 127–205.

3. Roi Ottley, *New World a' Comin': Inside Black America* (New Boston: Houghton Mifflin, 1943); and Walter White, *A Rising Wind* (Garden City: Doubleday Doran, 1945). A representative radical tract urging rejection of the Double V political philosophy is J.R. Johnson, *Why Negroes Should Oppose the War* (New York: Young People's Socialist League, 1939).

4. The liberal coalition for civil rights during these years is described in Patricia Sullivan, *Days of Hope: Race and Democracy in the New Deal Era* (Chapel Hill: University of North Carolina Press, 1996); and Michael Goldfield, *The Color of Politics: Race and the Mainsprings of American Politics* (New York: New Press, 1997), 176–230.

5. Mark Naison, *Communists in Harlem During the Depression* (Urbana: University of Illinois Press, 1983), 279–283.

6. Joan Shelly Rubin, *The Making of Middlebrow Culture* (Chapel Hill: University of North Carolina Press, 1992); Jane De Hart Matthews, "Arts and the People: The New Deal Quest for a Cultural Democracy," *Journal of American History*, 62, September 1975, 316–339; and Alfred Haworth Jones, "The Search for a Usable American Past in the New Deal Era," *American Quarterly*, 23, December 1971, 710–724.

7. Malcolm Cowley, "American Literature in Wartime," *New Republic*, 109, December 6, 1943, 800.

8. For an account that understands the black wartime press as a platform for social change, see Lee Finkle, *Forum for Protest: The*

Black Press During World War II (Rutherford: Fairleigh Dickinson University Press, 1975).

9. Ellington followed *Black, Brown, and Beige* with two other long works, these more specifically rooted in social criticism: *The Deep South Suite* and *New World a' Comin'*, which was ostensibly based on Ottley's book. The fullest account of the content and reception of Ellington's *Jump for Joy* and *Black, Brown, and Beige* can be found in a series of contemporary reviews, responses, and program notes in Mark Tucker, ed., *The Duke Ellington Reader* (New York: Oxford University Press, 1993), 146–179; while the story of *Freedom's Plow* is told in Arnold Rampersad, *The Life of Langston Hughes: Volume II, 1941–1967, I Dream a World* (New York: Oxford University Press, 1988), 57–58, 71.

10. There were dozens of such cantatas produced in America during the Popular Front and war years in America reflecting national and nationalist themes. In the spirit of the times, Robinson would soon write *Battle Hymn*, a cantata based on Franklin D. Roosevelt's life and ideas, and occasionally referred to as *The Roosevelt Cantata*. Robeson was invited to sing this work in 1942 at the White House, but his touring schedule would not permit it. Martin Duberman, *Paul Robeson: A Biography* (New York: The New Press, 1989), 655n; Barbara A. Zuck, *A History of Musical Americanism* (Ann Arbor: UMI Research Press, 1978), 139–198.

11. Quoted in *Duberman*, 259.

12. Quoted in *Duberman*, 647n.

13. Earl Robinson, with Eric A. Gordon, *Ballad of an American: The Autobiography of Earl Robinson* (Metuchen: Scarecrow Press, 1998), 96.

14. Luther Davis and John Cleveland, "And You Know Who I Am," *Collier's*, 106, October 19, 1940, 91.

15. Alain Locke, "Ballad for Democracy," *Opportunity*, Vol. 18, August 1940, 229 (emphasis Locke's).

16. Howard Taubman, "American Music Heard in Stadium," *New York Times*, June 26, 1940, 27.

17. *Time*, "I Hear America Singing," July 8, 1940, 46–47.

18. Barry Ulanov, *Duke Ellington* (New York: Da Capo, 1975) [originally published 1947], 250–251.

19. Robert Cantwell, *When We Were Good: The Folk Revival* (Cambridge: Harvard University Press, 1996), 107.

20. In "The Legacy of the Thirties" Warshow also criticizes Corwin by name as one of the period's major purveyors of a studied "'American' inarticulateness and diffidence." Reprinted in Robert Warshow, *The Immediate Experience* (New York: Atheneum, 1971), 3–16.

21. Michael Denning, *The Cultural Front: The Laboring of American Culture in the 20th Century* (New York: Verso, 1996), 115–118.

22. Marie Seton, in her 1958 biography of Robeson, quotes a 1940 *Collier's* profile:

> Paul Robeson is America's Number One Negro Entertainer. His performance in *Emperor Jones* fixed him that position as a dramatic actor; his performance in *Show Boat* settled the matter of his place as a singing actor. Meanwhile concert audiences had named him their favorite Negro singer. (Marie Seton, *Paul Robeson*, London: Dennis Dobson, 1958, 107).

See also John K. Hutchens, "Paul Robeson," *Theatre Arts*, 28, October 1944, 579–585.

23. Michael Rogin, *Blackface, White Noise: Jewish Immigrants in the Hollywood Melting Pot* (Berkeley: University of California Press, 1996), 168, 175–177, 183, 192; and Eric Lott, *Love and Theft: Blackface Minstrelsy and the American Working Class* (New York: Oxford University Press, 1993).

24. During the Paul Robeson Centennial Conference on February 28, 1998, at Long Island University, I had the opportunity to watch and listen to a live performance of *Ballad for Americans* by a large youth orchestra accompanying the New York City Labor Chorus, the spiritual descendant of Earl Robinson's American People's Chorus. I sat with individuals who had known both Robeson and Robinson. The performance was absolutely stirring; but lacking Robeson's admonishing vocal presence, it was far easier to be persuaded of Robinson's unalloyed optimism about the American prospect.

25. Robinson, 100.

26. Norman Corwin, interview with author, January 31, 1998. Corwin was quoting from an introduction he had written to one of the plays in his collection, *Untitled and Other Radio Dramas* (New York: Henry Holt, 1947).

27. Norman Corwin, interview with author, January 31, 1998.

When Paul Robeson Sang to Me[*]

LEAH ZAZULYER
Rochester, New York

In the decade after World War II, once a month my parents went to meetings of the Jewish People's Fraternal Order, and the Brisker-Vicinity Aid Society. Members of the two organizations were the mainstay of their social life, links between a *Fiddler on the Roof*–type past and a post–Holocaust American present. Although many of the same people belonged to both groups, and sometimes activities were jointly sponsored, each organization was unique.

The Briskers were men and women in the Los Angeles area who had emigrated from shtetls in the province of Grodno near the city of Brest — then Russia, sometimes Poland, and now Belarus. They had formed themselves into a group in order to send food, clothing, money, letters, and moral support to whomsoever from their villages had survived Nazi persecution in general and the death camps in particular. It was a region they knew all too well — a swampy, pogrom and poverty ridden cor-

ner of the Pale of Settlement from which they had fled either before World War I or between the two wars, or where they had barely survived World War II as partisans or prisoners.

Chief among the Briskers' fund-raising techniques was the concert or lecture, alternating with holiday get-togethers. These were secular events usually held in small dingy rented halls. Traditional religious rituals had long been replaced by fervent social action, which the Briskers devoutly believed would mend or restore the world, *and*, of course, teach their children how to be good, secular Jews.

On the other hand, the Jewish People's Fraternal Order, a division of the International Workers Order, was initially set up as a means to provide life insurance, burial and death benefits — plus a kindershul — for its many working class members who did not have union benefits or wanted more. Since it was nationwide, given the flavor of the times, it soon developed a

This paper, presented at the Robeson Conference, first appeared in Jewish Currents: A Progressive Monthly, *which holds the copyright. Reprinted by permission.*

political action agenda as well. The JPFO campaigned tirelessly for Franklin Delano Roosevelt, exposed the virulent Detroit-based radio anti–Semite Father Coughlin, a Hitler apologist, and gave fierce attention to the great civil rights issues of the day, which often pertained to black Americans, and ranged from protesting lynchings to supporting fair employment practices.

Is it any surprise then that both Jewish organizations soon found themselves denounced as subversive during the full deflowering of democracy known as the McCarthy era, and each earned a place on the attorney general's long garden variety list of Communist or pinko organizations? Jews were in good company in those days, sharing media vilification, costly court appearances, and disemployment with Paul Robeson and many another defamed American who still believed that politics and commitment had virtue.

Before they were forced by court order to disband, I was taken to most of their parties, concerts, and lectures during my pre-teen and early teen years, since I was too young to be left at home alone, and too old for a baby-sitter. Besides, I grew up in one of those many Jewish households in which children were definitely to be seen, heard, included in conversations, and taken to events in order to listen, ask, and thereby learn. Mostly I liked going, even though right then in the midst of the fastidiousness of adolescence I had already been called a dirty Jew by some kid at school, and by then I had repeatedly heard talk about an international Jewish conspiracy — whatever that was!

What I had the most trouble with was just being reminded that I was Jewish, which I understood to be problematic and somehow unfortunate, because why else had Hitler almost succeeded in killing all of us? Frankly, it was all beyond my comprehension, and I suspected it was even be-

yond the comprehension of the adults, judging by the answers they offered me. So I preferred to just skip the whole topic.

Yet the homemade delicacies brought to these events and sold before or at intermission to help defray costs certainly helped, if not to resolve my feeling about being Jewish, at least to momentarily push them deeply down. After all, as the Yiddish proverb I had so often heard explained, "A sick person you ask, a well person you give."

My parents were at their best those nights, even dressed up a bit, my lovely but too hard-working mother's fine brown braids a crown across her head, her large hazel eyes dancing about as she laughed and visited with other shop girls and friends. Even my artistic and intellectual father was connected, stimulated, and almost animated on these occasions. If only they had all spoken good, unaccented English! But Yiddish was primarily the language of these events, or broken English, which was not something I could easily reconcile with my zealous English teacher's fanatic approach to "proper" grammar, pronunciation, and spelling.

Often I was among the youngest in attendance and therefore treated to much attention, patting, praise, and questioning merely for being that wonderful creature, a child! Didn't I look pretty? What grade was I in? How was the piano playing? What did I want to be? Was I a good student? Braces on or off, pigtails cut or not, I knew these people cared, and that perplexed me even more.

Since it was feared that complimenting one's own children might visit bad luck upon them, my parents busily complimented the children of their friends. Meanwhile, their friends in turn lavished compliments on me, and everybody eavesdropped on everybody else — all this in Yiddish, that gutsy language full of diminutions and endearments. Despite their terrible English, and everything else about them that was, if not un–American, certainly non–American, when people called me Layala, or Layechke, I loved it as much as I hated it. Though when they said I had a Yiddishe ponim, a Jewish face, I worried that they meant my nose and not my soul.

But the night Paul Robeson was to perform, both the announcements and the introductions were cut relatively short. What restraint! We were merely given to understand that he and we were comrades in the fight against McCarthyism and oppression everywhere in the world — and in the interests of time, only some of the everywheres were enumerated.... The man who was giving the pitch for money could barely contain his excitement at having Robeson in the wings. He kept peering stage right, as if to make certain Robeson was still there, which caused him to forget what he wanted to say and repeat himself.

The programs were always organized on a domino theory. One person, promising to be brief, introduced the next speaker, who also promised to be brief but introduced yet the next speaker at length and with elaborate heartfelt plaudits, and so forth until the stage and the air were heavy with fraternal extravagances, pleas for money, and laudations for what was, interminably, to come...

I could hear the main introducer's voice quiver with pride as he congratulated the audience, "this little band of Jewish working class people," for having sacrificed so, having scraped together by contribution and raffle ticket just enough, barely enough, gelt to bring Paul Robeson! (This same Robeson I would later learn was unable to work because of blacklisting within this country and the government's refusal to issue him a visa to travel and work abroad. Jews probably put a little bread on his table in those times, but surely he came cheap!)

The introduction concluded: "And now, I present to you, the Jewish people of Los Angeles, this great man, this magnificent artist, this citizen of the world" ... is what he finally got around to saying, followed by a long list of Robeson's various credits, degrees, and accomplishments. I wondered could the deep-voiced person on my parent's scratchy old 78 rpm records be THAT special?

Suddenly, slowly but deliberately, a huge black man — maybe, in fact, an actual giant I figured — entered and immediately took possession of the stage. For once the voluble audience became totally and instantly silent. Smiling broadly, Robeson approached center stage; everyone leaped up and clapped hard!

He smiled on, nodded, spread his hands for them to sit; they clapped again, loudly! When I asked my parents why they were clapping so hard when they hadn't heard a single song yet, they were too busy clapping to answer. Was it possible that all these people, the whole audience, knew this man? Who was he anyway? Why had the introducer with the thick Yiddish accent said that no matter how big Robeson was, he was with the little people, the common people of the world? And why was everybody so excited about a black man when this was a Jewish occasion?

He was the biggest black man I had ever seen, but not the first. Maybe, just maybe, he was a male angel, something like the mysterious one in the real full name of Los Angeles, Our Fair City Queen of the Angels, which I had recently learned about in school. If so, why had he come here now? Or was this really Elijah? After all, it was almost Passover time. Had I missed something, some explanation given in Yiddish, which, when I couldn't understand it, tended to make me daydream? Meanwhile, his accompanist, Laurence Brown, a man of ordinary size who had been lovingly introduced by Robeson, came on stage and arranged himself at the piano expectantly. Another black man. More applause.

At first Robeson spoke, in his astonishingly deep voice, which resonated along the stage boards, out and up through the soles of my feet, until I, like a deaf-mute, I could both see and feel his presence. His voice was carried through both my ears and my skin to every nerve ending. He spoke simple words, of his travels, of Jewish life flowering despite all odds around the war-torn globe, and of his deep conviction that a new day was dawning for mankind.

Then he actually sang. Okay, I recognized he was good. Better than Frank Sinatra and Nat King Cole. More like Jan Peerce singing *Kol Nidre* for the dead, or Jascha Heifetz and Yehudi Menuhin on the violin, certainly different than Pete Seeger. So I sat back and listened.

First came his songs, the songs, as he said, of "my people." Funny how one was called "Go Down Moses." Go figure that. "Deep River." "Old Black Joe." "Michael's Boat." *Porgy and Bess.* "Sometimes I Feel Like a Motherless Child." Sometimes I did too, when I had done wrong!

Next he sang songs of other lands or other times, but each in its original language, in Chinese, Russian, Spanish, an African language, and more! How many languages were there in the world anyway,

I wondered? Every song was prefaced with a story about where he had learned it or when he had sung it in that country. I was still trying to figure out how the audience knew so many of these songs, and when he invited them to join in, did so—and why he raised his hand to cup his ear when he got to the lowest notes or the softest parts of songs—when, to my utter amazement he began to sing all the Jewish songs I had ever heard my Mother sing to me at bedtime, or softly to herself at the kitchen sink!

He who spoke perfect English was singing in Yiddish, and it was okay! "Tumbalalika," my favorite riddle song about love or life or both. "Raisins and Almonds," the lullaby about saying goodbye to the old world. "Freiheit" and "Zog Nit Keynmol," which he explained showed the world that the Jews were more than victims. Gently irreverent songs about rabbis, about Jews who finally could own land and run tractors and cream extractors. Songs of willful girls who wanted to marry for love, and did!

As he sang, I forgot. About Hitler, about McCarthy. As the Yiddish proverb says, "He crawled into my heart with both feet," and in so doing displaced much, somehow making room for me to forgive my enemies, love my parents, their friends, their stories, their language, and myself.

Legacies

"Americans Through Their Labor": Paul Robeson's Vision of Cultural and Economic Democracy

MARK D. NAISON
Fordham University

Paul Robeson is the most complex and challenging African–American cultural figure of the twentieth century. During the 1930s and 1940s Robeson had the international stature of a Michael Jordan or Michael Jackson. He was not only the best known African-American performing artist of his era, he was also one of the world's highest paid commercial entertainers. Robeson's prodigious talents spanned the spectrum of the performing arts, ranging from classical and contemporary theater to film, radio, and the concert stage. At the peak of his popularity in the mid–1940s, Robeson was commanding over $2,000 per concert, making his annual rate of pay higher than that of Joe DiMaggio, and had an international audience for his films and music that extended into Africa, Asia, Europe, and the Soviet Union. Among African Americans he was also widely admired as one of the greatest college football players of the first half of

the twentieth century, and as the valedictorian of his class at Rutgers University. Throughout the 1940s he was far and away the best known person of African-American descent in the world, far more widely recognized than his closest competitor, the great heavyweight champion Joe Louis.

Yet within a span of ten years, 1947 to 1957, Robeson was virtually erased from historic memory. In response to a coordinated effort to impugn his patriotism, which extended from the FBI and United States State Department to congressional and state investigating committees, Robeson was barred from the commercial theater, the Hollywood film industry, radio and television, and from the concert stage. During those years no major concert hall, stadium, or amphitheater would sponsor a Paul Robeson concert, and two of his largest concerts held on private land, his Peekskill concerts of 1949, were the subject of mob attacks spurred on by veterans' organizations. The American establishment also tried to erase the record of his achievements. His trophies were removed from the display case at Rutgers University, and he was excluded from the Football Hall of Fame. Many prominent African Americans, under pressure from government security agencies, felt compelled to denounce his ideas. The NAACP and the Urban League, which had once treated him as the most honored of black Americans, excluded him from their meetings and from the pages of their publications. Even private individuals felt compelled to hide their respect for his ideas or attachment to his music. During the 1950s, possession of Paul Robeson records, or books and articles about his life, could mark a person as a security risk and get people hauled before loyalty boards if they were government employees.

In a country that called itself democratic, that proclaimed itself the "leader of the free world," it is sobering to think that a person of Robeson's talents and stature could be silenced and marginalized so quickly, strictly for his political beliefs. What does it say about America that the most talented African American of the century—a scholar, athlete, artist, and human rights activist, a man whose singing voice sent chills through those who heard it, and a man who mastered twelve languages—could be turned into a nonperson by the hysterical manipulation of public opinion? Paul Robeson broke no laws. His crime, to those who attacked him, was that he refused to denounce the Soviet Union as the major source of evil in the world and to sever ties to American Communists he worked with in civil rights organizations, labor organizations, and campaigns to end European colonialism. The political and cultural leaders of the United States were so threatened by Robeson's political outlook and his utter lack of deference to the leaders of white America

that they decided to make an example of him that would redound through the ages.

In the last thirty years Paul Robeson has been slowly rehabilitated. His trophies have been restored to the display case at Rutgers, his recordings have been reissued as CDs, books and articles have been written about his life, and he has been the subject of several museum exhibitions and documentary films. He is now mentioned in college history texts, and a few cities have even named schools and community centers in his memory. But Robeson still remains far less known in the United States than in England, Germany, Russia, China, and South Africa. In the course I teach on the 1960s, which begins with a section on the Cold War, less than five of the forty students in my class had heard of Paul Robeson before I gave a lecture about him. Compared to the other great African-American activists of the twentieth century—Booker T. Washington, W.E.B. Du Bois, Marcus Garvey, Martin Luther King, Jr., and Malcolm X—Paul Robeson remains a shadowy presence, someone that many African Americans, not to say Americans generally, are still reluctant to claim as a hero.

Why this ambivalence? Marcus Garvey held ideas that were extremely controversial in his time and was arrested, persecuted, and deported by the American government, yet he is respected by scholars and the general public as the leader of a mass movement that exerted great influence on African-American life. But, Robeson is, in some ways, a far less accessible figure. There are things about Paul Robeson that Americans in 2001 find very difficult to grasp, and, frankly, very difficult to identify with.

First of these is Robeson's connection to the Soviet Union and American Communism. At a time when most people believe that Communism is a failure as a social ideal and a political system, it is hard to understand why a person of ability and intelligence would sacrifice his career for such a flawed principle. But we need to look at the world as Robeson saw it when he began gravitating to the Left in the 1930s. We have to remember that Paul Robeson left the United States in 1929, only to return in 1939, because he no longer wanted to subject himself to American racism. American society, the golden child of global capitalism, was poisoned by white supremacy. Not only were the southern states zones of political terror where people of African descent could not vote, serve on juries, or run for political office, but the rest of the country had apartheid-like social relations that humiliated black people at every turn. Even in liberal New York Robeson was barred from service in most restaurants, hotels, and night clubs, was confined to balconies in most theaters, could not live in most neighborhoods, and could not work at most occupations. The other major centers of capitalist power — the nations of Western Europe — were less color conscious than the United States, but held the colored peoples of the world as colonies, denying them political independence and the right of self-determination. When Robeson became politically conscious under the influence of European and African radicals he met in England, he began to see that everywhere global capitalism had influence, it generated patterns of racial inequality or imperialist control that kept people of color in poverty and transformed them into cheap sources of labor. The Soviet Union, and the parties under its influence, appeared to be the major force in the world challenging this system. When Robeson met Communists, whether in Europe, the Soviet Union, or the United States, they described the ending of racial prejudice and the freeing of colonial people as one of the more important consequences of their war against capitalism. It also impressed Robeson that

when he visited the Soviet Union in 1935 he was welcomed with uninhibited enthusiasm by the Soviet people and experienced a complete absence of color prejudice. So impressed was he by the egalitarian atmosphere in this predominantly white but multiracial society, that he decided to send his son to be educated there.

When Robeson returned to the United States in 1939 he gravitated to people and organizations connected to the American Communist Movement because he presumed that Communists would be the Americans most opposed to racism and imperialism. At that point in American history his judgment was sound. Communists were an embattled minority in a conservative nation, but their movement was virtually the only organized group in American society — political or religious — that forced white Americans to confront and overcome their own racism. Not only did the Communist Party and its affiliated organizations — which included trade unions, peace organizations, fraternal societies, and cultural organizations — have many African-American leaders, but the Communist Party's social life was proudly and militantly interracial. Communist social clubs, summer camps, resorts, and housing developments welcomed African-American participation and actually encouraged interracial socializing, interracial dancing, interracial dating, and interracial marriage. In a society where interracial intimacy was seen as a source of shame and illicit desire, the Communist Party, virtually alone among political movements, insisted that fraternization across the color line was a natural and inevitable component of the practice of racial equality, something that would help, not hinder, the struggle for social injustice. For Robeson, being connected to the American Communist Movement not only meant that his cultural and intellectual achievements would be respected, but that his family and friends could socialize among people of different races, free of insult or suspicion — something which was not possible in any other setting in the United States at that particular time in history. Robeson's connection to Communism was not, in short, irrational; it was part of a principled protest against a worldwide capitalist system that appeared to promote the exploitation and social ostracism of people of African descent. While capitalism today may not have such a firm connection to racism, we can hardly blame Paul Robeson for responding to the world as he perceived and experienced it.

Another aspect of Robeson's legacy that confuses current generations was his working class internationalism, his conviction that there was a powerful commonality in the experience of working class people that crossed lines of color and nationality. When Robeson returned to the United States in 1939 he rarely performed concerts that only featured African-American music. Rather, he sang African-American spirituals and work songs in the context of a presentation of songs of the common people of Europe, Africa, and the Far East, as well as immigrant workers in the United States. At the high point of his fame, Robeson was an artist with a political mission, someone who was determined to devote large portions of his time and energy to helping workers of different races and nationalities fight for their economic and political rights. Robeson always expressed great pride in his African ancestry, and presented the cultural legacy of the African-American people with unprecedented eloquence and power, but he felt that to deal with black issues in isolation was to weaken their force. At a time when the American labor movement was reaching out to black workers for the first time in its history, and when independence movements were arising through the colonial world, Robeson believed it would help

African Americans to see their struggle as part of a worldwide movement of oppressed peoples of all races. In particular, he saw African Americans having a strong affinity with the peoples of Africa, Asia, and Latin America who were oppressed both as workers and as victims of European and American imperialism.

Paul Robeson's record of fighting for his political beliefs, of giving substance to his vision of working class solidarity, was quite simply unparalleled by any other cultural figure in American history. From 1939 to 1956 Paul Robeson sang before more audiences of working class people, representing people of more racial and ethnic backgrounds, than any American artist, whether folk, classical, or commercial. He did so, at great financial sacrifice, when he was at the height of his commercial popularity, and he did so when he was an outcast in his native land, unable to find a commercial concert hall that would rent him space. He sang to African-American tobacco workers in the Carolinas in schoolyards and Baptist churches, around the campfires of Filipino and Japanese pineapple workers in Hawaii, to black and white stevedores and factory workers in union halls in Memphis, to Jewish-American garment workers in Catskill bungalow colonies and Bronx social halls, to Finnish miners in their social clubs in the Mesabi Range of Minnesota, to Mexican-American miners in Colorado and Arizona, to black Panamanian government workers assembled in a stadium in Panama City, to crowds of thousands of auto workers outside of factories in California and Michigan, to an audience of Canadian miners and metal workers on the border between Washington State and Canada, to congregations of his brother's AME Zion church in Harlem. He marched on picket lines in the Bureau of Engraving with black workers seeking to gain access to the skilled trades, and with black and white housing activists seeking to open the largest privately financed housing development in the Bronx to black tenants. He was an honorary member of labor organizations, such as the Fur and Leather Workers' Union, the National Maritime Union, the Food and Tobacco Workers Union, the International Longshoreman and Warehouseman's Union, the Mine Mill and Smelters Workers Union, and the United Public Workers Union. He performed regularly at pageants and festivals of the International Workers Order, the left-wing fraternal order that had insurance societies among twenty-odd language groups, including Puerto Ricans, Mexican Americans, Chinese Americans, Finnish Americans, Japanese Americans, African Americans, South Slavs and Jews. Because of his commitment to performing for and *among* workers, and his ties to unions that were trying to organize the most persecuted and marginalized of American workers, Robeson experienced the American working class as multiracial and multicultural. Although his deepest emotional connection was to the African-American tradition, Robeson understood that the United States was not simply a black-white society, but had peoples from Asia, the Pacific, and Latin America doing much of its agricultural and extractive labor, especially on the west coast, and that their contributions to the building of American society, as well as their sufferings, had to be recognized and understood. At a concert he gave in 1947 before a convention of the National Maritime Union, a multiracial organization that had an Afro-Caribbean secretary-treasurer, Ferdinand Smith, Robeson told his audience: "This is the reason I have come into the struggle, so that I can go back today to the people, to the Negro people, to the forces of labor. Speak to them not from the Carnegie Hall stage ... but in their small meetings, in their churches, wherever they may be — and it is with

them that I will stand until the final victory."

Did Robeson's internationalism and his laboristic ideology dilute his civil rights activism? Did his concern for the suffering of workers of other nationalities make his fight for the rights and dignity of the African-American people less powerful? To arrive at an answer to this question, we must take a closer look both at Robeson's concert repertoire and the theory of American nationality that infused all his spoken remarks, whether formal speeches or commentary during his performances. Robeson's concerts were a living embodiment of his profound belief, shared by a small number of other progressive intellectuals, that beauty derived from labor and that virtues such as courage, solidarity, compassion, and endurance found their highest expressions among the lives of the common people. Robeson's intonation, his diction, the timber of his voice, the controlled emotion he placed into each note, and his extraordinary physical presence made his audiences, especially those of working class background, feel they were in the presence of something that ennobled them and gave their lives new meaning. Those who heard Robeson sing in the intimate setting of a union social hall or African-American church rarely forgot the experience. One of the most courageous people I have ever met, the radical minister and union organizer Claude Williams, a person who had been beaten, tarred, feathered, and whipped, run out of three states because of his efforts to organize black and white Southern workers in interracial unions, told me that the highlight of his life was being in the same room with Paul Robeson. I have seen a sixty-five-year-old musicologist, a head of the music department at the Library of Congress, start crying unashamedly when trying to describe to younger scholars what it was like to listen to Paul Robeson, telling us we could not have a Paul Robeson exhibit without hearing his music. I have spoken to a seventy-year-old schoolteacher from the Bronx who told me that her most vivid childhood memory was of sitting on Paul Robeson's knee while he sang a lullaby to her in the social hall of a Jewish workers' bungalow colony in Peekskill. If the purpose of great art is to allow us to feel a higher sense of our own possibility as human beings, then Paul Robeson was perhaps the greatest artist of his time, someone who found beauty in lullabies, work songs, the chants of road gangs, prisoners of war, peasants, and soldiers, the music people sang in churches and on picket lines, making those whose work received little recognition feel that *their labor* made civilization possible.

And where did African Americans fit in Robeson's pantheon of laboring peoples, this musical celebration of those whose labor built America and the modern world economy? They were at the center, the core; they were the people whose experience would ultimately be the test of whether America would reach its potential as a democratic country. Wherever he sang, Robeson placed the songs of the Negro people in the most prominent position, using them as the base of his entire concert repertoire. "When I sang my American folk melodies in Budapest, Prague, Tilfis, Moscow, Oslo, the Hebrides or on the Spanish front," Robeson told an interviewer, "the people understood and wept and rejoiced with the spirit of the songs. I found that where forces have been the same, whether people weave, build, pick cotton or dig in the mines, they understand each other in the common language of work, suffering and protest.... When I sing, 'Let my people go,' I can feel sympathetic vibrations from my audience, whatever its nationality. It is no longer just a Negro song — it is a symbol of those seeking freedom from the dungeon of fascism."

Robeson also insisted that his audiences recognize the centrality of African-American labor, paid and unpaid, to the building of American civilization. "The great primary wealth of this land," Robeson told an audience of Canadian miners assembled at the Peace Arch in the border town of Blaine, "came from the blood and suffering of my forefathers.... I'm telling you now that a good portion of that American earth belongs to me." With a power that has remained unmatched to this day, Robeson insisted that African Americans were foremost among the diverse laboring peoples whose work and suffering made America a great nation. "Who built this land?" Robeson proclaimed. "Who have been the guarantors of our historic tradition of freedom and equality? Whose labor have produced the great cities, the industrial machines, the basic culture and creature comforts of which our Voice of America spokesmen talk so proudly about? It is well to remember that the America we know has arisen out of the toil of many millions who have come here seeking freedom, from many parts of the world: the Irish and Scottish indentured servants who cleared the forests, built the colonial homesteads, and were part of the productive backbone of our early days; the millions of German immigrants of the mid-nineteenth century, and the millions more from Eastern Europe whose sweat and sacrifice in the steel mills, the coal mines and the factories made possible the industrial revolution; the brave Jewish people from all parts of Europe who have so enriched our lives on this continent; the workers from Mexico and from the East — Japan and the Philippines — whose labor has helped make the West and Southwest a rich and fruitful land; and through it all, from the earliest days — before Columbus — the Negro people, upon whose unpaid toil as slaves the basic wealth of this nation was built! These are the forces that have made America great and preserved our democratic heritage."

What did African Americans, and indeed all Americans, lose when this voice was silenced? One way to answer this is to try to imagine where Paul Robeson would be today in an America where even our most perceptive, class-conscious young people sing "It's All About the Benjamins" and "Cash Rules Everything Around Me." He would be in the sweatshops of New York and California, where women from Asia and Central America are making garments for Kmart and J.C. Penney. He would be with the Nike workers of Vietnam. He would be with dishwashers from Guatemala and El Salvador who work 18 hours a day in the kitchens of our restaurants. He would be with housekeepers and janitors in universities throughout the country, trying to help them win union contracts. He would be with African-American women in chicken processing plants throughout the South, helping them fight for better wages and working conditions. He would be with the people of all races in New York City, protesting the police execution of Amadou Diallo. He would be with homeless families and former welfare recipients who fill the food pantries in our cities and towns. And he would be at our prisons and penitentiaries where hundreds of thousands of African-American men, denied decent work at living wages, are being confined and humiliated, treated like parasites in the land their ancestors toiled so hard to build. In his time, Paul Robeson was the conscience of a country that feared the very democracy for which it claimed to stand. We need to incorporate his vision and example into our personal lives.

Paul Robeson: Icon or Hero?

JEFFREY CONRAD STEWART
George Mason University

During the 1930s Paul Robeson was very likely the best known American abroad. Robeson was the most popular American concert singer in Europe, because his bass voice had become, for critics and the listening audience, the preferred sound of the increasingly popular spirituals. That voice also had become the voice of European freedom and self-determination, because in the early 1930s Robeson had added English, Scottish, French, and Russian songs of labor and resistance to his concert program. Robeson's face and magnificent body were seen throughout Europe in not only American-made movies such as *The Emperor Jones* (1933) and *Show Boat* (1936), but also the European-produced *Song of Freedom*, *King Solomon's Mines*, and his favorite, *The Proud Valley* (1940). Robeson was one of the most photographed Americans abroad, as his picture was splashed over dozens of European newspapers, his enormous presence dominating coverage of concerts, exhibit openings, fancy dress balls, and receptions for the rich and the famous. As if that was not enough, Robeson invaded the European stage, becom-

ing the first Black man since Ira Aldridge to perform in Shakespeare's *Othello* in England in 1930, and returning several years later to critical acclaim in Eugene O'Neill's *The Hairy Ape*. Robeson became an international icon of what it meant to be an African American and an American.

But in the process of gaining such popularity, Robeson began to struggle with the issue of representation — of how he and other African Americans were portrayed in the media. He began to question his value as artist when he observed how his image was used and manipulated on the stage and in the movies. While most African-American actors regurgitated stereotypical roles in Hollywood movies, Robeson began to criticize racist imagery in films and eventually refused to act in American movies. At a time when American singers and actors routinely performed before segregated audiences, Robeson, in 1940, forced the play *John Henry* to open in New York rather than perform the title role before a segregated audience in Washington. During the 1940s and 1950s Robeson took his status as America's beloved football All–American; its renowned Harlem Renaissance actor, singer, and motion picture star; and its symbol of African-American opportunity and used it to advocate for socialism and the Soviet Union.

In the ensuing post–World War II struggle over Communism in America, Robeson became the symbol of resistance to the House on Un-American Activities Committee during the McCarthy era and called its members the "real un–Americans." In that struggle Robeson became what conservatives and liberals alike lament we have too few of today — an American hero who is willing to trade material success for moral and political significance. For Robeson gave up his status as an icon of popular culture to become America's first politically-engaged black performing artist and its most outspoken critic. As a consequence, he sacrificed the wealthy and glamorous lifestyle he had gained as a celebrity and became to many Americans by 1950 a pariah, because he rejected the rewards of American success. Much of America responded by all but erasing his name from the history books, the popular media, and much of the internal memory of the black community.

As if Robeson himself was responsible for the consequences of his activism, many voices, black and white, have asked — Why did he do it? In his biography of Robeson, Martin Duberman suggests that being abandoned during the 1930s by a white woman who had promised to marry him transformed Robeson from a celebrity icon to an anti-racist and anti-capitalist hero. While this incident certainly hurt, I doubt that such a monumental life change can be explained by one such personal experience. At most, that incident served to highlight that the "freedom" he supposedly enjoyed as an international icon was illusory. And in that sense it merely attached itself to a deeper, longer-termed process of emerging self-consciousness about his limita-

tions as a black artist and his destiny as a heroic figure in America and the world. Sometime in the 1930s, while still a beloved American icon, Robeson recognized that he could not transform the racist representations of African peoples on stage and in motion pictures unless he undertook an activist struggle to transform the system of international capitalism and racism that sustained those representations. Robeson answered the hero's challenge by attacking not merely the obvious obstacles to his success as an artist, but to underlying degradations of the humanity of all African peoples.

Robeson could come to such an analysis *because he was a performing artist* at a crucial moment in American cultural history, when technological innovation transformed entertainment in America from a participatory to a consumer culture industry. Robeson was part of the transformation in American culture whereby the primacy in our culture moved beyond the manipulation of words to manipulation of images. As a performing artist he was more sensitive to and directly dependent on the economics of cultural production in the motion picture, concert, and legitimate theatre world than, for example, a historian like W.E.B. Du Bois, or a philosopher like Alain Locke. In the 1930s that dependency opened Robeson's eyes to the ways in which he and his art were used to advance racial and class agenda he rejected. When he shifted the emphasis of his public career from cultural production to the interrogation of the social formation that underlay it, Robeson risked the future of his career as an artist on the willingness of workers, black and white, to support his heroic activism.

Robeson's problem was that the class conscious basis for such activism, i.e., the willingness of white workers to join with black workers in a sustained attack on the capitalist system, was never strong in

America and probably reached its peak in the late 1930s and early 1940s. It evaporated during the McCarthy-led anti–Communist campaign of the late 1940s and early 1950s; and that government-led capitulation to anti–Communism destroyed Robeson's career as one of the top performing artists in the world. The cosmopolitan experience of his international celebrity had remade his identity on a globalist basis, but most of the working and middle class Americans who were his natural audiences had not had that experience. In that sense, he would be handicapped as a political leader by the individualistic and elitist character of his challenge to the American political oligarchy. At his best, he created the first truly integrated, interfaith, and interracial audience for progressive change in the United States. At his worst, the solitary nature of his heroic challenge to the American system made him an easy target of a campaign to tar him with a welter of negative media caricatures. An icon who had been created, in part, by twentieth century media — the American theater, music, and film industry — Robeson could be remade by a media — this time the newspaper, radio, and political mouthpieces of anti–Communism — by the middle of that century.

Ironically, Robeson's dethroning as an icon did not obliterate his name from twentieth century American or European culture; it gave it a new life as an international symbol of dignity in the face of oppression. All along, Robeson had also worn another mantle, that of the hero of black America; and during the 1930s he had also become a hero to Leftist Americans and Europeans of all races. Finally, during the 1940s and 1950s he became a hero to the victims of anti–Communism and the defenders of constitutional rights to free speech and freedom of assembly in America and the world. In a sense, Robeson today is more known as a hero than an icon, because the former replaced the latter just as surely as his life as a political activist replaced that of a motion picture actor. Indeed, one can argue that the still simmering hope of a revival of the progressive movement in America today is linked, in part, to the messianic heroism that Paul Robeson brought to that movement from the 1930s on.

What was it about Paul Robeson that made him such a compelling figure? How was it that a son of a slave could rise so quickly in America during the early twentieth century and become a popular American and international star? Why did he strike such a powerful chord with thousands of people in Europe and the Soviet Union? And what can his case tell us about the plight of talented African Americans, especially athletes and entertainers, who also, sometime in their lives, face a moment of decision as to whether they will use their celebrity to advance a social agenda?

I believe that Robeson's success during his time and his continuing grip on our imaginations comes from the way in which he challenged the process by which successful African Americans have become both icons of American success and heroes to the black community. The hero, as a narrative, is deeply inscribed in African-American history. Indeed, today, when most academic American history has left behind the concept of the American hero, the notion, best articulated by Carlyle in his nineteenth-century classic *The Hero in History*, that great men make great history is still a powerful narrative in African-American popular history. It is most obvious in the African-American fixation on writing histories of the first black man or woman who has broken the race barrier in some occupation or profession. That admittedly nineteenth-century tradition has persisted, because success for many blacks has continued to require overcoming some racially-imposed obstacle. In this narrative the quintessential African American is Frederick Douglass, who became a black hero because he taught himself to read and write, whipped Covey, the feared Negro breaker, on a Maryland farm, escaped slavery to freedom up North, and became the finest public speaker in America during the nineteenth century. Douglass became an American icon because, as Nathan Huggins pointed out in his fine but neglected study *Slave and Citizen*, Douglass's story epitomized the American narrative of self-help and self-made men. Douglass remained a black hero and an American icon in the post–Civil War period because he embraced the mantle of the self-made man, in part because he did not or could not mount a serious challenge to the system that replaced it. Typically, a person was first a black hero, and then became an American icon through a process of commodification that emptied out his blackness. Robeson had the audacity to reverse that process, to become an icon, and then seek to become a hero of resistance to the very system that had created him.

I believe that what distinguishes the black heroic tradition from that of Carlyle's ilk is the issue of gender. For, while much of the black heroism has been narrated in terms of hypermasculinity, the role of black women as active agents in the freedom struggle has undermined the gendered vision of Carlyle and the British imperialist tradition out of which it emerged. Yes, there is Frederick Douglass; but there is also Harriet Tubman; and while the former is more widely known than the latter, Tubman occupies a unique space of selfless liberation in the freedom struggle that even Douglass does not inhabit. For Harriet Tubman physically liberated dozens of others, rather than simply herself. And there is also Sojourner Truth, who becomes not only a runaway slave but a fearless abolitionist and a Women's Rights

Leader. It may be that part of the success of black women in the African-American heroic tradition is that they are able to wrap themselves in the same hypermasculinity that black men grab on to. In some cases they are more masculine than the men. I can never forget my mother narrating to me her belief that Harriet Tubman always carried a pistol with her on her caravans northward, because, invariably, in my mother's telling of the tale, there was always some slave man who wanted to turn back to the comfort of old master's plantation. And Harriet, again in my mother's voice, would say, "Either you come with us or you die here!" And who can forget that on the abolitionist circuit in Indiana, Sojourner Truth was such a vocal force and spiritual symbol of resistance to apologists for slavery? And gender was part of that story in an unavoidable way: She was challenged on numerous occasions with the charge that she was not a woman, but in fact a man. And at one stop she reputedly answered such challenges by pulling down her shirt to show her breast to the white men assailing her from the audience, and asked them, "Here's my breast — do you want to suck?" In the history of the black community, in part because of the challenges facing black men, in part because of the way the black community in the urban ante-bellum North encouraged black women in spokesperson roles, black women could anoint themselves with the heroic role and enter our history as heroes and, at times, as icons.

Becoming an icon is also part of African-American history. But it usually requires something more than simply the agency of an individual black person or the celebratory zeal of the black community. To be black and a national/international icon requires the knack, the luck, the manipulative genius to attract and hold the gaze of the white public in such a way that one transcends not only the black masses, but also the individuality of a particular life to become symbolic of the best there is in black and white popular culture. There is always something almost religious in the ascendancy, as when Jesus Christ moves from his heroic victory over death to become an icon reproduced in thousands of paintings, tapestries, stained glass windows, church banners, and little crucifixes hung around believers' necks. There is much that is good in such symbolization, such as the identification of the individual self with something more noble, more poised, more fundamental to all that life means, something that transcends even as it embodies the best of the self. But there is also something atrophying, reifying, and possibly dangerous about the reduction of a life to a representation, to the sequestering of all the multiplicity that is any personality into a thing, a token, an artifact that can be worshipped in place of a person. It is not for no reason, therefore, that the Bible has the prohibition against worship of graven images. This is particularly relevant today when so many of our icons are mass produced and mass marketed emblems of status, comfort, and taste. And when one adds the work that must be done to anyone or thing that is black, which starts out as the "Other" in our society, to transform it or him or her into something almost universally loved in an otherwise racist society, then one has something remarkable indeed. That transformation from a talented young black boy from New Jersey into a world-revered statesperson is a process that occurred with Paul Robeson.

Paul Robeson was the first twentieth-century African American to be both a popular culture icon and a black hero, to become a commodified symbol of blackness that whites felt comfortable consuming, and to become a hero of the black community's desire to have a leader who would not give in to white authority and oppression. I want to interrogate the popular notion that to be an icon and a hero is the same thing. Why would someone be considered both an icon of popular culture and a political hero? Robeson did that even before Ronald Reagan. How did this happen, and why does this conjunction of the popular and the heroic continue to confuse our assessment of what constitutes heroism in the African-American — and the larger —community. For example, in a television commercial that ran during Michael Jordan's self-exile from basketball, Jordan asked the camera, "If I did not play basketball, would I still be your hero?" Implicit in this question is the idea that because Jordan plays basketball, is perhaps the best basketball player ever, and is a media and advertising industry darling, he is a hero— and a black hero at that. I want to contest that notion in the following analysis by showing that Robeson was a hero precisely because he was willing to sacrifice his fame and fortune to fight for principles in a way that is completely foreign to Michael Jordan. Yet Jordan's question also suggests something of the poignancy of his and other black athletes' position in American culture that is also important here: their status as icons is incredibly tenuous. If I did not play sports, a spectacle for you, the consuming audience, would I be anything but "another nigger?" As the story of Robeson shows, the iconic status of Black athletes and actors can very easily be removed if they stop being commodified performers and become actors on the historical stage.

Jordan's question, ironically, could have been posed by Paul Robeson to the country in 1950 when it began to ban his records, cancel his concerts, remove his name from the list of All-Americans, and treat him like a non-person. "If Paul Robeson ceases to play football, entertain you on the stage or on the screen, will I remain your hero?" The answer from the majority of Americans was no. But the answer from a significant minority of black Americans and a smaller percentage of white Americans, plus thousands of Europeans, Russians, and other nationals was yes, and it continued to be yes in the 1960s and 1970s. Robeson became a hero for many people precisely because he was not like Michael Jordan — a yes man for corporate America — but a challenge to the system that exploits African Americans for profit. Robeson was thus a hero because he stood up to the FBI, the State Department, and President Harry Truman's campaign to stop his criticism of American racial and human rights violations. The price he paid for that stand was enormous— his career, his health, and his peace of mind. Why did he do it? Part of the answer came from his relationship with his father.

William Robeson was born on a North Carolina plantation, which he escaped from in 1860, returned to during the Civil War as a member of the Union Army, and left again to attend Lincoln University. By learning to read and write English and Latin, earning a college degree from Lincoln University, marrying Maria Bustill, a woman from a prominent black family, and becoming a respected minister in the Presbyterian Church in Princeton, the elder Robeson became a hero in the tradition of Douglass and in the manner of Booker T. Washington — someone who had lifted himself "up from slavery" to become a success in his community. Washington refined and expressed what was already a prominent strain in African-American life, that to become middle class was a heroic kind of success for a former slave. But what Washington did was to empty out of the slave-as-hero narrative the demand explicit in Douglass that the former slave was a hero because he or she was a kind of moral conscience, a fearless critic of the ideas, attitudes, and institutions that made the gross exploitation of human beings

possible under slavery. The elder Robeson, in this sense, was more in the tradition of Douglass than Washington, because after he became a prominent minister in Princeton, he was not willing to indulge the paternalistic fantasies of Princeton whites who believed that "their" African Americans ought to continue the deferential traditions of the South. William Robeson discovered that he was resented in that community because of some violation on his part, now lost in history, of the community deference norms. For this he was criticized as an unfit minister of his church, and was removed from his position. This was the challenge that is visited upon true heroes, and as a true hero, William Robeson accepted the challenge, refused to kowtow to whites or feel self-pity, but moved his family around until he could find new employment. The family experienced deep privation and discomfort, but in the end Robeson found a new church and provided for his family, which included Paul, two brothers, and a sister, with dignity. It was because of this specific incident that William Robeson became a hero in Robeson's eyes and a model for his own later resistance to oppression. But why?

Surely, no matter how romanticized this heroic story of his father's "standing up to the man" became, the truth must have been that, for such a young boy, his father's dismissal scarred him, for it suddenly catapulted the family into poverty. That fear must have been heightened because it also coincided with the death of his mother when he was six. Simultaneously, he was wrenched from his mother's nurture and the safety of a middle class black life in an upper class white community. What hurt the most, he recalled, were visits with his mother's family, Bustills, who made snide remarks about his family's newfound poverty and his father's poorer relations.

Early exposed to the butt of class

conflict, Robeson sided emotionally with the working class: He would become their defender, in part because he carried within him the pain of having lived in a virtual paradise of a black childhood at the turn of the century and having lost it. But defending the working class was also his way of psychically defending his father: The two would become fused in the mature Paul Robeson, so that his defense of workers in later life would carry with it the energy of his psychic defense of his father. Paul Robeson was left with a kind of double consciousness about success in America.

We can unpack something of the feeling by considering what the Presbyterian church his father pastored — which may still be seen in Princeton, New Jersey, on "Paul Robeson Place" — with its beautiful structure and its accompanying house, must have meant to Paul, especially when he was forced to leave them behind. On the one hand, the church was a splendid example of the middle class respectability that William Robeson had achieved. But that church also represented the sacrifices, the concession, the compromises required of a black person to have such a house in Princeton during the Jim Crow era. Such images must have carried for Robeson a profound sense of irony and a message: black people could not construct their identity through the possession of property, because America would ultimately take it away from them. Furthermore, one risked exposure to the brunt of middle class antipathy and the former slaves who did not run away, such as Booker T. Washington, who advised black men not to behave like men but like freed slaves.

The fine houses of Princeton remind me of the photographs taken of "the Beeches" in Connecticut, which Robeson himself bought at the height of his popularity and fame in 1944. With its enormous and imposing pillars, Robeson's mansion reminds me of a plantation of the type that his father had been forced to leave behind. This and other photographs of this house, with Essie, Paul's wife, and Paul, Jr., his son, as a smiling happy family sitting on its steps disguise the price such a possession cost Robeson, the many compromises he had to make to keep such a house and prosper in a system of cultural production that increasingly disgusted him. Robeson could do that — pose for smiling pictures, live the celebrity lifestyle — until the society made the compromise explicit and demanded that he choose, in the late 1940s and early 1950s, either to stop criticizing America and defending the Soviet Union or lose his celebrity lifestyle. Then he would return to the internalized image of his father, his model of heroism in Princeton and the message of his loss of his parsonage — that the black man's identity was built on the heroic tradition of the runaway slave who left house, home, family, and plantation in the pursuit of freedom. At such crossroads Robeson would conclude that, faced with oppression, the heroic black man must choose resistance and deprivation over compromise and negotiation.

Robeson's bond with his father strengthened as Paul met the challenges of race in school, particularly at Rutgers College, where he enrolled in 1915. There his experience in football was formative. Trying out for the team, he was stomped, beaten, and gang tackled by white team members determined to discourage the "giant" Negro from joining the team. In one sense, this was simply the fact of segregation in American life in the 1910s, but it was also something more: College sports had emerged by the second decade of the twentieth century as a site of masculine conflict in which white men proved their Darwinian superiority over other men. By 1915 the masculine ideal in popular culture was no longer the Victorian gentleman,

Witherspoon Street Presbyterian Church, William Robeson's Princeton, New Jersey, church, photographed by Betty Millard in 1952. Courtesy of Lloyd Brown Collection.

Two views of the Robeson family — Paul, Eslanda, and Paul, Jr. — on the steps of "the Beeches," the home they purchased in Enfield, Connecticut, in 1942. Photographed by Frank Bauman. Courtesy of *Look* Magazine Collection, Museum of the City of New York.

but the muscular and aggressive football player, whose ability to endure pain, destroy the opposition, and work together with other players epitomized the notion that life was a field of organized conflict between blindly goal-centered, muscular men. And here was Robeson, a six foot, two inch, two hundred and fifteen pound man who was muscular, swift, and aggressive, an excellent catcher of the football, a superb blocker, whose body was hard as nails—a masculine ideal, who had to be kept out of the arena lest he overturn the notion that whites were biologically superior to blacks. After one practice, during which players had broken his nose and dislocated his shoulder, Robeson went home severely injured and thought of quitting the team. But the male coterie of his father and brother emboldened him to return. And to the inner Paul, the father's image of courage had been internalized: He would not bend, he would not be broken. When his hand was stomped on during the next day of practice, he began knocking players to the ground and picked up one with the intent to body-slam him to the ground. Then the coach yelled, "Robeson, you're on the team." Robeson's active response also manifested the character attributes of the new masculinity popularized by Theodore Roosevelt and his "rough riders," that the true man exhibited courage in the face of enormous odds. By fighting back, Robeson dispelled white supremacist notions that because they had been slaves, all blacks were cowards. Thus, Robeson's response was deeply rooted in his father's steely determination to succeed despite oppression.

But it was also something more—Paul Robeson had taken the next step beyond his father's quiet resistance, beyond running away from slavery to actively fighting the white man—as Frederick Douglass had done with Covey—to counterattack against oppression. In this step,

Robeson's action embodied the generational consciousness of the "New Negro," and anticipated the "fighting back" attitude of Northern blacks during the attacks on their communities by whites in the 1919 race riots. In this step, Paul Robeson had become the hero.

Something of the tension of Robeson's struggle to make the team is apparent in the first photograph we have of Robeson with the football team. Although he is ensconced in the middle of the team photograph, there is the feeling of begrudging acceptance of his presence. Later pictures of him, especially those after the 1917 season in which Robeson played such a crucial part in the victorious Rutgers' teams of that season, show greater camaraderie, greater ease, and a sense that this is now a team of men together. It was in that 1917 season that Robeson moved from being a hero for his family to becoming a hero of the team and the school. His performance in the 1917 game against Naval Reserve wrote his name into football legend, as he completely dominated the play of the team. That success brought him to the attention of the media and he became the subject of numerous campus articles and cartoons, whose representations of him show how the commentators struggled to find racial formulas to report what was happening on the field. "The Giant Negro" dominated all play, wrote one commentator, enlarging Robeson's stature to unrealistic proportions, presumably as a way of explaining how a black man could dominate the play of average sized white men; but Robeson was only six feet two inches tall—taller than most, but not towering above all opponents. Another commentator began reportage of a game with the intro—"A dark cloud descended on the field"—as if Robeson was a storm that swallowed up the rest of the players. All this was necessary to try and communicate to readers what his impact was on the

Paul Robeson with football team, c. 1915, Special Collections, Rutgers University Libraries.

field in racial terms and not simply suggest that Robeson was superior in talent and skill to the white players he faced. Even the venerable Walter Camp called him a "superman" when he named him to the 1917 All-American team; but in 1918, when Camp chose his all-service team (since no All-American team was picked that year because of the war), he was able to put racial characterization aside and state what Robeson meant to football — that he was the best all-around player in college football and the prototype of the future tight end. The famous photograph (see page 207) of Robeson standing holding a football created a new icon for an African American in 1918: Here was a man who was tall, muscular, and fit, but also proud, centered, and resolute in his sense of purpose. The photograph also showed him as an individual, which was rare in popular representations of African Americans in

the period, someone whose image communicated that he could stand alone and accomplish something solely on his own ability. This 1918 photograph, reproduced widely at the time and since, made Robeson a football icon, a masculine ideal for all the nation, a person and an image that transcended traditional representations of African Americans to become a representation that could appeal to both black and white Americans.

The two psychological forces — to be heroic, to honor his father and his race and to become a popular campus and national success story — meshed nicely in the Rutgers environment. He was a black American hero because he overcame and faced down racism, and a white American icon because he was a football and social star of Rutgers College. His success symbolized the "talented tenth" segregation of the early twentieth century, a system in which

Robeson lined up with football team, c. 1918, Special Collections, Rutgers University Libraries.

a few exceptional blacks would be allowed to get excellent educations in integrated institutions of higher education while millions of other blacks were excluded. And his success and his acceptance at Rutgers narrated a larger American story — that everybody can make it in America, that the son of a slave can grow up to become valedictorian at Rutgers College. Not surprisingly, Robeson left Rutgers with a great deal of optimism about America. His senior thesis argued that with the passage of the Fourteenth Amendment, the Constitution was finally made whole, finally rendered a just document because it finally defined citizenship in a way that made the travesty of the Dred Scott decision (the decision of the Supreme Court in 1857 that decreed blacks were not citizens of the United States) no longer possible and opened the door for bestowing all citizenship rights on all Americans. In his valedictory speech, "The New Idealism," he

optimized about the prospects for a new generation of African Americans after World War I who now realized that their success lay in their hands and not in white America's. His performance inserted this one caveat: White America would have to meet the Negro half way and refuse to deny Robeson and others like him the opportunity to rise to the highest aspirations of their character in modern America.

Robeson's willingness in the 1940s and 1950s to sacrifice all of his success to protest against America's failings was directly related to this "idealism," to how much he believed in the American Idea. The power of that idealism was evident in 1919. One observer of his valedictory speech recalled that moment as a time when Robeson had the entire nation in his hands, could have done anything and become anything he wanted — a lament the observer issued from the perspective of 1949 when he could not understand why Robe-

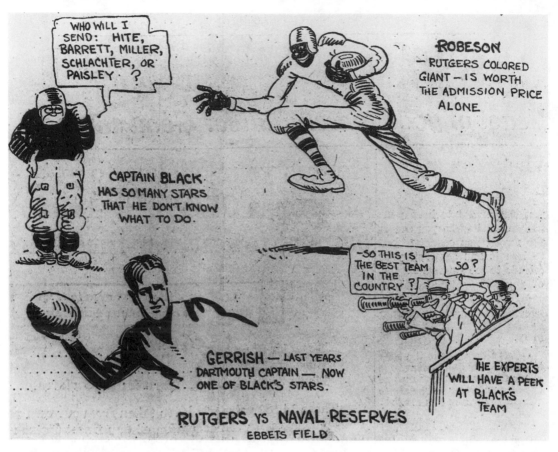

"Rutgers vs. Naval Reserves, Ebbets Field." Cartoon, November 25, 1917. Photograph by Jack Abraham. Courtesy of Robert Smith Collection.

son had turned on America and declared (as falsely reported) that blacks would not fight for America against the Soviet Union. Regardless of the observer's flawed sense of Robeson's possibilities, this white Rutgers graduate had stumbled onto a connection: The observer had felt Robeson's powerful optimism for the American Idea — that every person can rise to his or her level through ability — on that valedictory stage in 1919 and linked it, as a contradiction in his mind, to Robeson's later rejection of unswerving loyalty to America. What the observer had left out was the segregation, disfranchisement, and discrimination that was the daily barrier to such aspirations in the life of all African Americans, including Robeson, after they left college.

In some people this contradiction between the American idea of inclusion and the American practice of exclusion and exploitation did not burn as hotly as in Robeson. They were the black cynics who never believed in America anyway. But Robeson believed all that stuff about America, believed, à la Booker T. Washington, that one could rise in America to the limit of one's bootstraps; that merit would be recognized in America; and, most important, that any migrant could come to America from anywhere and become an American, a respected citizen of this country, an integral part of Americanness, in a way that was not true in any other country. And the idealism of Robeson's speech epitomized the Enlightenment optimism of an entire

generation of young New Negro intellectuals, writers, and artists who would
create the literature and art of the
Harlem Renaissance, the Black Arts
Movement, of the 1920s. But what the
observer failed to see lying hidden in
the breast of this young African American was the rage that would be expressed when America's promises were
not kept, a rage that would be expressed in the summer of that same
year when those other "New Negroes,"
the largely southern born, working
class, also idealistic African Americans
who came to northern cities during
World War I, were stoned, beaten, and
murdered in the northern city streets
by whites in the 1919 race riots. Former
black sharecroppers and their youth
fought back against white rioters with
a ferocity and viciousness that frightened whites and seemed to declare that
if America was not intended to include
blacks, then blacks would tear it down.
In that sense, Robeson's anger (and that
of others of his generation) shows how
powerful and dangerous it was for a
generation of African Americans to actually believe the American Idea. For
such anger led directly to the kind of
revolutionary rage that had inspired
the Founding Fathers to overthrow
their government because it did not
live up to its promise.

During the 1920s Robeson became
receptive to a variant of the American
idea in the Harlem Renaissance, the
cultural pluralist ideology that says that
people can choose their identity in a
marketplace of ideas and practices. His
success as an actor, a singer, and a film
star was related to the rise, during the
Harlem Renaissance, of a sense of pride
among Negroes in being Negro, of
singing spirituals, the music of black
people, and the rise among white liberals of a sense of respect for African-

**Paul Robeson, Rutgers' All–American, c. 1918.
Courtesy of Robert Smith Collection.**

American folk culture. This self-respect was reflected in the singing of the spirituals, and that recognition meant that playwrights like Mary Wiborg and Eugene O'Neill wrote plays about the black theme in race relations, and the black character as a dramatic figure, for the first time. Philosophically, a dualism developed, which we still struggle with today: We are all Americans and we are part of the same national identity; but we are also different culturally and we can choose to celebrate a distinct ethnic identification — a black person rather than "someone who happens to be black." Robeson articulated this most clearly in an interview in which he speaks of his possibilities after completing his successes in the O'Neill plays: "I believe that I can accomplish more for my people just being an artist than any amount of protest and propaganda can accomplish." It is good to remember this interview to remind ourselves of a very important fact — Robeson was a developing African-American mind and reflected the thought and opinion of his times, opinion shared broadly by such other Harlem Renaissance figures as Alain Locke, Langston Hughes, and Zora Neale Hurston, a group in rebellion against the protest-obsessed cadre gathered around W.E.B. Du Bois.

Those Harlem Renaissance ideas — that you can be black and successful without confining your life to protest — helped Robeson be successful. He was also helped by the cultural changes of the period, that he emerged at a time when dark skin color — being black and proud — and identification with Africa and with the folk of the African-American community was in the ascendance in American cultural life. Such changes were the result of Marcus Garvey's Universal Negro Improvement Association and his nationalist construction of African-American identity, and, to a limited degree, from the rise of primitivism in white bohemian American life. The black face and narrative of civilization became popular during the 1920s and 1930s, and Robeson was able to find work during this period in dramatic roles which he would have been unable to do even a decade earlier in American theater and concert stage history. But it is through this experience, believing in its transformative ability to change American racial relations, that Robeson got an education that others, who were not performing artists in white contexts, did not experience. It was during this period when Robeson attempted to act out this agenda that he came face to face with the problems of representation as a Black artist: being owned by the means of cultural production in America and England, the resultant cultural products lacked representativeness. Robeson's confrontation with his cultural impotence then took his consciousness into its third phase.

After 1935, and the horrendous experience of the release of *Sanders of the River*, Robeson moved beyond liberal pluralist politics to become an advocate of a class struggle and a radical critique of establishment culture. Robeson remained an advocate of what would be considered African-American cultural pride — as signified by his lifelong performance of the spirituals in his concerts, his advocacy of African independence and self-rule, his interest in African affairs, and his definition of himself as an African. By becoming a member, for example, of the West African Students Association in London, Robeson also realized that his individual choice as a black artist was limited by the range of possible options allowed him in a film industry that was a multinational capitalist institution. And he began to realize that without some fundamental change in the worldwide economic structure that supported the film industry and racial practices in America, he could never find fulfillment as an artist. As such, Robeson realized that our identity is socially constructed by others, and he therefore accepted the notion that he must reveal and transform those social forces to achieve his freedom. He realized, as Toni Cade Bambara stated many years later, that "I do not think that literature [for Robeson, artistic performance] is the primary instrument for social transformation but I do think that literature [read, art] has potency. So I work to celebrate struggle...." In taking on this mantle, Robeson entered the African-American tradition of "truthtelling," of speaking the truth to power.

I believe that it is during the 1930s that Robeson realized the difficulty of being both an icon and a hero, an artist and a citizen, and that the marriage of the two during his Rutgers years, which was largely due to the hypermasculine setting of the football field, was over. His ability to retaliate physically was removed from him and he became subject to a gaze which both heightened his black masculinity yet attempted to deny it. Robeson's agency did not disappear, but the very nature of that agency shifted. On the football field he might be Teddy Roosevelt; but on the stage he was much closer to Eleanor Roosevelt. In a series of particularly difficult roles, such as the lead character in the film version of *The Emperor Jones,* or as Jim, the Sambo character in *Show Boat,* Robeson's role was written in such a way that his power either remained absent or was used against the heroism of his character.

But rather than abandon the marriage of icon and hero, Robeson tried to tilt it towards his new values. Rather self-consciously and publicly, he tried to use his artistic prestige, his status as an American icon, to bring about fundamental social transformations, such as the defeat of fascism, both in and out of the United States, and thereby become a new and more potent kind of hero, not only for the black community, but for the international Left community as well. Once again, and re-

markably I think we have to say, Robeson was successful in being both an icon and a hero, now in a new way: He was able to become someone who was loved by the general American public for his accomplishments as an artist and as a "superlative Negro," and simultaneously be respected by the masses of blacks and leftists who saw him as a force of transformative social change.

By 1946, however, the strain of balancing the relationship began to tell on Robeson, as symbolized by his decision — in order to relieve some of the tension — to stop performing in films and on the dramatic stage. He limited his concert singing as well, confining himself to a few singing engagements, so that he could turn most of his energy towards his heroic quest of becoming a "primary instrument for social transformation"—a political activist to bring about a democratic, multicultural America. In reality, of course, it was not Robeson but the United States government that ended the marriage for him. For despite his declining film and dramatic career, Robeson had remained such a powerful icon, such an international symbol of courage and accomplishment, that the United States felt he had to be brought down, had to be disciplined (in the language used by Michel Foucault in *Discipline and Punish*) into another kind of symbol, a sign to others that if they too "stood up to the man" (in the narrative of slave resistance that the historian Eugene Genovese discusses in *Roll, Jordan, Roll*) they would be crushed.

Robeson's harassment and confinement, after his passport was taken from him in 1950 and before it was returned in 1958, constituted a system designed to connote to observers that the state has the power to control, to observe, to demean, and humiliate whomever it wishes whenever it cares to. But the reality was far more complex. Unlike the official story of his destruction by the state, Robeson continued to lecture, to speak out, and to challenge the system that metaphorically imprisoned him and all those who spoke their minds in the 1950s. Robeson was active during the early 1950s as the still-standing hero who lectured to labor unions that would have him, colleges and universities whose student bodies wanted to hear him, and to smaller collections of progressive people, sometimes gathered around him in living rooms throughout America. Mary Cygan, in this collection, graphically tells how such activity went unreported in the public press. When his passport was returned, Robeson left the United States for Europe, where he was welcomed throughout the continent. He returned to the Soviet Union and a hero's welcome, and basked in the glory of someone who had stood up to imperial power and lived. But Robeson also had paid a terrible price during these years. Not only his physical but his mental health was damaged, beyond repair. He encountered, struggled with, and succumbed to depression — it would be surprising if he had not — and ultimately terminated his active speaking career after he returned to the United States in 1963.

Some have wondered why this withdrawal occurred. Robeson suffered greatly because he was no longer an icon. As a performing artist, his living was performing — connecting with and being reinvigorated by an audience. Robeson's tank was refilled by performing. And when he could no longer per-

form before the kinds of audiences whose response had meant so much to his psyche, he began to collapse under the pressure of state-induced isolation, silence, and, ultimately, media irrelevancy. Some kind of decline, of course, is experienced by most actors, singers, and performers in American popular culture. But the decline is usually gradual, often the result of some random force, such as the preferences of Hollywood executives, or some obvious

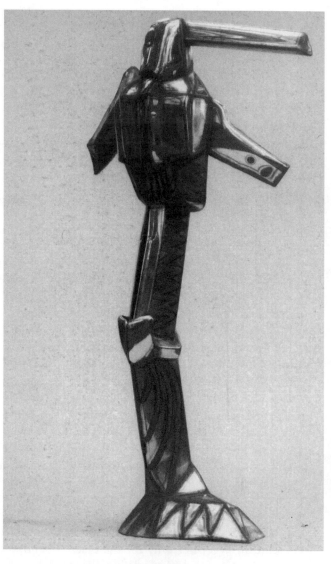

Ed Love. *Monument to Paul Robeson.* October 1, 1974. Welded steel. 85". Private Collection.

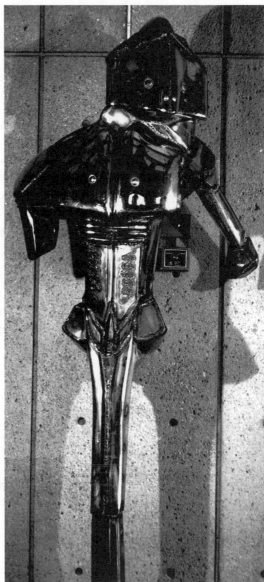

Ed Love. Two views of *Robeson Totem 2nd Variation*. July 27, 1975. 96". Photographs by Jeffrey C. Stewart. Collection of the University of the District of Columbia.

personal failing — intense egotism, decline of ability, and family dysfunctionality. In Robeson's case, at the height of his artistic and professional powers he had his iconic power taken away from him. It is not surprising that a man who had drawn strength from crowds was devastated when he was cut off from them. Robeson had faced the choice of whether to be an icon or a hero with courage, but the choice destroyed him.

But Robeson was not destroyed as a heroic figure. Part of the continuing attraction of Robeson, I believe, is the way in which his story connects with universal narratives of the heroic. Like many an ancient Greek and Egyptian hero, Robeson had to leave home, had to go on a dangerous journey, only to return battered and bruised. He went off to Europe and the Soviet Union and experienced much as an icon that most Americans would not. He returned to his homeland with scars, like a modern day Ulysses—wounded, bent, and battered, but not bowed.

Two sculptures by Ed Love capture the tension I have been exploring in this essay. The first, *Monument to Paul Robeson*, portrays Robeson as an artist, whose genius, stemming from his head, made him the epitome of uprightness and style. The sculpture's elongation and bent leg signify the African tradition that meant so much to Robeson. But most significantly, his knees are protected by knee pads shaped like hearts. The artist, the icon, must ultimately bow down before the audience, if s/he is to retain his or her popularity. Ed Love thus shapes the pads as hearts, perhaps to express his love for Robeson's—and other artists'—sacrifice in such compromising moments.

The second sculpture by Love, *Robeson Totem 2nd Variation*, conveys a different message about Robeson. Here he is the hero, swathed in armor, who knows the score and is willing to fight. No longer does he need kneepads, for he is not going down to appease anyone. Robeson's head is turned a quarter turn to the right, as if about to ask, "What did you say?" Refusing to let any insult go unchallenged, this Robeson is well-defended by the chrome breastplate recycled from found automobile parts. That recycling suggests the return of a leader to his earliest moorings on the Rutgers College football field, where fierce self-defense was the essence of survival. The hero has learned a lesson that the icon never does—that one cannot live one's life in catered dependency, even for the sake of art. Having gone down for art, Robeson is now standing for justice.

The heroic narrative was completed in Robeson's life and was recognized by artists who followed in his footsteps. His survival vindicated that the hero can still live, even after the state has attempted to destroy him. Symbolically murdered as an American icon, Robeson was resurrected by those who revered him more as a hero.

Expanding the African-American Studies Curriculum: "Paul Robeson: An American Life"

Paul Von Blum
University of California, Los Angeles

For almost twenty years, since beginning teaching in 1968 at the University of California, I dealt regularly in class with the multifaceted accomplishments of Paul Robeson in many of my interdisciplinary humanities and social sciences courses. Because my focus has largely been on twentieth century cultural and political history, and because I have often emphasized the central problem of race and racism, my Robeson references have been both pedagogically appropriate and personally compelling. Paul Robeson is arguably the greatest Renaissance person in American history and one of the central cultural figures of the twentieth century. An exceptional scholar, lawyer, athlete, stage and screen actor, singer, and civil rights and political activist, he performed brilliantly in every professional enterprise he undertook. Few human beings have ever achieved his levels of excellence in even one field, much less several.

Yet despite his extraordinary accomplishments, he remains virtually unknown by millions of educated Americans. In my own work as a university teacher I rarely encountered students familiar with his many accomplishments. Indeed, most of my students, including African Americans, had not even heard of him. I often found it necessary to interrupt my regular course progression to inform students of Paul Robeson's life and work and to offer various explanations for the discouraging lack of public knowledge about the artist/activist and his colossal impact.

As a human being, I found this widespread ignorance disturbing and depressing. As an educator, I resolved to address the problem by initiating a new course that would simultaneously address this egregious educational deficiency and expand the curriculum in African-American Studies. My goal was to offer UCLA students a systematic opportunity to learn about Paul

Robeson and to provide, through a detailed examination of his life, a unique approach to study twentieth century history more generally. Because Robeson's spectacular talents in theater, film, music, and politics encourage students to understand culture in broader historical perspective, I also envisioned that the course would augment the interdisciplinary emphasis of African-American Studies—a perspective that distinguishes the field from the conventional disciplines that have dominated university life for many decades.

Believing that the time had come for a comprehensive examination of the man and his times for a university audience, I approached the UCLA Center for African American Studies. Quickly responding, the Center offered me the opportunity to present the upper division and graduate level course I entitled "Paul Robeson: An American Life" in 1988. Because the course has been well received by undergraduate and graduate students alike, I have had the good fortune to present it each academic year.

As I explain in detail at the first class session, the course attempts to accomplish several intellectual objectives. On one level, the inquiry into Robeson's life encourages students to understand more fully the psychology and sociology of human creativity. They are invited to comprehend how one person can accomplish so much so well. In addition, they examine the social conditions that both encourage and inhibit human potential, especially the extent and persistence of racism in American history.

At the outset, I also indicate that the course has a concurrent and deeper objective. For in many ways the story of Paul Robeson is also the story of America throughout much of the twentieth century. An intensive treatment of Robeson's life, focusing substantially on his artistic and political activities, yields valuable insights into the character of American society. Accordingly, the course uses biography as a window for a wider understanding of art, history, politics, and race relations. Through course readings, guest speakers, films, records, and personal research projects, students become more capable of understanding the complex and fascinating connections between the several disciplines in the social sciences and humanities.

During the ten-week academic quarter, the course focuses on each dimension of Robeson's life and its linkage to the historical currents of the times. I encourage students throughout the term to make connections between the past and the present, enabling them to appreciate the deeper relevance of historical inquiry. For example, when I teach about Robeson's difficult and unpleasant encounters with racism as a Rutgers undergraduate, I invite my present students to examine the extent of change (or lack of change) for contemporary African-American undergraduates at large, predominantly white colleges and universities. Similarly, when I present material about the racial hostility Robeson encountered as an award-winning athlete and later as a lawyer in a New York law firm, I compare his early twentieth century experiences with the more subtle persistence of racism in sports and in law in the century's final decade. This contemporary application, in fact, constitutes a major theme of the entire course and has been responsible for the high quality and robust discussion that has characterized each offering of "Paul Robeson: An American Life" since its inception.

The following themes represent the intellectual substance and direction of the course:

Introduction and Overview

At the outset, students explore the use of biography as an approach to historical and social inquiry. Several examples of major historical and contemporary personalities are briefly examined for breadth and perspective on this issue. I identify several strengths and limitations of such an approach. Thereafter, I present a specific overview of the life and multifaceted career of Paul Robeson. I begin the course with two video presentations, both widely available for educational use, in order to provide a biographical outline for students, providing a common knowledge base for the more analytically complex material to follow. I use the PBS documentary *Paul Robeson: Tribute to the Artist* and the play *Paul Robeson*, starring James Earl Jones as Robeson. These visual documents provide a glimpse into each aspect of his life treated in greater depth throughout the academic quarter: athlete, dramatic actor, film star, singer, and civil rights and political activist, all within the context of twentieth century U.S. history and politics.

The Early Days

In this unit, students examine Paul Robeson's early life. They learn, for example, about the immense influence of his father, an escaped slave. They also examine his early contact with racial discrimination in Princeton, New Jersey, and its implications for his future political consciousness. I discuss his lifelong reaction to the specific racism he encountered in his high school principal. I examine too the influence of his siblings, including that of his brother Reeve, whose emotional hostility to racism both precipitated his early death and provided an enduring legacy of militancy for his younger brother Paul. I then delve into his life and struggles as a Phi Beta Kappa student at Rutgers University. Similarly, I present material about his studies at Columbia Law School and his subsequent work as a member of a New York law firm. In particular, I examine the role of an African-American scholar and lawyer in a segregated society in the early part of the

twentieth century. Readings include substantial excerpts from Paul Robeson's own book, *Here I Stand*, Susan Robeson's book, *The Whole World Is in His Hands*, and Martin Duberman's comprehensive biography, *Paul Robeson*.

Robeson the Athlete

During the next segment, students learn about Robeson's athletic career at Rutgers. In particular, they come to understand his accomplishments in baseball, basketball, track, and football. I give extended attention to his record as an All-American football player. I also note his brief career as a professional football player. Most important, students examine why Robeson's athletic greatness still receives scant mention in contemporary sports circles. As a bridge to future themes in the course, I focus on his exclusion, until 1995, for political reasons, from the College Football Hall of Fame. Finally, I discuss his personal athletic accomplishments in light of the continuing use of racial stereotyping and discrimination in American athletics. Readings include additional excerpts from *The Whole World in His Hands* and various scholarly articles by University of California, Berkeley, sociologist Harry Edwards.

Robeson the Stage and Screen Actor: The Stage

This course unit investigates Robeson's highly acclaimed accomplishments on the New York and British stage. A brief history of the Harlem Renaissance serves as the background for Robeson's personal accomplishments as a dramatic artist in the '20s and '30s. Among the examples I cover are his work in *All God's Chillun Got Wings, The Emperor Jones, Show Boat, The Hairy Ape,* and *Othello.* I pay particular attention to *Othello,* because Robeson was the first major African-American actor to perform the role of the tragic Moor in the

United States. I play excerpts from his 1943 performance of *Othello* from a Columbia LP record; this is a relatively rare resource, but it can be found with diligent effort. Class discussions concentrate on Robeson's insistence that the central tragedy of the drama involved race and honor rather than mere jealousy. Students are invited to examine the racial implications of the play and, as usual, to draw whatever contemporary applications they believe are warranted. Readings include the entire text of Shakespeare's *Othello* and further excerpts from *The Whole World Is in His Hands* and *Paul Robeson.*

Robeson the Stage and Screen Actor: The Screen

Because Paul Robeson was also a star in eleven motion pictures, I also examine this feature of his artistic career in depth. Students view and discuss such films as *The Emperor Jones, Jericho* and *Songs of Freedom*, all widely available at present. A major emphasis is on his portrayals of partially strong black characters, which I compare to more stereotypical images of blacks throughout American film history. I also encourage students to think about the deeper reasons for Robeson's determination to abandon his film career because he was unable to obtain more positive roles about his people. Finally, students discuss the continuing problems that racial minorities encounter in the film industry and explore the limited options for both African-American actors and producers. Martin Duberman's biography provides the main reading for this unit.

Robeson the Singer: African-American Origins

A great bass-baritone, Paul Robeson excelled as a concert singer throughout most of his life. Because records, tapes, and compact disks of his performances are also widely available in commercial outlets, I use them so that students can listen to numerous examples of his concerts and other performances. In the first part of this two-week course segment, students explore the African-American roots of Robeson's singing career, concentrating especially on spiritual and freedom songs. While the main materials consist of musical primary sources, I also make available excerpts from Robeson's own writings on music and various secondary sources relevant to his musical career.

Robeson the Singer: Topical Folk Songs

Since many of his songs dealt with various struggles for racial justice and other social themes, this segment of the class is also especially useful in stimulating students to understand the connections between social life and artistic creativity. In particular, students listen to a wide range of Robeson's music with social and political content, such as the Spanish Civil War, labor struggles, civil rights, and related themes. I also investigate Robeson's place in the broader American tradition of topical music, and compare his work to that of such performers as Woody Guthrie, Pete Seeger, Leadbelly, Josh White, Odetta, Bob Dylan, and others. Once again, musical recordings serve as the chief source material.

Robeson the Political Activist: African Nationalism and Civil Rights

Throughout his entire life, Robeson was committed to the liberation of his fellow African Americans and to several broader struggles for human dignity and liberation. In this first week of the concluding unit of the course, I emphasize Robeson's specific work on behalf of international black liberation. I explore his deep commitment to African freedom struggles, using in particular Sterling Stuckey's essay *I Want to Be an American.* I also assign and promote discussion about Robeson's personal writings on this topic. Finally, I ask students to make an assessment of his role as a militant civil rights activist in the historical tradition of Nat Turner, Frederick Douglass, W.E.B. Du Bois, Martin Luther King, Malcolm X, and others.

Robeson the Political Activist: McCarthyism

From the end of World War II to his death, Paul Robeson was effectively blacklisted and unable to perform his work as a dramatic and vocal artist. During this week, students learn of his encounter with McCarthyism during this dubious era of the recent American past. In particular, I present such themes as the Peekskill Riot, the passport denials from the Department of State, and his appearance before the House Un-American Activities Committee (HUAC). I address the impact of this political persecution on Robeson's physical and mental health. My readings include excerpts from *Here I Stand*, Robeson's complete testimony before HUAC, excerpts from David Caute's *The Great Fear*, Duberman's *Paul Robeson*, and Eric Bentley's play *Are You Now or Have You Ever Been?*

Robeson the Political Activist: The Issue of Communism

For much of his life, Robeson had a close association with the American Communist Party and with the Soviet Union. Although denying personal membership in the Party, Robeson clearly knew, admired, and worked with many of its members and leaders. Moreover, he spent considerable time, personally and professionally, in the former Soviet Union and Eastern Europe. Robeson's acceptance of a peace prize from the Soviet Union during the reign of Joseph Stalin exacerbated his difficulties with U.S. authorities during the era of McCarthyism and strikingly split the African-American community. In this final week

of the class, students attempt to assess the significance of his relationship with domestic and foreign Communists. We explore its impact on his career, on his emotional life and difficulties, and on his broader public reputation. This final theme generates the kind of interdisciplinary fusion of personal biography and social and historical analysis that underlies the course as a whole.

I have found that the uniquely great life of Paul Robeson provides an exciting opportunity for students to examine deeper issues in African-American history, politics, and culture. The course's pedagogical appeal stems in part from students' intrinsic interest in the lives and struggles of real human beings. Robeson's extraordinary accomplishments in so many different areas, moreover, make linkage to historical currents especially easy. His encounters with racism in education, athletics, the theater, the film industry, and with various United States government agencies also encourage serious consideration of the contemporary problems of racism in these same institutions.

The easy access of multimedia presentations for the course similarly engages student attention. Viewing original films, listening to original recordings, and reading original documents add vitality to historical inquiry and motivate students to develop a deeper appreciation for historical knowledge generally. Interdisciplinary African-American Studies courses like "Paul Robeson: An American Life," moreover, encourage students to transcend arbitrary disciplinary boundaries and develop a more dynamic sense of the complex and fascinating relationships between various areas of human knowledge.

The Robeson course also has immense value for African-American students still struggling to overcome the pervasive and insidious effect of negative stereotypes in the media and popular culture. For the past nine years, many of my African-American students have commented on the profound role of Paul Robeson as a role model for young people. That one black man could do so much in the face of profound institutional obstacles is clearly a major source of inspiration. One of the most gratifying educational outcomes of the course over the years has involved presentations by my UCLA students to middle and high school students about the life and impact of Paul Robeson. Equally important, the story of Robeson's multiple talents and achievements is educationally beneficial for non–African-American students. Whites, Asian Americans, Latinos, and others also need to understand that excellence in any field is never determined by one's racial origins, an insight of particular significance in an era where the destructive mythology of race-based intellectual inferiority still has currency in many quarters.

This course (and many others following a similar pedagogical model) is easily adaptable in whole or in part in American colleges and universities. Although most appropriate to an African-American Studies curricular format, the course can be usefully presented throughout the humanities and social sciences. The wide availability of readings, films, recordings, and other materials should facilitate the more systematic educational treatment of Paul Robeson, an especially appropriate outcome given the recent centennial of his birth in 1998. Above all, my good fortune with this course at UCLA has reinforced my view that curricular developments in ethnic studies generally have made a major and progressive difference in higher learning, a durable legacy of the historic struggles for civil rights a generation ago.

Paul

STANLEY ISAACS[*]

The booming voice filled the air Tuesday night as the mourners hurried through the rain, shaking out their umbrellas before moving into the Mother AME Zion Church. The words of *Ballad for Americans* rang out from church loudspeakers onto West 137th Street in Harlem. Paul Robeson had come home. About 3,000 persons, a quarter of them white, were at the church to attend the funeral services of Robeson, the most famous and controversial black man of his time. "He was an ambassador of justice and equality who stood as a giant in a society racked by injustice," Bishop J. Clinton Hoggard said.

The AME Zion Church was the one at which Robeson's brother was the pastor from 1936 to 1963. Hoggard said, "In those days it was filled every Sunday just as it is tonight. And many times Paul came here to worship and to sing because he was always welcome here. Paul sang within these walls, 'Freedom, freedom, freedom over me, and before I'll be a slave, I'll be buried in my grave and go home to my Lord and be free.'"

The clergyman's voice rang as he repeated the words from the old spiritual. It stirred the crowd and people responded with an ovation, perhaps the most spirited of the evening. In that moment it was as if Robeson himself were saying the words. A sadness hung over the evening. It underscored the comments of the eulogists and it was expressed outside the church by a middle-aged citizen of Harlem. He said, "Robeson was a great man, but it's too bad all this came after he died. It's a shame that he hasn't been honored in his lifetime. He has been sick all these years and that's the time something should have been done to tell all Americans what a great man he was."

Robeson was ahead of his time. His admirers and detractors might have agreed on that. What Robeson said about injustice in the 1930s and 1940s are commonplace utterances today. But he was out in front by himself then, and at a time when dissent was equated with communism. Robeson was vilified. He was, as much as any victim of a shooting war, a casualty of the Cold War.

Robeson preceded Ralph Bunche, Walter L. White, Roy Wilkins, and Martin Luther King as a national spokesman for blacks. He said, "My father was a slave who

---

This is a reprint of a memorial column published in Newsday, March 1976, as a tribute following Robeson's death.

helped build this country, and I'm going to stay and have a piece of it just like everybody else."

A London critic once said of a Robeson singing performance, "He broke our hearts with beauty." That same voice could be strident in its passion for his people, and he incurred the wrath of many of his countrymen during the Cold War period when he said at the World Peace Congress in 1949, "It is unthinkable that American Negroes will go to war on behalf of those who have oppressed us for generations against a country [the Soviet Union] which in one generation has raised our people to the full dignity of mankind."

He said later that his statement had been taken "slightly out of context," but the comment was in keeping with the admiration for the Soviet Union that Robeson frequently expressed. (He always was treated with greater esteem in Europe, particularly in the Soviet Union, than in the United States.) This hastened the commercial ostracism that eventually ended his artistic career, broke his health, and forced him into seclusion over the last 10 years.

At the funeral eulogist Lloyd L. Brown quoted Frederick Douglass: "For he is a lover of his country who rebukes and does not excuse its sins." Brown then said, "Robeson transcended hypocritical concepts of patriotism."

That was not the prevailing thinking in the United States in 1949. Robeson's remarks so agitated a nation aflame with anti-communism that no less a figure than Jackie Robinson was trotted out before a congressional committee to attest to Negro loyalty. Robinson, while acknowledging respect for Robeson, affirmed the allegiance of Negroes to the United States. He later came to regret his appearance, and echoed militant beliefs about racial injustice which were in the Robeson tradition.

Eulogist Samuel Rosen said he always thought of Robeson as "Big Paul." Robeson, known as "Robeson of Rutgers," was an All-American football player, a four-sport man. In any historical roll call of American black athletic titans, the list would start with Jack Johnson, continue with Robeson, Jesse Owens, Joe Louis, Jackie Robinson, Bill Russell and Jim Brown to Muhammad Ali, and it should be recorded that all but Owens and Louis would come to be marked as militants who frequently incurred the wrath of many Americans.

It is a piddling footnote to the annals of sport that Robeson has not been voted into the College Football Hall of Fame.* The man left a mark far beyond the realm of sports, but such is the Neanderthalism prevalent in sports that guardians of the sacred precincts of the college football Hall of Fame have managed to keep Robeson out. They claim that "a man must have proved his worth as a citizen carrying the ideals forward into his relations with the community and his fellow man." Where is this Hall of Fame housed: At Rutgers!

Robeson made Phi Beta Kappa at Rutgers where a student lounge and the student Union at its Newark Campus have been named in his honor. There has been a drive by the students of the Livingstone College division of Rutgers to get the name changed to Paul Robeson College.

When the Robeson obituaries were published last week, a man who is in his 30s commented, "What a man he was. I never realized he did so many things." Eulogist Brown said, "He was a modern day black American with the manifold talent of a Renaissance man."

At the end of the services, as they carried the coffin draped in red carnations out into the pelting rain, the Harlem street was filled with the mournful strains of Robeson singing "Deep River."

*Robeson was inducted into the National College Football Hall of Fame in 1995 — The Editors.

About the Contributors

Sheila Tully Boyle is senior editor at the Houghton Mifflin Company, Boston.

Andrew Bunie is a professor of history at Boston College.

Mary E. Cygan is an assistant professor of history at the University of Connecticut–Stamford.

Joseph Dorinson is a professor of history at Long Island University.

Howard Fast has written more than 50 novels and an autobiographical memoir, *Being Red*.

Henry Foner, former president of the Fur, Leather, and Machine Workers' Union, has also taught labor history at a variety of colleges in the New York City area.

Kevin Jack Hagopian teaches communications and film studies at Penn State University.

Jerry Holt is a dean at Shawnee State University.

Joseph Illick is a professor of history at San Francisco State University.

Stanley Isaacs was a long-time sports and media columnist for *Newsday*.

Lawrence Lamphere is a dean at Cornell University.

Mark D. Naison is professor and head of the Department of African-American Studies, Fordham University.

William Pencak is a professor of history at Penn State University.

Lester Rodney, founding sports editor of the New York *Daily Worker* (1936–57), continues to write columns in California newspapers.

Robert Shaffer is an assistant professor of history at Shippensburg University.

Jeffrey Conrad Stewart is a professor of history at George Mason University.

Paul Von Blum is a professor of African-American studies at the University of California, Los Angeles.

Joseph Walwik is an assistant professor of history at Manatee Community College.

Leah Zazulyer is an educator and prize-winning poet.

Index